W9-CSC-842

Beatrix Potter's Americans:
Selected Letters

May 20. 27   Sawrey
                              ʋ Ambleside

Dear Miss Bertha Maloney,

Some months ago the "Hornbook" contained a paragraph relating how the writer and illustrator of the "Peter Rabbit" books lived in the district of the Westmorland Lakes in the north of England.

Peter Rabbit is not begging for himself — and he offers something.

"Beatrix Potter" has very much at heart an appeal to raise a fund to save a strip of foreshore woodland and meadow, near Windermere Ferry, from imminent risk of disfigurement by extensive building a town extension.

So many nice kind Americans come through the Lake district on their tour, some of them ask after Peter Rabbit. Do you think any of them would give a guinea (our £1.1.0) to help this fund, in return for an autographed drawing?

Alas! so many of our heirlooms — our pictures, our ancient books, even our old timbered houses — are crossing the Atlantic — would not American friends help to save a bit of our scenery?

It is only half-a-mile of Lake frontage; but it is right in the middle of Windermere; and it is near my home

yrs sincerely "Beatrix Potter"

Letter written to aid in the purchase of Windermere strip. *The Horn Book,* May, 1927.

Beatrix Potter's Americans: Selected Letters

Edited by Jane Crowell Morse

The Horn Book, Inc.
Boston, Massachusetts
1982

Printed in the United States of America
Library of Congress Cataloging in Publication Data

Potter, Beatrix, 1866-1943.
    Beatrix Potter's Americans

    Includes index.
    1. Potter, Beatrix, 1866-1943 — Correspondence. 2. Authors, English — 20th century — Correspondence. 3. Illustrators — England — Correspondence. I. Morse, Jane Crowell, 1922-   . II. Title. PR6031.072Z48 1982 823'.8 [B]   81-7258 ISBN 0-87675-282-2   AACR2

To Frances Atwood Crowell
and
Samuel French Morse
in gratitude

Contents

·~·~· Introduction ·~·~·

After her marriage to William Heelis in 1913, Beatrix Potter settled easily and happily into the country life of her beloved Westmorland, where she devoted herself to the raising of Herdwick sheep and the preservation of land for the National Trust. Marriage and her new career were so absorbing that she found little time for writing and drawing. She did not want to be known as Beatrix Potter, writer and artist for children, nor did she want to be bothered by visitors.

In the summer of 1921, however, she replied cordially to a request to visit from Anne Carroll Moore, well-known storyteller and Superintendent of Children's Work for the New York Public Library. Before Miss Moore left Sawrey, Mrs. Heelis had extended a welcome to "any of the storytellers in your children's libraries. I know they would be coming for the sake of the children and not out of mere curiosity." Miss Moore was so delighted by the visit with Beatrix Potter that she often recounted the story to friends. She also preserved the details of the visit in her book for children, *Nicholas and the Golden Goose,* and in her appreciation published in *The Art of Beatrix Potter.*

Anne Carroll Moore was only the first of many admiring American visitors. Families as well as librarians came to Hill Top Farm. They were lively, intelligent, well-educated people, who appreciated the privilege of meeting the creator of the Peter Rabbit books. The summer of 1921 also brought Mr. and Mrs. William L. W. Field of Milton, Massachusetts, their two daughters, Mary and Helen, aged twelve and fourteen, and Mrs. Field's sister, Miss Mary F. Gill. Their visit had its beginnings in the work of an informal organization called "Friendly Links," founded by the Unitarian Church in Boston. Both Beatrix Potter and Mary Gill were Unitarians, and they had exchanged letters for several years.

Unfortunately, Beatrix Potter's correspondence with Miss Gill and the Field family has been lost; but in her journal, "My Trip Abroad," Mary Field wrote, "In the morning we went rowing in Grasmere Lake. In the afternoon we went to Hill Top Farm to see Beatrix Potter. We saw the old farmhouse and some descendants of Peter Rabbit. I played with a descendant of Tom Kitten and he was just like Tom Kitten himself."

Helen Field recalls in a letter to Jane Morse that "we had been prepared for this call by repeated forceful admonitions to be polite, quiet, restrained, and not greedy at tea time, because we were told, Beatrix Potter *did not like Americans,* and it was important not to increase her prejudice by being bad-mannered children. The garden was recognizable to anyone familiar with her illustrations, and when I perceived a rabbit in it I was delighted, and said, Of course it couldn't be Peter, could it? She replied, A relative, undoubtedly, perhaps a descendant." Before they left, Helen and Mary received an inscribed copy of *The Roly Poly Pudding,* containing an appropriate message.

Mr. Field, headmaster of Milton Academy and a biologist, was impressed by the scientific accuracy of Beatrix Potter's drawings of fungi, lichens, and mosses. He thought their accuracy and detail made them worthy of publication in a scientific journal.

After her first visit, Mary Gill kept up a correspondence which led to a second family visit in July, 1924. Helen Field also remembers that at tea Beatrix Potter brought out a treasured possession to show her parents and aunt. "It consisted of two or three linen napkins with a C and a crown embroidered in one corner, more or less like this ⌣C . And B.P. said that when they came into her hands she wondered if Charles I had stopped at her farmhouse during his escape." At the end of the second visit, Beatrix Potter gave the girls two original preliminary sketches — one of Jemima Puddleduck and one of Jemima and the Foxy Gentleman. Later she sent Christmas cards to the girls. After the girls grew up, married and had children, Beatrix Potter sent Christmas cards and an occasional letter to their children giving them news of Squirrel Nutkin and Jemima Puddleduck.

These early visits led not only to letters but also to an ever-widening circle of acquaintances. Beatrix Potter discovered that she liked the "nice Americans." They were neither curiosity-seekers nor idle trippers, but candid, friendly, spontaneous visitors from across the Atlantic with whom she felt relaxed and able to share common interests.

Her reply in 1927 to Mrs. J. Templeman Coolidge's request to visit was by then a familiar response. "I am always pleased to see Americans; I don't know what I think of you as a nation (with a big N!) but the individuals who have looked for Peter Rabbit have all been delightful."

Peter Rabbit and her other cherished books most certainly brought Americans to Hill Top; equally important to the visitors was a sense of place and shared tradition. Like Mrs. Heelis of Sawrey, the Americans, particularly those from New England, appreciated "the memories of old times, the simple country pleasures, the old farmhouse, the sublime beauty of the silent lonely hills."

They were also bookish, serious about literature, eager to talk about and send her books which they admired and enjoyed. Their attitude toward children's books pleased her. To learn that the reading aloud of *The Tailor of Gloucester* (her favorite among all her books) on Christmas Eve had already become a tradition in many children's libraries and New England homes helped to dispel her disappointment that in England her books were often considered "toy" books by the shopkeepers and bought as "a convenient present" rather than for appreciative reading aloud.

The Americans were enthusiastic conservationists, too. It was very natural for them to respond to her desire to "save anything I can of our Lake country from being vulgarized." Coming from a nation which had undergone rapid growth and industrialization, they endorsed her belief in conservation and preservation: "as true education advances, the beauty of unspoilt nature will be appreciated, and it would be a pity if the appreciation came too late. . . . we wish to preserve some portions of wild land unspoilt for the general good."

They took notice of her fine oak furniture and china, and although she regretted that many good English pieces had to be sold at auctions, she found it "very pleasant" to meet Americans who also valued "old associations" and who would appreciate those "treasures" that had "to cross the seas."

The visits and friendships led Mrs. Heelis to say that the Americans had brought her "outside of herself." " 'I' always seem to 'me' to be comparatively dull, with not much to say, and with only very occasional flashes of amusement," she confided to Mrs. Perry, her closest American friend. Shy by nature, and at times considered diffident and a recluse by her neighbors, she found Americans easy to talk to and even easier to correspond with.

More and more letters were exchanged during the thirties, letters in which Mrs. Heelis expressed her growing concern about the changing economic and political events plaguing the world. She was "one of the sceptics who refused to sign the League of Nations Manifesto" and who was troubled by the plebiscite which led to the reunion of the Saar Basin Territory to the German Reich. As a stout Tory, she expressed her opinion candidly, "If they *will* fight, let them exterminate each other and hope that England, the Colonies, and the States may survive to see — rule, real rule by power, not by preaching — a better world."

By 1938, her fears had increased. "Can you hear Hitler over the wireless as far as America?" she asked Mrs. Perry. "Did you ever hear such a brutal, raving lunatic. I could not understand a word of his clipped rapid German; but the ranting note and smiling face in the telegraphed photographs are not sane. If Mr. Chamberlain believes in his promises he must be an incurable optimist. . . . The sheep sales are coming on; up to date they are bad, prices 5/ per sheep down from last year. Everything is in an upset way."

Most of all, the letters of the war years show her "strongly marked personality"; that she was a true descendant of the "Lancashire yeomen and weavers" of whom she was so proud: "obstinate, hard-headed, *matter of fact* folk." Outspoken and independent in her thinking, she liked order and having things run in a business-like way, be it farm or nation. Although she felt "anything — 'nearly' anything — may be better than war," she also believed it "not an honourable fear — and doubtful of any permanency."

When war finally came, she directed her energy to active farm work which had to be done, and yet she, too, became caught up in the excitement of war: the marvelous feats of the R.A.F., the indomitable spirit of the bombed-out citizen, and the uneasy thrill of finding bits of silvery Blitz material on the fells.

By 1942 when events took a turn for the better, she returned to her writing. At the insistence of Bertha Mahony Miller, founder and editor of *The Horn Book*, a magazine about literature for children, she wrote two essays and revised a short sketch. After rereading old letters in order to reply to questions Mrs. Miller had asked about the origins of her stories, she commented, "I have been surprised at the number and the friendliness of the packets of dozens of letters from the U.S.A.; and they are only a few tied up in bundles from amongst the numbers received through many years. I don't receive English letters like that — a good many from children, some wanting autographs, some enthusiastic grateful parents (also in U.S.A.). But never does anyone outside your perfidiously complimentary nation write to tell me that I write good prose!"

The letters written to Americans reveal that Beatrix Potter Heelis could write as well as draw with precision, insight, and conviction. They emphasize her identity as a Westmorland farmer and breeder of Herdwick sheep, her deep emotions about place, and show her love of accuracy of observation and detail. But this is not only a country correspondence, a record of wind and weather, sheep fairs and harvests, it is also her own record of her "purposeful life of achievement" between 1921 and 1943.

Jane Crowell Morse

Milton, Massachusetts
June 1981

～～～ Editor's Note ～～～

I should like to express my gratitude to all those who so generously made their letters from Beatrix Potter Heelis available to me for this selection, and most especially to Henry P. Coolidge, Richard K. Stevens, and Nonya Stevens Wright. Mr. Coolidge, through the auspices of Eleanor Sayre, Curator of Prints and Drawings at the Museum of Fine Arts in Boston, allowed me to choose for reproduction original illustrations from the watercolors and drawings Beatrix Potter had given to him. In giving this permission, Mr. Coolidge characterized the generosity of all the donors of letters and pictures when he wrote, "I feel they ought to be shared, and further that the Horn Book, if anyone, particularly deserves them." I am also grateful to Helen Field Rich and Mary Field Twombly, the nieces of Mary F. Gill; and to Elinor Hopkinson Barr and Joan Hopkinson Shurcliff, the daughters of Mr. and Mrs. Charles Hopkinson, for sharing delightful reminiscences of their visits to Hill Top.

Howell Heaney, Rare Book Librarian, Free Library of Philadelphia, gave permission for the selection of letters received by Mrs. James deWolf Perry and Alexander McKay, and assisted in obtaining the letters written to Mrs. Richard K. Stevens. The New York Public Library gave permission to use the Anne Carroll Moore letters. The Trustees of the Milton, Massachusetts, Public Library gave permission to reproduce an original drawing.

Joyce Irene Whalley, Assistant Keeper of the Library, Victoria and Albert Museum, allowed me to examine the Linder Collection, and appointed a junior colleague, Lynette Dalkins, who painstakingly searched the Enid and Leslie Linder papers for pertinent material. The late Cyril Stephens and Frederick Warne and Co. gave permission to use all of the letters Beatrix Potter wrote to Americans, as well as works of art reproduced in this book. The illustrations which have appeared in books by Beatrix Potter, and the other illustrations by Beatrix Potter, are reproduced by permission of Frederick Warne PLC, the owners of the copyright in all works by Beatrix Potter.

I also wish to thank Eleanor Sayre for allowing me to make use of the material prepared for the Beatrix Potter exhibition mounted at the Museum of Fine Arts in 1977; and also Karin Peltz of the Department of Prints and Drawings at the Museum of Fine Arts for her assistance.

Special thanks go to the Graduate School of Boston University for a grant-in-aid, and to Patricia Craddock and Harriet Lane, of the English Department, who assisted me in obtaining the grant.

Finally, I want to thank The Horn Book for its interest and support, and for allowing me to begin this project by reading the letters written to Bertha Mahony Miller. To Anita Silvey go thanks for her preliminary transcription of the letters received by Mrs. Miller. To Betsey Halbrooks, Karen Jameyson, and Lee Kingman go my gratitude for enthusiasm, sound advice, and much practical help.

The salutation and final complimentary close are omitted except in the first and last letters. The name of the correspondent is given only with the first of a series of letters; the absence of a name indicates another exchange with the same person. The address is given with the first and final letters or when the address itself changes. Brackets indicate editorial interpolations, usually factual, to clarify or explain. Dots indicate the editor's deletions. Explanatory notes have been kept to a minimum. Except for her indiscriminate use of the dash, and some casual errors, Beatrix Potter's phonetic spelling of multisyllabic words and punctuation have been respected. When a letter is signed "Beatrix Potter," not Beatrix Heelis, the signature has been retained to point up her wish to be identified as the author of the Peter Rabbit books. Peter Rabbit is considered a title only when it appears as a shortened form of *The Tale of Peter Rabbit*. All book titles have been italicized even though Beatrix Potter often used quotation marks or no identifying punctuation.

J. C. M.

xvi

~~~ Part I ~~~

"Come up early afternoon and stay for tea"
1921 – 1930

Anne Carroll Moore was the first American to visit Beatrix Potter in Sawrey. She had come to England from France, where she had been visiting children's libraries sponsored by Anne Morgan's American Committee for Devastated France. Since libraries were a prime concern in the restoration of French village life, Miss Moore contributed picture books for these libraries "which had been opened in wooden baraques on the ruins of homes and schools." In London, she ordered fifty copies of the French translation of Peter Rabbit and Benjamin Bunny from Frederick Warne & Co. to be sent to the library in Soissons. Then, because she was going to Grasmere in the Lake District, she asked Mr. Fruing Warne if she might see Mrs. Heelis in Sawrey. Mr. Warne gave her the address, but cautioned her that Mrs. Heelis did not welcome visitors.

Undaunted, Miss Moore wrote from Grasmere to Mrs. Heelis. In her letter she described both her work in France and the French children's love of picture books. Mrs. Heelis sent Miss Moore a cordial reply. Their meeting was an immediate success; and Miss Moore was urged to stay on for tea. Together they walked around Hill Top Farm and visited Beatrix Potter's study in Castle Cottage. There Miss Moore saw the original sketches, drawings, and watercolors from which the pictures in the Peter Rabbit tales were reproduced.

At tea, when Beatrix Potter suggested that she spend the night, Anne Carroll Moore realized that her visit "had turned into an adventure for Beatrix Potter, too." Miss Moore remembered that Beatrix Potter whispered, "I think the nicest way of having company is to ask them to stay on after they come instead of before. You haven't seen half of Hill Top and I want to look at the French pictures again and hear more about New York children. Please stay with us." The invitation included "Nicholas Knickerbocker," a wooden doll which Anne Carroll Moore carried with her wherever she went.

To Anne Carroll Moore

Sawrey,
Ambleside
June 24. 21

Dear Miss Moore,

We shall be very glad to see you. Can you come to lunch on Monday? It is not long notice, but a pity to miss fine weather; and we have not much hay cut at present. I wonder how you will get here — if you can combine it with motoring it is easy, and you could combine it with a sideways excursion to Coniston, either going (or coming back) by Skelwith Bridge. We are 1½ miles south of Hawkshead and about the same distance from Windermere Ferry. If you are coming by public conveyance the best way will be from Waterhead (Ambleside) pier to the Ferry pier.

My reason for these details is that our post town Ambleside is 7 miles away, which is rather misleading, and I should not like to think of "Nicholas" hopping along the dusty roads. My husband will be at the Ambleside office, telephone 74 Ambleside, from 11 to 12:30 tomorrow morning; if you could call him up, it would be best, as we have no Sunday post. And if you are to come by boat, I would send down to the Ferry.

Excuse a scribble I have just come out of the hay — It is uncommonly warm!

Yours sincerely,
Beatrix Heelis

[P.S.] I like the French translations, it is like reading some one else's work — refreshing.

Beatrix Potter obviously understood Anne Carroll Moore's attachment to Nicholas because the next letter is addressed to him.

To Nicholas

Oct. 22. 22

I am so glad to hear of you again — do you know you ran away without leaving any address, except a temporary one at Lancaster, so I could not send you Christmas greetings. But that matters the less as you have not forgotten me. Apparently *I* did forget the French books, very naughty of me after receiving the beautiful French photographs from Miss Saxby. I have asked Messrs Warne to forward a dozen, but I am afraid they would scarcely reach France before you left, the post has been slow for U.S.A.

Now we are enjoying an Indian summer, cold nights and sunny days. Better late than never; it has been an awful wet slow hay time. How hot it was when you came over the croft, along the dusty road, snug in Miss Moore's handbag. If you find you are coming north Mr. Heelis will meet you at Windermere any moment on receipt of a wire.

But it is getting late in the year, better come another time more leisurely on holiday.

I shall have a small book [*Cecily Parsley's Nursery Rhymes*] to send to you both at Christmas, for which you are partly responsible! Where oh where is your New York address?

We are all well here and with love remain dear Nicholas Ann Carroll,

[P.S.] How silly of me! I see there is a club address at top of this paper so I can send it there.

Charles Hopkinson, the Boston painter, his wife and their five daughters came to Hill Top in the summer of 1924. Later, in 1935, the two youngest daughters, Ellie and Joan, and a friend were biking and hiking through England. They called on Mrs. Heelis, who welcomed them cordially and invited them to stay for tea.

To Mrs. Charles Hopkinson

August 23. 24

Your guess at the locality of my dwelling is not far out of it! I have a farm at the Lancashire end of the Lake district; but we are within a long walk of the "Three Shire Stone", where Cumberland, Westmorland and Lancashire meet.

A good many Americans arrive; we had a pleasant party of friends from Boston to tea a few weeks ago. [Miss Mary Gill and the William Field family] They have stopped twice at Grasmere, and they call here when driving round by Windermere ferry, Hawkshead and Coniston. Keswick is the other end (Cumberland) of the district. We are 7 miles from Ambleside although it is the post town. But distances are nothing to motorists now.

If you could send me a postcard it would be just as well, though I am seldom at any great distance from home; at present we are struggling with a horridly wet hay-making. I should like to show your young people the old farm house where the kittens hid in the cupboards and chimney.

Sept. 2nd & 4th are the two local agricultural shows, when I may be out, if the hay is in.

Ask for Mrs. William Heelis, anybody will show you where we live.

With thanks for your kind letter, believe me, yrs sincerely,

"Beatrix Potter"

H.B.Heelis

As "Ann Caraway," Anne Carroll Moore became the heroine of the two books she wrote about Nicholas. She found the names in Walter de la Mare's Peacock Pie. *The first book,* Nicholas, A Manhattan Christmas Story, *describes his arrival in New York City from Holland, and his adventures in the city during the Christmas season.* Nicholas and the Golden Goose, *published eight years later in 1932, is a chronicle of the year 1921 when he and Miss Moore visited France and England. Chapter XI describes Nicholas's visit to Beatrix Potter.*

To Ann Caraway and Nicholas

Jan. 28. 25

What a delightful book you have made! It was a great surprise when I opened the parcel. I am sure American children will love it, and ask for *more.* Do let us hear about Nicholas in France. Ann Caraway need not fear the task; she can write a book that has wisdom, pathos and fun — tears and laughter. My favourite parts are about the Knicker-bockers and General Washington; and I think it is wonderful how cleverly Ann Caraway has worked in two real live — very gentlemanly

6

— young fellows as companions to Nicholas. ('Ben' being a small boy is easier.)

I had no idea that New York is so "Chrismassy" — a real old fashioned Christmas.

We have had a wet one here, wild windy and much floods; and influenza in the village; but so far my husband and I have escaped it.

I have no new book to send in return; there should have been a painting book for children to colour, but the engravers made a muddle of it.

With congratulations and very kind regards,

Bertha Mahony, whose recently received requests for information perplexed Beatrix Potter sufficiently for her to mention them in her letter to Anne Carroll Moore, was founder of The Bookshop for Boys and Girls *and founder and first editor of* The Horn Book Magazine. *In a letter to Margaret Lane she described her work: "There is in Boston an institution which would require almost a volume to fully explain, —* The Women's Educational and Industrial Union. *It came into being about 1876 when women were being forced out of their homes by new industrial conditions. After college, my whole professional life was spent there from 1906 on. It was a grand university for me, for I reported executive committee meetings and heard discussion of all the departments' work, all of which was vitally interesting to me. When, in 1915, I had a vision of my own for a bookshop specializing in children's books, the WEIU asked me to establish it as one of their departments. In 1916 The Bookshop for Boys and Girls opened; in 1921 it was moved to a very fine street floor location and built up interesting collections of grown-up books around its specialty. For twenty years it grew and prospered and became rather famous. In 1924 my friend and assistant, Elinor Whitney and I, started* The Horn Book, *a magazine devoted to children's books and reading, in an effort to do in a wider area the work we were doing in the Bookshop.* The Horn Book *was named for that early lesson book for children but then we adopted Caldecott's* Three Jovial Huntsmen *as our colophon and decoration to have the double meaning of blowing the horns lustily for fine books, searching for talent and excellence as the huntsmen follow the scent of the fox, all of it with humor and gusto."*

To Anne Carroll Moore

Dec. 12. 25

I do not know the home address of Nicholas; Peter and Flopsy want to wish him a very Merry Christmas and they hope that the Bookshop will be so kind as to pass the message on. We will read his book again on Christmas Eve and think of his merry doings across the Atlantic.

Here there has already been some old fashioned weather, 4 weeks hard frost, with skating and dry snow. But it thawed suddenly last Monday, and although the frost had been enjoyable and lovely to look at, I was not sorry to see green grass again. I wonder how the sheep live in countries like U.S.A. and Canada? Ours scrape and dig with feet and heads to get at the rough grass on the hillsides; but frozen snow soon means anxiety to the shepherd and hunger for the sheep. They are not now to eat hay; and there are too many to feed, many hundreds in a flock.

There have been two letters recently from Miss Bertha Mahony of the Boston Bookshop, forwarded through Messrs Warne; and also copies of *The Horn Book*. The letters which ask for particulars about "Beatrix Potter" are very perplexing. I have a most intense dislike to advertisement. (And I have got on quite well without it.) On the other hand, a mystery is silly, and it invites curiosity. And I object to being supposed to be the wife of Sidney Webb, a member of the last socialist Government. He married a Miss Bea*trice* Potter, no relation. There were photographs of him in the newspapers, it said his wife had written children's books. There has often been confusing between us. I thought it would be best to write this for Mr. Warne, to forward through the New York branch of F.W. Co. to whom Miss Mahony had applied: —

"Beatrix Potter is Mrs. William Heelis. She lives in the north of England, her home is amongst the mountains and lakes that she has drawn in her picture books. Her husband is a lawyer. They have no family. Mrs. Heelis is in her 60th year. She leads a very busy contented life, living always in the country and managing a large sheep farm on her own land."

I don't think anybody requires to know more about me. In the second letter Miss Mahony asks how I came to write the books. I used to write picture letters to a little invalid boy years and years ago, the eldest child of a friend. *Peter* was written to him in a letter. He is now a hardworked clergyman in a London parish and I believe he has the

8

letters yet. About 1900 there began to be a fashion for little picture books, and I thought Peter might be worth while publishing. But I could not find anyone else who thought so. It was refused by many publishers, and I got a small number printed for myself, with pen and ink illustrations like the scribbles in the original letter. That is the history of Peter Rabbit. I have never been able to understand what is the attraction of the book; but it continues to sell.

The Horn Book is pleasantly written, I wish all such books of gossip British as well as American, — were in equally good taste.

But I *don't* want to be exploited! And I am very grateful to Nicholas for his reticence. There have been several Australian visitors who have looked in on the old farm house as they passed, but no Americans this summer. It has been a pleasant sunny year — only we have had some family losses and illness of 3 of Mr. Heelis's brothers. But I am thankful to say my husband and I have kept very well. Has Nicholas been abroad again? With kind regards from us both.

After reading the copies of The Horn Book, *which Bertha Mahony had so wisely included with her first letter of inquiry, Beatrix Potter realized that Miss Mahony was not one of those who confused her with Beat*rice Webb, *nor was her intention to exploit the author of* Peter Rabbit, *and she replied to Bertha Mahony's letters. Her first letter was an appeal for The Windermere Fund. A packet of fifty original drawings, copied from four of the illustrations for* Peter Rabbit, *accompanied the letter. Bertha Mahony printed the original letter and her editorial comment in the August, 1927* Horn Book.

To Miss Bertha Mahony

May 21. 27

Some months ago *The Horn Book* contained a paragraph relating how the writer and illustrator of the "Peter Rabbit" books lived in the district of the Wesmorland Lakes in the north of England.

Peter Rabbit is not begging for himself — and he offers something.

"Beatrix Potter" has very much at heart an appeal to raise a fund to save a strip of foreshore woodland and meadow, near Windermere Ferry, from imminent risk of disfigurement by extensive building and town extension.

So many nice kind Americans come through the Lake district on their tour, some of them ask after Peter Rabbit. Do you think any of them would give a guinea (our £1.1.0) to help this fund, in return for an autographed drawing?

Alas! So many of our heirlooms — our pictures, our ancient books even our old timbered houses — are crossing the Atlantic — would not American friends help to save a bit of our scenery?

It is only a half-a-mile of Lake frontage; but it is right in the middle of the most beautiful part of Windermere; and it is near my home.

Yrs sincerely

"Beatrix Potter"

More Boston families came in the summer of 1927. The pattern of the visits was always the same. After finding lodging in nearby Grasmere or Keswick, they wrote to ask if they might come to see Beatrix Potter. Mrs. J. Templeman Coolidge and her son, Henry, were friends of the Hopkinson family.

To Mrs. J. Templeman Coolidge

Sept. 15. 27

I well remember a very pleasant visit of the Hopkinson *family* — it was most amusing — they were as numerous as dear little rabbits; first two were brought in by Mrs. Hopkinson; followed by two's and three's; possibly fours; waiting round the corner. I think they had friends with them.

I shall be very glad to see your boy, and I think you had better come too, and tell me about Fawe Park. It has a familiar sound.

Are you staying with the descendants of old Mrs. Spencer Bell, or is the house let or sold? I was fond of the place in old days thirty years ago.

Wednesdays, or Tuesdays, are convenient days to be in; Thursdays — Fridays, Saturdays are the least convenient to me. Shall we say Wednesday next if fine.

I see we are both on the telephone; do not come without warning as I am so often out in connection with farming affairs. The lamb sales are on now — and we are still in the corn and hay — a few days like today will make us quite cheerful.

I am always pleased to see Americans, I don't know what I think about you as a nation (with a big N!) but the individuals who have looked for Peter Rabbit have all been delightful.

[Sept. 21. 27]

We tried to call you back! They weren't autographed. So you *must* come again, to get my precious signature —

Thanks so very much for your visit —

Sept. 30th 27

Everyone is happy and satisfied. Henry P. is pleased, and so am I — pleased to have given pleasure and drawings to such an appreciative friend of Peter Rabbit's, and such a very charming young boy.

And it is not unpleasing to receive such a substantial return this morning! I do feel very gratified to be able to help the Windermere fund.

Your interest in my surroundings will encourage me to try to work up my desultory chapters this winter. It is not easy to explain my feeling about publishing them on this side of the Atlantic. Do you know the old rhyme? "As I walked by myself, I talked by myself, and myself said to me —" I have always talked to myself (out loud, too, which is an indiscreet slightly crazy habit, *not* to be imitated by Henry P.!) and I rather shrink from submitting the talkings to be pulled about by a matter of fact English publisher, or obtruded on my notice in the London Daily.

If they were printed in an American journal and looked silly in print — and were considered foolishness, I needn't see them at all. But I must say the New Englanders who have drifted over to Hill Top Farm have been singularly sympathetic.

They appreciate the memories of old times, the simple country pleasures, — the homely beauty of the old farm house, the sublime beauty of the silent lonely hills — and — blessed folk — you are not afraid of being laughed at for sentimental.

I can quite believe that when Henry P. was a very very small white headed baby he may have been acquainted with fairies, like I was, if there are fairies in New England.

With very kind regards and thanks,

Marian Frazer Harris was born December 3, 1866. In 1914, at the age of 48, she married James deWolf Perry, a widower and former rector of Calvary Episcopal Church, Philadelphia. The Reverend Mr. Perry died in 1927 at the age of 88. Mrs. Perry died February 18, 1960.

In a letter to Jane Morse, Mrs. Perry's great niece, Nonya S. Wright, describes her great aunt, called Andy by the family, a nickname for what had originally been "Auntie."

"Andy was interested in many things; English and Italian Renaissance history, and read a great deal in these subjects. She did the most exquisite embroidery, tiny stitches, beautifully blended colors. She had a wonderful collection of semi-precious jewelry; topaz, gold, coral, and tourmaline. She loved the beautifully crafted pieces of not great value.

"Andy loved England — the pace, the gentility, the courtesy of servants and employers, the gentle countryside. She and Mrs. Heelis exchanged titles often. Mrs. Heelis introduced her to Alison Utley's work and sent her The Country Child. Then Andy told Mrs. Henry Beston, Elizabeth Coatsworth, of these books, and she read them, too. These ladies all had time to read, enjoy and write letters.

"One place Mrs. Heelis and Andy differed. Mrs. Heelis dressed in clothing made from her own sheep's wool, serviceable, but not stylish. Andy was quite a fashion plate for an elderly, somewhat rounded lady. She favored mauves, light lavenders, light blues. She always wore a hat, even at Sunday lunch, and her hats were a delight! Fruit, flowers, ribbons. All these colors showed off her lovely clear complexion and rosy cheeks and snowy white hair, piles of it.

"World War II was of great concern and sadness for her. She had many friends and quasi-cousins who lived in England, and she was terribly concerned for their safety and well being. They were all very old and she was afraid they would either be bombed out (one was) or not get enough food. Andy sent dozens of packages throughout the war — food and warm clothing.

"Andy would entertain her visitor in front of the fire with tea (I don't remember anything stronger) and converse on a multitude of topics, the government, WWII, England, books, family history.

"One thing I've never quite figured out: Andy was in so many ways out of touch with life; she never had children; she never was poor, or washed dishes, etc. She led a sheltered life. Yet she had a genuine inter-

est in Life, and worked very hard for the Episcopal Church, and was a person to whom many family members brought their problems and joys. She was genuinely concerned with us, but had a certain detachment, a level head; a sense of honor, truth, and love; also a wonderful sense of humor; and she gave us all of that generously."

To Marian Frazer Harris Perry

Nov. 30th. 27

At length I am sending your three drawings, in a registered parcel to the Bookshop, with the remainder of those spoken for by Miss Mahony. Tell it not to other people but I've taken special pains with yours because you wrote me such a nice letter! The drawings are *not* the actual originals of Peter Rabbit, which I am obliged to keep because the copper blocks wear out. The engravers borrow the original drawings to re-engrave from. I cannot paint quite so delicately as I did twenty five years ago; but I can still draw. It has been a very great satisfaction to be enabled to help the Windermere fund to the extent of £100. The money is being entered in the subscription list as from "friends in Boston," it is pleasant to know that New Englanders value the old country. The land is safely purchased, and a dry gravel path is being made near the bank of the lake; the photographers do not do justice to the view, they seem to have been taken with a lens that does not give any idea of height. The remaining debt is nothing serious now; people have been so kind in helping. With many thanks for your kind letter,

PS. I have pencilled your name on the drawings so that you may be sure to get them — it would be least trouble to send the money to Miss Mahony to be processed with the rest.

To Mrs. Charles Hopkinson

Dec. 12. 27

I mislaid your address which has been supplied anew by your friend, Mrs. Coolidge, so I am able to send Christmas greetings to you and your family. Mrs. Coolidge came over twice while she was staying at Keswick; if you happen to meet Henry P. he will be able to tell you all about us, that boy doesn't miss much! I enjoyed making their acquaintance, I am so glad you sent them.

There has been an alarming visitation since, an American publisher who took the trouble to come all the way from London in search of a book that does not exist. Alexander McKay. He produces very beautifully illustrated books, there is no question about that. It would vex my old publishers very much, and I don't like breaking with old friends. Possibly I may arrange to have published something in America for the American market only. That was an odd book you sent. I couldn't thank you because I had lost the address, and I did not know whether I liked the book or not! I respect dogs to a certain extent; but I don't think they are moral characters — leastways I have been acquainted with some rascals. I know my favourite she-colly is looking out for a chance to quietly remove my favourite tabby cat. She has already killed a semi-tame fox belonging to the shepherd; but it was no loss, a snappy little beast.

With kind regards to you all (are the girls all quite grown up?)

To Marian Frazer Harris Perry

Feb. 10. 28

I am sending you the receipt slip from the treasurer of the Windermere fund. Whenever I cross the ferry and look at the pleasant green banks I will think of the good friends across a wider stretch of water — who still believe in old England, and all she has stood for in the past. I too believe in the future. It may be a long time before the world recovers from unrest; but it has survived other upheavals. I think in this country there is decidedly a better spirit arising and a strengthening of the moderate middle-classs weight of opinion. If I have done anything — even a little — to help small children on the road to enjoy and appreciate honest simple pleasures — of the sort that leads to becoming Boy Scouts and Girl Guides — I have done a bit of good.

And I'm sure I am doing good in trying to save anything I can of our Lake country from being vulgarized; for, as true education advances, the beauty of unspoilt nature will be appreciated; and it would be a pity if the appreciation came too late. We do not wish to interfere with house building in suitable places, but we wish to preserve some portions of wild land unspoilt for the general good, and above all to avoid the erection, of perhaps *one*, unsightly building; which might destroy the beauty of a whole wide landscape. The glebe land estate is quite secured now; there is only a small debt to wipe off, and it will be thrown open to the public next summer — to the great pleasure of strangers from the Lancashire mill towns who like to picnic beside the lake; and also the extension of the park and playing fields will be a great boon to the young people in Bowness and Windermere.

I hope your sore throat has not proved serious. There has been much illness in this district and most inclement weather — gales, rain, wind, thunder, but fortunately not much snow.

Thank you again for your kind and cheering letter and believe me, yours sincerely,

[P.S.] It was kind of you to write when you were ill in bed. I hope you are well again. I have kept free from cold — but the poor sheep are suffering, never dry.

During 1928 and 1929 when Beatrix Potter was rewriting earlier stories and planning the book which became The Fairy Caravan, *she sent the first chapter (*"Tuppenny"*) to both Henry P. Coolidge and Bertha Mahony. Miss Mahony published the tale of the long haired guinea pig in the February, 1929 issue of* The Horn Book, *as* "Over the Hills and Far Away." *The copy to Henry P. was accompanied by the following note, dated June 29. 28.*

Keep this if you like, as I have another copy. I have written perhaps six pieces of this length, but there are connecting pieces that I am not satisfied with yet; and I want another fairy tale (partly invented) to round off this collection. And I do not wish to include one or two that I sent to your mother last autumn; because they belong to Cherry Tree Camp. You see — you and I take our fiction *very* seriously. The circus did *not* get as far as Cherry Tree Camp during this first part of their wanderings. They only have 4 camps (1) in the stone quarry, (2) at the Ellers Ford, (where they met with the flock of sheep) (3) Codlin Croft farm where Paddy Pig was seriously unwell, (4) after a journey through the woods, to a camp on the moor where they met the Plopfoots. They were hearing and telling stories all the way, so their progress (and mine!) is slow.

Yours sincerely,
Beatrix Potter

To Henry P. Coolidge

June 28. 28

I have taken such a long time to answer your two letters that I am almost ashamed to write! I hope the bantam hen did her duty more conscientiously than Jemima Puddleduck, and hatched her eggs successfully. Things have "hatched" badly here this spring; which is in part my excuse for not writing sooner. There are seasons when things go wrong; and they just have to be lived through; like the old inscription "Good times and bad times; all times get over." It is strange where all the rain comes from; after such a wet winter of rain and sleaty snow we *did* hope for a fine summer. All my spare time last winter I was working at the guinea pig story. I became so much interested in it — it grew longer and longer, and I kept re-writing earlier chapters. In spring, before lambing time I came in sight of a halt (or convenient pause) in the tale; but before I could finish off the series of stories up to that point — the spring work outside commenced — and various disappointments and annoyances; so that I had no time to "finish" the adventures of the caravan. Besides being out of tune and cross. The wanderings of the circus company go on and on without end or "finis"; next winter I hope to write out carefully a sufficient number of varied tales up to a point that is a convenient breaking-off-place. I could have finished it after a fashion; but I like to do my work carefully. The yellow-and-white Mrs. Tuppeny-guinea-pig is such a beauty, she looks twice the size now. The little dark one died in the cold weather, I do not think it was the cold though. It was rather badly treated by the others, and always seemed scared and thin. Nip my favourite colley has a promising puppy, a blue gray coloured dog. I have not started to break it in yet for sheep work. I was very much pleased with the way you wrote about your visit here; it was well done in every way, no word too much nor anything one could dislike; and it made me understand so well the sort of interest that the readers of the books feel when they see the real place. A very pleasant account of the old house. I wonder what you had for tea — was it pear jam I forget! This cottage is nearly smothered with roses, the rain has weighed them down over the porch and door. There was a spell of fine weather early in the spring between Easter and Whitsuntide. Tell your mother it was pleasant to see the holiday makers sitting on the grass on the new recreation ground; the walk beside Windermere lake is much appreciated. We had a jolly camping party of girl guides at the farm. They brought 5 tents.

I will send you a copy of the first chapter of "Over the Hills and Far Away"; but you must understand there is not so much exclusively guinea pig in the other later chapters after Tuppenny joins the caravan. I don't know what Miss Mahony is thinking of my delays — but I *can not* write if I am out of humour. I hope you have been well, as we have —

With kind regards to your mother and you,

[P.S.] and thanks for *The Horn Book* which I will always keep.

Yes, it has been a lovely spring of blossoms. The hawthorn bushes were like snow, and the bluebells like a bit of sky come down.

To Mrs. J. Templeman Coolidge

Nov. 20th 28

I am in disgrace not answering letters. I had a very kind one from Mr. Alexander McKay a month ago, and now he has written a short line again. I am writing both to him and Miss Mahony by this post. I have not absolutely committed myself to his offer because you said I might avail myself of the helpful advice of the Women's Union. I feel no distrust whatever of the publisher, but I want to know a little more of what is implied in a copyright agreement in the States. I was surprised when he offered a percentage agreement, as I had rather thought it likely to be a lump sum — out and out purchasing the American rights. A royalty agreement is more satisfactory for authors; provided there is no fussy doubt about small details. Do you remember the German tale of Kluge Else? and her train of imaginary accidents that set her weeping in the cellar while the beer jug ran over full ?! I am rather given that way. I want Miss Mahony to tell me whether Mr. McKay takes all the risks, including possible law suits in America. Sometimes I feel I don't want to print the stories at all, just keep them for the private edification of Henry P. and me. I guess we will keep some of them private and unprinted; they are more and more peculiar; I wonder what makes me spin such funny spider webs.

It is raining again here, storms and floods day after day. One of the shepherds had a narrow escape; they were driving a flock of sheep over a narrow stone bridge and the last 10 jumped in and the man after them, luckily he was swept against the bank; several sheep were drowned.

Henry P. will be grieved to hear that I have had to dismantle the dear old house where Tom Kitten lived — one incident in a season of worries — but I hope at the end of three years I may be able to put my pretty things back; some are squeezed in here, and others lent out amongst friends in the village. I have left the big dresser; and also said firmly that the present occupiers must put up with the kitchen fireplace; they do not appreciate either Tom Kitten or Samuel Whiskers. I was maliciously pleased to hear that Sam had been upstairs and made himself a nuisance.

They are quite nice young people; but I regard them as cuckoos. I never thought I would be giving up the old house to anybody.

The guinea pig is flourishing, such a big fat pig. They were both females and had no families. I hope Henry P. and you are very well and with kind regards remain

[P.S.] A curiously developed boy; he said something in his last letter to me about the beauty of Spring and straightway I wrote down my memory of spring in Birds' Place where we children used to look for the little sleepy dor-mice in their nests — that is the sort of sentimental chapter that I am disinclined to print. I will send it to Henry P. some day.

Dec. 10. 28

Tuppenny and I wish you a Merry Christmas and Happy New Year. We are well, but we are very cold. It has been bitterly cold all day, and now there is sleet blowing from the low east, which is our dreaded direction for heavy snow and drifts. — The poor King! the weather has not given him much chance; cold winds and fogs can do harm even in a palace. I wonder if you will like this piece describing Spring ["Springtime in Birds' Place", Chapter VII in *The Fairy Caravan*]; I like writing about things I remember long ago, and Birds' Place was so lovely if I could do justice to the recollection. If I were putting it into the story I would shorten it; there is too much description for the amount of interest. I have written some amusing chapters about Paddy Pig's adventures; he lost the caravan by wandering away into a wood, and by the time Pony Billy found him — he was ill through unwisely eating toadstool tartlets. Mind you don't eat too many mince pies (if you have those indigestible delicacies in U.S.A.)

With all good wishes,

[P.S.] Also herewith a calendar, which has fallen flat! People like it, but the shopkeepers did not, so there are not many on sale.

To Marian Frazer Harris Perry

Dec. 17. 28

I am so sorry I never sent you those further drawings that you asked about — the Spring out-door work came and I had to stop, though there was still a little wanted for the fund. Now it is all paid for, and it was a great satisfaction to me to have been able to help the fund through the kindness of my friends in America. I wish the treasurer had sent me some spare balance sheets; there was only one sent to me, so I can only repeat the detail in writing — "Per Mrs. W. Heelis' Friends in Boston USA £42.3.0, Mrs. T. Coolidge Boston £25, Friends in Boston £10.10.0, Friend in Philadelphia £3.3.0, Friends in Boston £15.18.0 Friends in Boston £7.7.0 = £104.1.0." It was a great help, as the last few hundreds were difficult to collect.

A dry, but unobtrusive, foot-path has been made, along the meadow and through the wood, beside the lake; it has given very great pleasure both to the residents of the town (or large village!) and to visitors from a distance. And what especially pleases me — a large space quite out of sight behind the wood has been set apart as a parking place for cars — both private cars and these horrible motor charabancs that have done so much to spoil the Lake district. One cannot grudge the inhabitants of manufacturing towns an outing and it may do them good. (those that come to see the scenery!) but it is much pleasanter to have some central place for the "charis". There are all sorts; many of them are thoroughly appreciative; other trips bring a barrel of beer with them! It is quiet enough for 9 months of the year; at present we have a fine sunny day and snow on the ground. Perhaps another time I shall be begging again. There is a strong desire amongst thoughtful people to preserve what is possible before it is too late.

I am sending you a little almanac, most of the pictures were done years ago; it was a way of using up odds and ends.

With all good wishes for the New Year for yours sincerely,

"Beatrix Potter"

Alexander McKay was the president of David McKay Co. of Philadel-phia.

To Alexander McKay

Jan. 18th 29

Thank you for your cablegram. I herewith return the signed agree-ment with Clause 10 deleted. Our nephew has witnessed my signature. I will send the corrected mss of the story as quickly as possible. (the more so, as there is beginning to be a bit of influenza) The story is longer than *The Farm Twins* [Lucy Fitch Perkins]: but that very charm-ing book could have held more matter in it; so I do not suppose you will object — besides I could always cut bits out.

I will assume that the coloured illustrations are to be of a shape that would go comfortably on a *Farm Twin* shape of page. Size is immaterial. I have usually worked for ⅓ reduction; but I do like to work to a well proportioned margin.

I can cash the cheque now. The book is workable now; but I want to round it off nicely.

I remain with thanks,

To Marian Frazer Harris Perry

Feb. 17. 29

I am most interested! put off the visit as late into April as you can, for the wild daffies do not like the winds of *March* in the north. Spring is the most beautiful time of year. The large hotels do not open till Easter; there are many — middle sized — ones that are comfortable, and very quiet in Spring; they have got the district a bad name for extortionate charges though! With the one drawback of an 8 mile drive from station, I should advise you to go to the Moss Grove at Grasmere; it is far the best centre, as you can do day-tours over the whole district — (with the exception of Wastwater and Buttermere.) I have never seen Wastwater myself. A great many Americans stay there, and it is comfortable, and in a pretty sheltered village. Windermere and Keswick are large dull towns, away from the water.

The railways have never been allowed to cross the middle of the district; so you have to leave the train at Windermere, or Keswick. The latter is on the north edge; better to come to Windermere station when arriving. There is the station hotel, "Windermere Hotel," large plain comfortable with a dull outlook; or there is Lowood hotel 2 miles north; edge of Windermere Lake, very comfortable; a mile further on there is a small hotel, Wateredge Hotel, Ambleside, a small hotel — then 8 miles from station there is the *Moss Grove, Grasmere*. There is also the Old England Hotel, Bowness on Windermere, beside the Lake. Keswick I consider an awfully dull cold town — if I were staying there I would rather go to the Derwentwater Hotel, Portinscale or to the Lodore Hotel, Borrowdale; but they are not good centres for doing anything except round Derwentwater.

I wish I could have invited you to stay here — there's no use mincing matters! I have only a daily servant and how can one invite strangers to sleep in cold weather when one has to get fires and breakfast oneself! During the day I have a good servant, and I shall be delighted to see you and show you my drawings — it is a pleasure to look forward to. Life has been trying lately; burst and frozen waterpipes, influenza, and intense frost.

There are many old fashioned farm lodgings, delightful for families on summer vacation, but I should hesitate to recommend them for early spring. From either Windermere, Ambleside or Grasmere you can take a pretty circular drive taking in Coniston, and passing through Hawkshead and Sawrey and returning over Windermere ferry which carries cars across.

There is no difficulty in getting on from the station anywhere; public buses and taxis meet trains, as well as the hotel private bus. Remember that rooms have to be booked well in advance for *Easter* week; after that there is no crowd until the summer holidays commence.

[P.S.] You must *telephone* to me, because I am often on the fell with the shepherds. I have a big flock of sheep.

To Alexander McKay

Feb. 28. 29

Enclosed please find sample drawings. You will see a bit of paper tacked across the coloured one; it seems too tall, for *The Farm Twin* shape — and a more square picture is better of the caravan subject?

I just happened to have this old design in the outline; it belonged to Miss Louisa Pussycat's Mouse Seminary.

I am afraid that book is like the curate's egg when he breakfasted with the bishop — "parts of it are excellent!" Some of it is awful; and this colour drawing is *smudgy* — will it process? My eyes have lost the faculty of seeing clean colours.

I did *not* like the way F.W. & Co. blocked pen and inks into the text of the *Patty Pan*; don't you think black and whites look better top or bottom? I can do the pen and inks easily. I will do plenty and you can use what you select. They should be reduced a lot *smaller*.

I found a stray page after posting that stuff, so I am sending it for fear there is one missing, page 182 or 3. The weather has been terrible; we picked up a little dead roe deer, hence these sketches.

March 28. 29

Thank you very much for your cheque for £100 and letter enclosing sample page. It is clear good type — a few errata — 'cats' should be 'rats'.

I have found no assistant yet. I wrote to an art school which did not even reply, and lost time. I think you said 8 coloured; I have 3 more on hand, and another designed. Should you get 2 or 3 designed in America? *How long have I?*

F. Warne & Co. are very jealous of my passing over the NY branch, and wrote me rather an unpleasant letter. It was *not* personal to you, as I had not named David McKay & Co, only told them I was "intending" etc. They sort of apologized afterwards; but endeavored to frighten me about 'pirates'. There are black sheep on both sides of the Atlantic; I might have retaliated about people in glass houses. It is evident that the English copyright must be secured by me. I told you — in our back yard — that I am shy about publishing that stuff in London. My real wish and present intention is to have 100 copies semi-privately printed by the Ambleside printer — a small local publisher — just a paper-backed thing. A few would have to be sold over the counter, and there are certain formalities about depositing copies for registration purposes. I should have to know the exact date when you propose to publish in U.S.A. and I wonder whether you would do me the favour to let me have a few sets of the colour plates? Not necessarily 100, but enough to register the copyright.

I cannot imagine that it would be to the interest of a decent American publisher to do me an injury — apart from being a gentleman! —

But their unpleasant letter may be correct in saying that my publisher in U.S.A. could not prevent others doing wrong.

One design I think I will get engraved in England; it is rather peculiar and may be too small in detail — especially the fairies. Would you mind cabling *me size in inches of colour illustration plates*; and approximate date for *me finishing*? I can do these — but I am slow and this inquiry for help loses time. I doubt they are too grand to work to order, these artists.

It looked rather well in *The Horn Book*. She should not print too much, because of this copyright bother.

I never really wanted to print at all; but the money has been useful.

To Marian Frazer Harris Perry

April 25. 29

What a charming little bunny you have sent me! He is just the image of the original Benjamin when I brought him home (surreptitiously — if that's the way to spell it) — from a London bird shop in a paper bag. His existence was not observed by the nursery authorities for a week. Little young rabbits, and foxes have snub noses at first. We have got two live fox cubs about 3 weeks old, pretty but very cross. One of the colleys killed their mother; she had been taking lambs.

I enjoyed the afternoon too. It's very pleasant to meet appreciative Americans, and to feel that you value old associations and will take care of our treasures, that have to cross the seas. When Americans are willing to give £50,000 for a single Romney portrait, it is better that it should go. I think there are very few left in this district; there is a fine portrait of a man with powdered hair, hanging in the dilapidated mansion on that island that you see from Windermere ferry. And I remember that there used to be perhaps half a dozen at an old hall in the Graythwaite woods, but they were sold years ago. Romney was born at the southern end of the Lake district, and came home to die. One always looks out at farm sales where there is "portion of household goods;" not that there are many bargains now; but old canvases sometimes get repainted over. One cannot remember everything one might tell people, not in a hurry. I saw you took notice of a fine carved chest in our dining room; it came out of "Thimble Hall." I was sorry to move it; but the new tenant had children; and poor old Mrs. Hunt who was leaving, begged me to take it way and take great care of it — poor old body; it had been in her mother's family, probably for hundreds of years, she said it would be sold when she died, and she "might as well have the money," but she would not sell it to a stranger. There is a fine dated piece in another cottage belonging to me.

Yes, Hawkshead is like a fairy tale, especially in winter moonlight and snow. The pronounciation of names is often a clue to their meaning; the natives call it 'Harksead' and 'Ammelsead' — Ambleside — which probably are Norse names, Haco seat, Hammel's seat; 'Seater' is I believe still a Norwegian name for a farm steading.

The queerest name in the district is Seatnabannig.

I hope you will not hesitate to come and see me again — if I cannot be in — I cannot, and will say so! And you can send any other very nice Americans. I forgot to ask whether you happened to know the Fields of Milton, Mass.? They have been here two or three times, and sent other carefully selected visitors. Indeed I have never had any of the loud inquisitive type that one reads about. I shall look forward to reading the book. Miss Gill, Mrs. Field's sister, sent me one I liked, *Faith Gartney's Girlhood*, [Mrs. A.D.T. Whitney]. It is very cold here still, snow showers. I am glad you liked our Nurse. The Queen's nurses are splendid women, gifted and chosen for character, and Nurse Edwards is one of the best type. A war widow who instead of living idly on her little pension, gives her strength gladly to good work, and uses her money to apprentice a fine big son to engineering. She has to work till he goes to sea.

To Alexander McKay

Sunday June 30th [29]

I was relieved to get the dummy book on Friday evening — a week after your letter. It was impossible to complete without more particulars, as some of the line blocks already are wrong size, but luckily they don't cost much (perhaps 2 or 3).

Thank you also for sight of color blocks at last — mine are terribly yellow, it must be some peculiarity of aged eyes! Or else — I must stop using aureole yellow — possibly the preparation of that paint has changed in the last 70 years; it used to be very expensive and it has become cheaper, and has some harsh quality.

24

I think the legends should be brief. I will write you again about dummy — possibly cable about one point I do not quite understand. In haste to catch Sunday post.

[P.S.] I will write a forward — a few lines — strictly on approval. If *you* are writing it — don't put in *please,* anything of the nature of a puff or flourish — let the book stand on its own merits — it ain't so bad after all. Please note whether the legends want type correcting. There is a comical mistake in chapter headings. *Pond* instead of Pound.

After a struggle with wording for the preface, Beatrix Potter chose:

"As I walk'd by myself,
 And talked to myself,
    Myself said unto me —
Through many changing seasons these tales have walked and talked with me. They were not meant for printing; I have left them in the homely idiom of our old north country speech. I send them on the insistence of friends beyond the sea."

July 28. 29

I am ashamed to have over-looked some corrections when going over the first proofs. I have marked them also on the dummy book which I am posting today 29th.

Mr. Hunter has all the designs. I suggested that he should send the last straight to you; I have indicated the subject in pencil on the dummy. I almost wish I had them to do again! I like the little tail pieces; but several of the full pages should have been stronger. They don't make much show for a lot of work. Unfortunately I *did* some on softer paper — the blacksmith's terrier, the *smithy,* Miss Pussycat's shop have not photographed well, but it is not the fault of the engraver. (Except I wish he had sent installments, instead of waiting for 30 at once!)

I am very sorry to have been slow, but indeed I have worked at them.

Dedication — I suggest "to Henry P." leaving out Coolidge. I don't know whether my pleasing visitors were related to your late president; but I think the surname complicates unnecessarily.

Preface. When a sentence gets into my head I cannot get it out. I quite thought "that New World which is the old" was a quotation; but

25

it ain't where I expected to find it; and I begin to doubt whether it is sense! What I mean, and have felt strongly, in the case of New England visitors is that they have more understanding and appreciation of old English traditions than the bulk of English people have. Doubtless you have all sorts too. The pleasant quiet-loving type come to the Lakes; they seem to me to have lived and stayed behind in those old fashioned times and places, which this 'old' world is rapidly obliterating.

I doubt meddling with the color proofs. If the yellow block is *weakened* — it will upset the greens; probably upset the whole printing. They look more yellow by comparison with the other artist's pictures than they will do in the bound book when they are scattered. Let them go as they are.

English Copyrighting. I think of getting the first "folder" — (don't know right word) = up to page 18 — getting it printed over here with a new (English) title page; preface and dedication omitted. I will get a few line blocks from Mr. Hunter. Probably redraw Keswick market place.

What words do I use on title page "Copyright in United States of David McKay and Co"?

Now would you very kindly sell me 100 sets *unbound*? then I can have as many of them as I want bound with the English first 'folder' in front. For copyrighting and private circulation.

If the book makes a hit, I foresee that it will have to be reprinted in this country. But I don't want it at all; it is too personal. Let me know earliest date when *I* may copyright. Cool request after keeping you waiting so long!

July 30. 29

These are just too late for the dummy, and it is rather a risk of confusion for me to guess at them now. I have wired to him to dispatch blocks.

I am still puzzled about the foreword
'friends in that New World which still is Old.'
    'that New World which still yet remembers the Old'.
'that New World which remembers the Old.'

If you don't think the one posted yesterday is sense — perhaps 'remembers the Old' is best. 'Appreciated' is not a pleasing word; and I regret to say — "loves" — would be inappropriate; as near relations frequently bicker.

26

To Alexander McKay

Aug. 23. 29

I shall be pleased to sign the sheets as you suggest, as soon as they arrive here; it is a good idea — may I take advantage of it for two friends in the States? Probably you would without my asking send to Henry P. Coolidge, 106 Beacon Street, Boston — Miss Anne Carroll Moore, 476 Fifth Avenue, NY, and Miss Bertha Mahony. A very pleasant girl who came here with Miss Moore was Miss Mary Haugh Fordham Branch of the N.York Public Library, but I'm not sure if she is still there, having lost touch. She told me the American children were short of Christmas stories, she might like "Demerara Sugar" [Chapter XIV in *The Fairy Caravan*]. Other 2 librarians who drifted here were Mary Gould Davis and Mabel Williams 476 Fifth Avenue NY City (?) seems as though same address as Miss Moore? I'm not sure whether Clifton Adams, Nat. Geog. Society Washington deserves one! He rushed through the district with a most charming baby; but he didn't say he would put my *address* in the geographical magazine — resulting in 2 parties of Americans on one Sunday.

My special friends for copies are *Miss Gill 378 Canton Avenue Milton Mass.* and *Mrs. J.S. Steel 1342 St Lawrence Avenue Bronx NY.*

I have got a piece set up by the Ambleside printer, and made inquiry about registering at Stationers Hall. It seems to be unnecessary according to the new British Copyright Act — but Mr. Heelis thinks it is very desirable to register, as it is an absolute proof of date, in case any body tried to pirate it by alleging that they had registered first.

Another American family and very pleasant people; but bless Mr. Clifton Adams. The season will soon be over.

[P.S.] Will the 100 copies be a big *slow* parcel? It takes 3 copies to register — for Stationers Hall, Br. Museum, and Bodleian. I am sorry to seem fussy or suspicious; it was F.W. & Co. that put it into my head there might be risk in delays.

Sept. 13. 29

Thank you for your letters; by one received this morning I am much interested to hear the book is in the press. It would not be wise for me to sell the coloured drawings, in case an English edition were required at some future time; it makes my eyes so sore trying to paint colours

27

I would not like to have to do a set of new ones for it.

I am very glad to hear that the orders for the book have pleased you. We have taken a number of first prizes this summer with the sheep — at all the local shows; and I think we could have gone to the "Royal" as we beat Willie Wilson with lambs yesterday at Ennerdale, and he has held the field as many seasons as Herdwick king. It is lovely weather and our hay and bit of harvest is in, so we are enjoying the 'shows' with a clean conscience — no *circus* — but dogs' racing, horses jumping, and prizes for cattle, sheep and foxhounds which you would think a funny mix up — worthy of the Caravan!

May I trouble you with just one more address? Mrs. James de W. Perry, School House Lane, Germantown, Philadelphia. She has called here at times when she has been at the Lakes, and gave me some American books — a pleasant acquaintance, and seems bookish! With kind regards and thanks for your letters.

Oct. 11th 29

The book parcels arrived this morning Oct. 10th; following your letter. I think it is beautifully printed. I like type, paper and all. And Mr. Heelis and I are very much obliged to you for leaving out those overdressed soft boys. I didn't like to say so, but the bride was not good either. I wish I had had courage to try, for I would have done no worse, and they were pretty sketches.

There might have been more line blocks; there are big slabs of print not illustrated — but then, I never would have finished it if I had not been rushed, and the rushed drawings are the best. My favourites are Tamsine staring at the fire (a 7th family arrived next day!) and Dolly trotting over the shadows.

I am taking copies to be bound. You will *let me know when I may register!* Thank you for turning out such a handsome book, and I hope it will give satisfaction to both of us — and I may add — to my most exacting critics — my own shepherds and the blacksmith. I do not care tuppence about anybody else's opinion.

There are 3 mistakes: p. 103 "spinning" and same page Whisht — (and you a Scotchman?!) and on page 99 I should have copied it "to meet my love in the gloaming. She left her etc."

Take out a few feeble pages — the book is none so bad.

Oct. 20. 29

I sent off the signed sheets on same day received Oct 16th. I would like one copy to keep — at least Mr. Heelis would much like to have one — and I intend sending you one copy of English binding, with an extra line block — and perhaps it might be of interest to pencil the localities on the margins. Could I buy 12 copies of the unsigned American edition?

It's a nice thing to be smuggling it into this country myself! but I've my doubts whether my extremely limited edition will go round all the shepherds and the coachmen; and I would rather give several American copies than make my own edition numerous by more printing than the hundred. Part of the 100 I intend to hoard, taking experience by the disappearance of the first editions of *Peter*.

To Henry P.

Oct. 27th 29

I hope by this time you have received your copy of Our Book! I have gotten my English copies bound in gray paper backs; it looks well. I am already in trouble — I cannot give the correct name and ownership of the horse waiting at the smithy. It is obviously not really "Maggret", because she was a pony, belonging to Joe Taylor, and Maggret and his master have been dead for many years. If it is a white horse it would be Ambrose Martindale's. But to the best of my recollection the animal was brown, when I sketched the smithy — so it's either John Kirkbride's or William Pottlethwaite's. William is quite enough in the book being owner of Fan, and Dick, Duke, Sally; but he wishes to claim that horse. Sally was white in old age; a grand wagon mare but a kicker. In fact it was always suspected 'Sally' had 'done something' in her youth; William bought her so cheap it was suspicious. I did not intend to draw a white horse. I left it light to try and look as if its hind quarters were in the sun.

I hope you and your mother are very well. This year has been hard work, (apart from drawings). I shall be glad of a quiet winter when the last fairs are over. We are selling 300 sheep at Ambleside on Tuesday; and the same day my stirks go to a Scotch sale at Newcastleton. Prices have been good up to now, and we had a grand hay time and harvest. The weather has been wild and rough. Today is glorious, after a white

29

hoar frost. The autumn colours are still splendid. After dinner Mr. Heelis and I are going to Coniston. There is a lovely stretch of mountain and valley to sell there and the National Trust are trying to buy it. Did you drive that when you came here I wonder — past Tilberthwaite and Yewdale. I am very interested because my great grandfather had land there and I always longed to buy it back and give it to the Trust in rememberance. I was very much attached to my grandmother Jessy Crompton and said to be very like her, "only not so good looking!!" according to old folks. Perhaps I will be able to help out of this book — it would be like a fairy tale, would it not? I would be glad to hear from you and your mother how it is received. Mr. McKay seems quite satisfied with the advanced sales.

I have 52 copies bound here with the English title page and copyright notice.

I remain with kind regards to you and your mother,

[P.S.] Tuppenny is flourishing — Charles is having a severe moult; but I hope to nurse him through. He is very old, but still fighting. I had to hold a young cockerell this morning and let Charles give it a good kicking. He will get killed someday I am afraid.

To Alexander McKay

Oct. 31. 29

I am much gratified to hear that the book is making such a good start, and what a charming review you have sent me! They are usually stupid, but Miss [Alice M.] Jordan [Supervisor of Work with Children, Boston Public Library] has just understood and picked out the characteristics that I like myself — not merely the funny bits.

I will send back one of your half-bound copies with some corrections, and some other outline designs. There are two I do not like — the caravan unharnessed by the water, which does not illustrate that page. And another with the little dog swimming in front is poor. Should have done them today, but was obliged to meet someone about moss drains. We were much upset to hear of a ghastly accident to the hounds; our Brilly and 8 others tried to jump some spiked railings, the fox having squeezed through; but the hounds got hung up. Brill has been stitched, the spikes only went through his legs; but two were horribly injured.

As for me — I got into one drain up to my knees in water, and then proceeded to wrench an ankle in another — so perhaps I may do some drawing with my foot up tomorrow!

It is indeed a good start when you had only published a week.

I have copyrighted the English edition, and deposited a copy at the British Museum. Miss Moore's approval will be a help. I am so glad. It has been received with acclamation by the men — only they are all claiming bits, and disputing whose who.

[P.S.] I posted you a copy of the English edition, two days ago.

To Mrs. J. Templeman Coolidge

Dec. 9. 29

It has been a great pleasure to receive such kind *understanding* letters from you and others in America. And it is appreciation that is worth having. I feel that you take me seriously! The Peter Rabbit books have been an immense success and popularity; but I have always been irritated that *The Tailor of Gloucester* was the least popular and successful — irritated a little because it was my own favorite, but still more so because I know that it was less generally cared for *because* it was less *comic*. I think the vogue of children's books in this country is far too much governed by the shop keepers; and mine have always been toy books — not literature. Certainly my English publishers consider the pictures first; and the words a poor second. The shop keepers like something comic and showy; I used often to buy stray copies in London, and encourage perplexed shop keepers to say how strange it was how they were asked for! There is nothing like *The Horn Book* or like Miss Moore's organization of storytellers to direct the choice of children's reading in this country, and it does seem such a pity that children should be encouraged to like things grotesquely ugly.

I am sure the average Londoner would care nothing about Herdwick sheep! That chapter made my old shepherd cry with pleasure; that is appreciation worth having. I don't feel at all as if I want to reprint it in this country. I had about 80 copies bound with an English title page.

Now I am very glad that you and Henry P. and Mr McKay — amongst you — extracted the book! It would have been rather a pity if I had shuffled off this mortal coil with most of those chapters inside my head. And it surprises myself that some of the late written chapters are as good as any, for instance the sheep anecdotes, and the woods by moonlight. It seems that I can still write and invent. I think that I had better write down some more — not necessarily for publication, but to preserve them. It is most kind of Miss Mahony to take trouble again about selling drawings etc., in a good cause. I sent her a parcel at once in case they might arrive in time for Christmas sales, but I doubt it. There were some misprints in the *Caravan*; I sent a list of 'errata' to Mr. McKay for the second edition. Miss Mary Gould Davis of the NY public library seems to say the book is going to be a permanent favorite. Very funny, I could not judge it in the least. Sometimes I thought parts of it must be real fine. Other times I thought it was dreadful rubbish. I like the pig the least. He was rather an after thought; his losing himself and [his] illness was used to string the chapters together. I hope Henry P. has a good long vacation to stretch his mind and his legs at Christmas time! Here we have shocking weather; but the stock is under cover, except the sheep and they can get down to the woods. The fells are very white and the gates are open. We are having a party for the folk dancers on Monday night. Now with love and best wishes for Christmas and New Year, believe me,

To Alexander McKay

Dec. 17th 29

Thank you for yours of Dec. 6th, we are always here, and will gladly put you up, if you can spare a longer call than the first one — about 25 minutes! At all counts — get out of the train at Windermere Station — (unless you are in an express that does not stop at Oxenholme Junction).

I am glad to hear that the *Caravan* has done so well.

I will think things over. Only you must remember that I am *not* a prolific scribbler. I wrote myself out on the rabbit series. We must talk over the future of the *Caravan* and consider where its wheels can travel without upsetting — not "most haste worst speed." My present inclination is to appease the English public and publishers with an inferior book next season; and make a sequel to the *Caravan* the year following, if spared; which would give time for more adequate illustrations.

If I made another *Caravan* for autumn 1931, it would be rushed; and there would be a blank in 32. You will let us know — approximately — lest I should be on the hill tops or stuck in a bog, when you arrive.

With all good wishes from Mr. Heelis and myself for Christmas and New Year,

To Henry P.

Jan. 1. 1930

I am glad to hear that the dedication has given you pleasure; and you show discriminating appreciation (as Louisa Pussycat might say) in your choice of favorite pictures. I was perplexed what to do with the hair brushing picture till I had a sudden inspiration about pig tails. But do you notice it should have been Xarifa who *"brushed* behind"? And on p 183 Jenny Ferret should have worn spectacles.

The coloured plate of the blue bell wood is bound into a wrong chapter; Pony Billy is without the caravan; I intended it for the chapter where he goes back alone to look for Paddy Pig, and hears a faint tingle ringle of laughing from thousands of blue bells in the wood.

Now for the old words — *sneck* is the sort of door latch that lifts open by pressing a flat thumb piece ⊣⊢ ⊣⊢ . All our cats from generation to generation learn the trick; Tamsine jumps up and opens the door into the kitchen. She tries the house door if she is left loose at nights; it is rather weird and troublesome, but I usually shut her in the granary. I had a dog, old Fleet, who "went one better." She used to open a similar latch in the iron garden gate, and what's more she (standing on her hind legs) holding the latch used to step backwards pulling the gate open towards herself. I could never teach her to close it; I have heard of a fox-terrier which would shut the door obediently. *Midden stead*, a 'stead' or place where farm-yard manure is heaped. *Clothes swill.* Swills are flatish baskets ⬗ woven out of interlaced thin broad parings of oak wood. *Uveco* a cattle food, yellow flakey rolled indian corn, from which the oil has been extracted. It is a waste product and comparatively cheap. *Lish*, active, supple, energetic; an expressive adjective; an old man who has preserved his youth and worn well is said to be "as lish as a lad." *Coppy* stools, three legged stools such as used for milking. *"Shippon"* a stable-like building containing stalls — or 'boosts' — for tying up cattle. *Ring widdie* the double ring,

33

with a swivel between the rings ⊃⊂ which slides loosely up and down on the rett-stake ⬚ to which the cow is haltered. It would be possible for a ring ⬚ widdie to "clink" on the stone floor of the bruist (rough bed or shelter); but "clink" is *not* the right word for a very pleasing sound. When anyone opens the shippon door, there is a sort of scraping noise of the rings, usually followed by a gentle 'moo', if it is feeding time. There are new fangled ways of tying up cows, but I prefer the ring widdies. 'Keshes', wild parsnips, tall coarse plants — does not Shakespeare speak of "rude kecksies-burrs"; burrs doubtless were burr docks = teazles. Wither [shins or] "widdershins", contrary way — there is an old verse "The stars shall gae wither shins Ere I will leave thee". *Demerara* sugar — a soft sugar not much refined. I suppose in old times it came from Demerara. What would you guess if I had put the puzzling numerals of the old sheep counting,

"Yan tyan tethera methera pimp (is it 'pimp' or dick) 'bumfit' is 15.
     1   2   3   4   5

Very interesting words they are, for they are supposed to be one of the few remains of the old Celtic language. Sheep have been kept in this district from early times. A fragment of woolen cloth was found in a "barrow" or ancient burial mound with a funeral urn, and bronze implements. I guess the stone men who set up 'Long Meg' and the stone circles had sheep. Now I wish you and your Mother a very Happy Year. Tuppenny is still flourishing; and we are all pleased with the success of the book —

To Alexander McKay

Feb. 24. 30

Thank you for your letter with the agreements, and also for the book by same post. It is a beautiful book. There are other verses as good as "Trees" — almost. The last verse of "Folly"; and "The Fourth Shepherd". And it is a pleasure to read the sonnet on "Waverley". I cannot understand what satisfaction people derive from modern novels. There is a highly successful modern novelist came to reside near Hawkshead; I was told I must read his books; but a dozen pages, beginning and end, were more than enough to leave an unpleasant memory. I have gone back to Scott's novels with never failing pleasure. Mr. Kilmer sometimes echoes Matthew Arnold; but M.A. wrote so very little poetry, it is no disadvantage to J.K.'s readers; rather a pleasure to be reminded of a vanished hand.

I have at last got the typewritten *Pig*. I think I shall spread the last two or three chapters a little; they are abrupt.

I hope you received the list of corrections. Probably the *Caravan* is like *The Tailor of Gloucester* — not everybody's book — but much favoured by a few. *Pig Robinson* is plainer; and provided I can do good illustrations it should be a presentable work.

We congratulate you on having caught the Irish Mail! Local trains can be so awfully slow that you might have registered a vow *never* to call upon us again! Which we would regret. With kind regards from my husband and myself,

Miss Helen Dean Fish was the editor of children's books for J. B. Lippincott Company.

To Helen Dean Fish

Apr. 30. 30

Most welcome! I always tell nice Americans to send other nice Americans along. Perhaps 'understanding Americans' would be a better adjective than 'nice'. You come because you understand the books, and love the same old tales that I do — not from any impertinent curiosity. I did not answer (your) letter right away because I was laid up with bronchitis, but I am about again, and making up arrears of work. It will be a lovely time to see the Lake district. If the bluebells are over, the foxgloves will be in flower — and I will show you the real woods and lanes. What a pity Miss Davis is not coming too.

You and your friend will be near Windermere ferry, and there is a motor bus up the hill every hour — which the fairies do not like; but undeniably it is convenient for mortals. *You must be sure to telephone.* I have a few fixed engagements, but I am often out of reach, amongst the sheep, if I am not warned of callers.

[P.S.] Come up early afternoon and stay tea — and if we continue to be friendly, we will take another bus on to Hawkshead and call on the Miss Pussycats and the old Grammar School.

To Alexander McKay

June 21. 30

Are you going to use the same type as in the *Caravan*? I presume so. But I wish I could see yours, *set up*; because of ends to chapters. If F.W. & Co. use another size of type — there may be more — or less space in the British edition. In the meantime I have no print at all; and I dislike typewritten matter. Probably it is my fault for having said I would extend the last chapter; but I am so much "at sea" on land; upon the subject of boats and desert islands, that I find it prudent to concentrate upon Robinson's Devonshire adventures; and I am sure everyone will be tired of him before the last chapter.

Minor corrections and alterations I could make on the galley — if I had it. I am putting in a sentence after passing Styford mill to bring in the big dog called Gypsy who barks, but the big dog smiled and wagged his tail at Robinson. And please put your children's names on the dedication page if it would please them.

I have done a great many illustrations, and I think they are fairly good but I had a disastrously slow start, getting bronchitis. I was not really bad but it left me so dull and lazy for a long time and ever since I have been desperately busy, indoors and out.

F.W. & Co. have a good drawing (2 copies plain and coloured) of Robinson, for the cover. They submitted an ugly design — doubtless they will send you the *Pig*, and you will make your own framework, for U.S.A. It seems as though they want all my blocks before setting up any copy; I must write to them also, I have no idea how many pages.

I remain with kind regards,

July 8. 30

I cabled to you that I would send extra (drawings) and that F.W. & Co. do not want ends, by which I mean heads and tails of chapters. They have returned the typewritten stuff yet again; with a selection of my illustrations placed, and they say they only require 2 more. This scheme is going to leave out a number of illustrations which I consider the best; but I hope you may care to include them in the U.S.A. edition, and let me have a few copies for my own private satisfaction.

Mr. Heelis wants me to argue the point; but I'm blessed if I'm going to! F.W. & Co. have always been inclined to save expenses at the expense of the appearance of the book. I remember you said you would like "ends" with sea landscape, — you were looking at one of my old sketches — and I relied upon them to give local colour.

My idea is that the story is short compared with the *Caravan*, but can be largely padded out by full page pictures, after the example of *The Farm Twins*. They are going to use 6 full page colour, 1 inset colour for wrapper, 22 full page line.

Counting ends, I have about 2 dozen more, some finished, others part done — What a waste?!

July 15. 30

I send with this 10 full pages and 16 heads and tails of chapters none of which appear in the English edition except 4 marine subjects which I have redrawn more compactly for inside the book-covers, by suggestion of Mr. Stephens.

It is difficult to judge one's own work, but I think myself that some of the chapter ends are the best drawings of any. I hope you may care to include them. There is one proof that they don't want, as the subject is illustrated by another drawing. They have 22, full page pen and ink.

It is a good book to illustrate. I should quite enjoy doing a few more! If you want any to fill up — just tell me the number of the (type-written) pages and I have kept the duplicates.

I got this typed from the altered copy; F.W. & Co. will be setting up letter press like enclosed.

About the cheque — would you please keep it back just a bit — I shall be re-investing something presently, and I will ask for it later on.

I am thinking it might then go direct to Messrs. WH Heelis & Son who invests clients' money for them.

I wonder how you make hay in hot weather in America! There was a run on the *barrel* last Saturday — we had a grand day, with lots of helpers; refreshments were gobbled up.

With kind regards from us both I remain,

[P.S.] I am not very particular about illustrations coming exactly opposite words — you may find them rather in bunches.

Betty Harris was the niece of Mrs. James de Wolf Perry. She and her aunt visited Beatrix Potter in August, 1930.

To Betty Harris

Sept. 4. 30

I am extremely amused with the snap shot — had there been a third victim — the (tea) caldron is there alright! Your long-suffering aunty looks rather like an elderly sheep. But I am more like a good tempered witch than a cow. We had speeches at lunch, at the Hawkshead Agricultural Show, and an old jolly farmer — replying to a 'toast' — likened me — the president — to the first prize cow! He said she was a lady-like animal; and one of us had neat legs, and walked well; but I think that was the cow not me, being slightly lame.

We had our pretty little Baa's at Ennerdale Show last week, and yesterday at Keswick; on perfect autumn days — still, sunshiny mists. The Buttermere fells were in golden haze. We did not try the 'passes'; we took the road to Cockermouth.

The sheep have been very successful in the female classes; 16 first prizes and several shows yet to come. Including Loweswater.

It is raining again this afternoon, but the fine hot week has been most acceptable for finishing hay and harvest.

I don't know whether you are still in England, but will send this on the chance. Hoping to see you and Mrs. Perry again some day,

To Alexander McKay

Sept. 9. 30

I return these by first post. You may possibly have received suggestions for *legends* already. They do not suggest anything specially bright. I agree with all your corrections, except possibly "fatter er"! Of course there is no such word; but it is expressive! If you don't like it, say "fatter and fatter and more fat." It requires 3 repeats to make a balanced ending.

I like the appearance of the book *extremely* — the head and tail pieces give it much more character than the English edition; and it is grand print.

It *might* make a hit. It is much more concise and understandable for children than *The Fairy Caravan*. If such a thing should happen, — a future edition would be improved by a few more illustrations, as some chapters are rather bare. I think Pig Robinson looking into a shop window is the best black and white I ever did. I feel most grateful to you for turning out such a handsome letter press and general set up.

When it is convenient to you to send me another cheque would you please draw it to W.H. Heelis and Son, that is the name of the firm. W.H. Heelis and Son, Hawkshead, near Ambleside.

Trusting you will receive the parcel promptly,

To Helen Dean Fish

Sept. 19. 30

I received the most amusing quaint book by the same post as your letter; and I take you solemnly to witness that it is my first acquaintance and meeting with Dr. Dolittle and his fascinating ship's company! *I* also have taken a voyage, in imagination; and sent my Pig Robinson to the southern seas; but I think my adventures are cribbed from *Robinson Crusoe*, 'per' Stevenson's *Kidnapped*. There is nothing new under the sun; and in the making of many books there are bound to be coincidences; it is probably that many plagiarisms are quite involuntary. It's a most amusing clever book (the Dr. I mean to say!)

You and Miss Street were enjoyable visitors — and I won't forget the short fish and the long street. There were some English visitors turned up yesterday and said they came ten years ago — and were rather offended I couldn't remember them; and I was inclined to say they could wait ten years more before they came again — very inquisitive; and completely uninteresting. However it happens, the class of Americans who take the trouble to call, are quite different to the English.

I had such a delightful day with Mrs. Perry and her niece Betty Harris, from Philadelphia; she has been here several times and this year they were touring in a car, and we went to Keswick and Buttermere together. A fine day as it happened.

It has been a wet season all through. There was one fine week when we got our little field of oats safely housed, so this farm is in better case than many others, where hay is still lying out. I do hope Miss Mahony will find an opportunity for an English visit sometime.

With kind regards to you and Miss Street, and thanks for the Dr.

[P.S.] The Coniston estate is being taken over by the National Trust this month. It is very gratifying — and I have a personal gratification — they have asked *me* to manage it for a time, till it is in better order; the farm rents will enable repairs and replanting to be undertaken this winter — interesting work, at other people's expense!

To Alcxander McKay

Oct. 27. 30

I should be very much obliged if you can send me 1 dozen copies of *The Fairy Caravan*.

I am looking forward to your edition of *Robinson*. The London edition is only moderately pleasing. Mr. Stephens writes that 2500 were ordered before publication, so it has started well here.

Nov. 5. 30

I received the parcel, unopened and safe and I am delighted with your edition of *Robinson*. I like the large type; and the paper and general appearance reminds me pleasantly of old favourites of nursery days. F.W.'s edition, with 45 less pages, and less pictures, does not look as good money's worth. This is a more likely book to sell than the *Caravan*, which was an indigestibly big mouthful. I hope you will have reason to be satisfied with this one.

As regards another book I have let myself in for a troublesome business; a book about the Lake District. Messrs. Warne brought out a rather handsome volume about the next county, Yorkshire; illustrated by R. Smith, and Mr. Stephens asked me if I would care to do one. I have always had rather a fancy to do a Lakes-guide-history-description. But now I am shying at the job — it is a task for one's declining years! not a job to do in a hurry; it would entail much "reading up". I tried to back out of it; but Mr. Reginald Smith turned up here with some very good pictures. I do wish they would get someone else to write it. It would be useless to you; besides it is their own idea, and they would claim it.

There are a good many other stories of the Caravan in existence. I will think the matter over. One book or other will have to wait. Several of the Cherry Tree Camp stories are not suitable for publication, especially a disgustingly realistic version of Bluebeard, told by the "second cousin mouse." Perhaps if it were deleted and a more pleasing fairy tale put in — I will think it over. I would like to do another volume some day; but I would not put so much crammed into it, as there was in the first one. And perhaps more pictures.

In the meantime how to get rid of Mr. Reginald Smith's illustrations? He has just this moment telephoned to say he is sketching at Grasmere. I am afraid I ought to do the guidebook first. It ought to be written by three or four people, agriculture, history, sport, scenery; I wish I had turned it down decidedly right off at first.

I am obliged for your kind wishes for a 'pleasant winter'! The weather has been atrocious, and personally I have been in bed with a chill. But it is a fine dry frost today.

With kind regards from us both,

[P.S.] Don't count upon a volume please till you hear again.

To Marian Frazer Harris Perry

Dec. 14. 30

What a very pretty bag you have sent to me from Florence, and it is none the less pleasing that it reminds me of the bugs, baskets, tea cosy — various parafirnalia of our picnic. It was very interesting, in spite of my leading the car such a dance into wrong roads; I enjoyed it thoroughly, and your niece Betty proved herself a capable driver anywhere — do you remember squeezing past the charabanc.

It stands out in my memory as one of the few fine days and real holidays of the year. I am very sorry and sympathetic to hear you are not well. I have been in bed twice this winter already with bad colds — not serious, but just sufficiently bronchial to make me afraid of bronchitis if I live to be as old as my mother, which is unlikely. I hope you have a good doctor and friends within reach if you are going to be laid up in a foreign land — it sounds alarming to one like me who lives always in one place. But it must be rather nice to get away from the raw weather. Yesterday was so beautiful — snow on the fells, hoar frost on the trees and grass and bright sunshine — now today it is almost dark, and big flakes of snow amongst *rain*. We have had no dry snow yet on the low land. The cattle are still out of doors in the day time; but it is raw, and every field is drowned in mud — a wet Yule. William (not Edward) had hoped to go shooting with friends, but they have telephoned putting it off. I was amused with our spaniel last time — she is not a well trained gun dog. One pheasant that she should have retrieved, vanished mysteriously; and later in the day's shooting — Spot was observed burying a pheasant privately under a hedge! I wonder if you will like *Pig Robinson*. From what Mr. McKay reports it has not taken so well as the *Caravan* in U.S.A. Which rather pleases me in one respect — *I* like *fairy* tales, and so do American readers. The London shops want nothing but comic toy books. *Robinson* is selling very well in this country.

I am posting you the American edition as it is better got up. Mr. McKay wants more Caravan stories — it would be rather a rush to do a volume this spring.

I can imagine Betty enjoying a walking tour, a fine athletic young woman — and such a nice wise like young person! I liked her very much —

Now I do hope your indigestion has passed; and I remain with our kind regards and very good wishes for 1931,

[P.S.] How lovely the border is, and Fra Giovanni messages of hope and faith.

~~~ Part II ~~~

"A world of beauty will survive"
1931 – 1940

To Marian Frazer Harris Perry

I often think of our drives and our tea party. I can assure you *I* enjoy your visits like you do yourself. And please tell Mrs. Clark how much I appreciate the *Shadows on the Rock*. I think I never read a more beautifully written book. The atmosphere, and character drawing are perfect. Certainly, one should try to write *one's* best, for American readers. But not many can write such clear cut sentences in so polished a style without its becoming cold or finicky.

That is to say — another fit of scribbling has taken possession of me: and I am trying to make a frame work to hold some more of the surplus stories that were left over from *The Fairy Caravan*. It will not be so pretty as the first volume, I am afraid. The frame seems plainer; and the stories rather long.

We have a very green Yule; accompanied by measles and influenza in the villages; but both very well here, I am thankful to say. And hoping for better times next year. Things have been very anxious, and it will take a long time to work trade round. The sheep farmers are holding on, only one or two giving up; but another bad season will try them. I am in a stronger position through farming my own land; no rent.

There has been snow on the fells but it has gone again. I was up at Tarn Hows on Tuesday, all silent, and very beautiful; the water as still as a mirror, and blue black like ink. We must try and get the car-turning-place improved before another summer season. There are un-employed in plenty, but no money to spare for the work. The district is very quiet and deserted. Fox hunting, (on foot); and folk dances in the winter evenings. Our village has the dance tomorrow night; parties will come from 10 to 15 miles around. What a pretty little bunny basket you sent me! and the round lined one is more useful when I go to shop in Windermere. The Italian bag is too pretty to use, it is always hanging on the cupboard door as an ornament.

I hope you are quite cured from indigestion and that we may have another (very *many*) pleasant drives in the unknown times to come.

With best wishes for Christmas and New Year, believe me,

To Henry P.

Dec. 15. 31

How is the algebra? Still troublesome? or have you mastered it? I have got along fairly well in the world without ever having acquired the art of doing sums! Never by any chance did they come right. What is the old rhyme?   "Multiplication is vexation,

> Division is as bad.
> The Rule of Three it puzzles me,
> And Fractions drive me mad!"

But I fear *you* will have to learn to understand Euclid — bother him!

I am struggling with another volume of the *Caravan*. I think of calling it "Cherry Tree Camp". There are a number of stories that were not used for the other book — though I do now think I was rather extravagant in using up all the prettiest in one volume. This collection does not wander amongst the hills. It is in a sunny pasture, surrounded by woods. As a matter of fact the site is where the Girl Guides camp in summer, and the Scouts. We had such a number for the August holidays, over 80. And one troop arrived in such a downpour that they could not get their tents up so there were 30 sleeping in the barn and cooking in our small kitchen, for 2 hours.

The country is very lovely and deserted now, in winter. Last week one of the shepherds, searching for stray sheep, found the bones of a poor man who had been missing for many months.

The sheep sales have been bad this autumn, disastrous prices. I am fortunate in not having to pay rent, as I farm my own land. The tenant farmers are having a severe struggle; if things don't improve next year many of them will have to give up. There has been a sprinkling of snow twice on the top of the fells, but none in the valleys, and it is very mild and muggy weather. We are quite well here (amongst measles and influenza epidemics!) I hope you and your mother are well, and with all good wishes for Christmas and New Year,

[P.S.] I hope we will meet again in more prosperous times. Very few Americans have been to the Lakes this season.

I wish someone would tell me how to address the friends in the U.S.A.! Do you put Esq. or Mr. on the envelope? I am always puzzled if I write to Mr. McKay.

To Mrs. J. Templeman Coolidge

Ap. 29. 32

Thank you for your interesting letter. I can read that "Henry P." is still the same eager unspoilt boy. Students in these later days have to absorb such an enormous range of knowledge, that it is pleasant to know that he has energy and time and strength for subjects outside the regular routine of school learning. I can believe he will make a good editor; he had originality and an inquiring mind.

Talking of editors — a curious thing has happened about my next book. I wrote out so many chapters and posted them. I never have much control of my subject; it ambles along, like the *Caravan*. By way of variety (and my own inclination) I made this sequel book more of tales told by, than of adventures happening to, the little animals. I remarked to Mr. McKay that the book seemed likely to be over weighted by the tale of the Second Cousin Mouse; an absurd and grisly version of *Bluebeard* which grew to a big length; I suggested throwing it out. Which he has done. But he suggested printing it first as a separate book under the title of *Sister Anne*; and "eliminating the mice". Alright; it will suit me well. Only if the mice are "eliminated" the tale becomes deadly serious. I am recopying it and trying to improve the writing; but I am uncertain whether it is a romance or a joke. It certainly is not food for babes. He will get it illustrated in USA, which will relieve me from the difficulty of trying to illustrate human figure scenes. I think it had better have a blood curdling picture on the cover to warn off the babes! As it stood originally, the mice afforded comic relief; for instance after Fatima's discovery, the chapter ended — "Then the First and Third Cousin Mice with nerves and fur on end, fell upon the Second Cousin Mouse and bit him". I leave the responsibility entirely with Mr. McKay. But I am not sure whether he is right. It wanted alteration, taking out of the frame work of the *Caravan*; but I am not sure how it will stand by itself. I wonder what Miss Mahony will think of it, it will be a queer book. I am glad to have more time for "Cherry Tree Camp".

Trade is so bad there may be other reasons for delaying a larger book. I should like to do a set of fairy tales in thin volumes; "Habbitrot" [Chapter XI in *The Fairy Caravan*] might be reprinted, with a coloured illustration for one of them; and I have others more or less written, for instance a version of *Cinderella*.

Mr. McKay sent me the *Epic Of America*, [James Truslow Adams], a fine brave book, face the facts. Your task of regeneration is even harder, for your country has not a background of centuries of developing character. But every country is suffering from the same complaint of coming on too fast; all the world; not only America — forces and knowledge that are out of control; a curse instead of a blessing. Free education has not done much for this country. Clever children could always get educated in the past; and shallow education without character is proving to be a snare. It is a pity all those unstable young people of both sexes have votes. The National Govt. has such an immense majority, it should last this Parliament out, but I fully expect they will lose most bye elections that crop up — that is replacing vacant memberships.

We have had a mild wet winter, a dry early spring; and a heavy snow shower at the end of April. The leaves are coming out and the country is beginning to look lovely. The shepherds are very busy. In spite of tempests we have lost very few lambs.

I hope we shall meet again in better times. I have the pleasantest recollection of your visits with Henry P. My husband and I have kept well; we don't grow younger, and always almost over busy; but one must do one's bit.

With our kindest regards,

To Alexander McKay

June 3rd 32

I received your letter tonight. I am ashamed not to have posted sooner. I could go on for ever re-writing sentences. The mice were interrupting; but without the — "au grand serieux" — it requires better writing? I sometimes wonder whether it is wise to cut them out entirely? but I leave it to you.

I would only suggest this much mouse, (preface) —

"Three little mice sat in a window to spin. They were cousins.
Said the First Cousin Mouse to the Second Cousin Mouse,
"Tell us a story, to pass the time while we spin".
"What about?" said the Second Cousin Mouse.
"About cats," said the First Cousin Mouse.
"About a cupboard," said the Third Cousin Mouse.
"Very well," said the Second Cousin Mouse, and thus commenced —
(And after Fatima's discovery, and end of Chapter 6)

48

"Then the First and Third Cousin Mice, with nerves and fur on end, fell upon the Second Cousin Mouse and bit him."

If you think anything of this suggestion, put it in quite different smaller print, or italics. I am glad I am not doing the pictures for I don't know how I would have got them done.

We are both very well, in all sorts of weather — snow in May after a warm winter. Always busy.

With kind regards from both and apologies from me,

[P.S.] I came across a pleasing dog story lately. A friend of ours Joe Gregg was cutting hay out of a stack in his barn, with a hay knife; he got too far, undermining the hay, which toppled over and pinned him. He was able to shout; his dog rushed into the barn and *dug him out!*

To Anne Carroll Moore

Dec. 3. 32

You have sent me a delightful book; alive and vivid. And although the description of the French villages is pathetic, it is hopeful. I turned to Chapter XI with some trepidation — quite unnecessary! Even "Wm." — who was once offended by being introduced to somebody as "Beatrix Potter's husband" — says it is harmless. It is sufficiently intimate to be interesting to children, and perfectly tactful. You remember more than I; I'm glad you survived my cooking comfortably! Poor Semolina Duck, she deserved to get into a book. The last of the older generation of animals has been put to sleep, the old cat Tamsine aged 16.

This card I am sending is intended for the dance that Tappie-tourie and Chucky watched on Christmas Eve in the snow. I had hoped to have a short story [*Sister Anne*], but I have had no news of it, perhaps the publishers are deferring printing till better times — which are slow of coming on both sides of the Atlantic.

I read in the papers that there has been a display of children's books in London. I think your own good work has borne fruit. There have been classics such as *Alice in Wonderland* and the *Water Babies*; but in the main children's literature has not been taken seriously over here, too much left to the appeal of gaudy covers and binding, and the choice of toy sellers.

With very kind regards from my husband and myself,

49

To Marian Frazer Harris Perry

Dec. 3. 32

It has felt quite lonesome — not <u>one</u> American Friend has been here this summer. I suppose it is the result of bad times. People are hard up over here. But we must pay our debts honestly. I wish the Treasury had called up gold a while ago.

One used to lament the export of old furniture, and even historical houses; that trade is slack; but the dealers and jewellers buy up any sort of gold ornament greedily. I think they might call in what is left for the Treasury.

We keep very well; but grumble of course! Sheep have been sold for 1/ each, but mine have not done quite so badly as that; they have averaged about 7/6 a head. Things cannot go on as at present. There seemed to be a sudden slump in farm stock at the time of the autumn fairs.

It has been such a fine summer, and a fine autumn, with wild interludes. Any weather is lovely at the Lakes. I went to Buttermere, on sheep business, one stormy day when the mist was rolling along the fells, with gleams of light breaking through onto Crummock Water, and it was just as beautiful as on the clear day when I went that pleasant trip with you and Betty.

I wonder — is there any little one arrived or on the way? I hope you are well — not troubled with indigestion or rheumatism, and I do hope to see you again sometime. Do not fail to telephone when you are coming, for I am so often out unless I know before hand. There should have been an absurd book — *Sister Anne,* but I cannot hear anything of it; perhaps Messrs. McKay have delayed publication till a better season.

My husband and I keep well.

With kindest regards,

To Alexander McKay

Dec. 18. 32

I am agreeably surprised with *Sister Anne.* The magenta is a crude color; but it is only a wrapper. The illustrations are fine; Katherine Sturges has conveyed the sense of giddy heights so well in the outdoor subjects; and the black backgrounds give an effective air of mystery.

Brother John who "rode light" could not possibly have scrambled up and down a dry ditch in heavy plate armour; but that is a mere detail.

The women's figures are beautiful, especially Fatima on horseback behind the Baron, and Anne coming down the cellar steps.

She cannot draw dogs — but no more can I. I should have sent a photograph of a wolf hound; they have *not* flap ears.

I should like to have the draft sent direct to me; not to Brown Bros.

I hope you and your family are having a Merry Christmas. I am *not*. My old mother is refusing to die. She was unconscious for 4 hours yesterday, and then suddenly asked for tea. She cannot possibly recover, and she suffers a lot of pain at times, so we hope it will soon be over; but she has wonderful vitality for any age — let alone 93.

With kind regards,

To Marian Frazer Harris Perry

Oct. 18th 33

Thank you for sending me *Miss Delicia*; [*Miss Delicia Allen* by Mary Johnston] she is delicious, a sweet book. And thank you for your letter.

I wonder sometimes what is the secret of attraction?! "I" always seem to "me" to be comparatively dull, with not much to say, and with only very occasional flashes of amusement. Anyway, it was a true pleasure to both of us to meet again, and I wish we could have met oftener. I always have just too much to do, though it is mainly useful work that takes me into pleasant places.

The afternoon in Yewdale was perfect; and it is no less perfect now in driving showers and mist, with gleams of light and waterfalls tumbling over rocks. My old drainer man is drowned out of the low meadows, onto higher ground. I have made acquaintance with the bride, described by the proud bridegroom before I met her, as "half a head taller and bred to it!" i.e. farming. She looks very suitable for the position, not too young, good looking, and big enough to take a stick to "Tommy" if he does not behave himself.

They have been courting 12 years; a very capable sensible person; and she has got the floor clean which is more than could be said for the departed sister, Bessy. It used to be one of the houses where offer of a cup of tea was embarrassing.

Mrs. Jackson at Yew Tree is almost too smush. I rather like a genuine farm kitchen. Next time you come I will take you to the sheep farm, at

Troutbeck; it is a fine old house, only deficient in oak. Probably burnt
out in the old times. Do come again some day.

With kind regards from us both believe me,

Nov. 17th 33

I am amused to hear that the Sergeant has done it once too often! —
provided you are not put to inconvenience in giving evidence against
him; he deserves a number of convictions; and term following term,
to keep him out of the path of enthusiastic American visitors who want
to see the xxxxxx of xxxxx review the troops, next season! Too bad
altogether; but very entertaining, as related by Miss Riley.

Yes — the Italian sunshine must be seductive. I have got lumbago;
but if one went anywhere warmer, it would feel still colder on coming
back. So I take a cup of hot mustard and milk at bedtime. Anyone with
muscular rheumatism should try mustard — half a teaspoon as hot as
you can drink it; it is not as nasty as it sounds.

By the way I had no idea that elderberry jelly is so good; I made a
little, and will make more another year.

I have not read any of the books you mention; I shall be delighted to
have them.

We have just been reading the *Gold of the Egypt*; those Italian divers
must be fine men, brave and clever.

If you come across a certain Miss Rebecca Owen in Rome — she is
an American who has lived for a great many years near Hawkshead —
a remarkable old person, must be nearly 80; lipstick, pink nails, a
handsome car, and lives in a large old house *alone*. She has beautiful
silver, books, and furniture; it never seems very safe the house is so
lonely. She is a clever old woman, very well read, with an eccentric
temper. She was groaning very much about the rate of exchange last
time I saw her. I am very glad it has not affected your plans.

I look forward very much to seeing you again next year. April this
year was lovely; sometimes it is dry and just too soon for the Spring
beauty of the Lakes. We have a white cap on the fells today, but warm
in the sun.

Dec. 13. 33

I thoroughly enjoyed *The Country of the Pointed Firs*. It is wonderful writing. I thought *Shadows on the Rock* was perfect; but this book is still better. I have read it repeatedly, trying to understand how it is done. The style is artless and simple; yet it is perfect as a work of art.

I have had time to read — can you imagine *me* wasting nearly six weeks, with a sick chill? I suppose you did something of the sort yourself; and I was pleased to see you looking remarkably well and rather younger than ever when I encountered you in Smith's Library! The doctor says there is nothing the matter with me except lumbago, so I expect the weather has a good deal to do with it, and it takes time for the organs to recover from a chill. We have had a fine winter, up to yesterday, when the first snowfall arrived; very wet horrid half thawed snow, freezing again at night. It will be pleasant to welcome Spring; the snow drops are already pushing through the earth. Cattle and horses under cover for the winter months; and sheep in very good condition. They can support hard conditions of cold and scanty grass provided they commence the winter favorably.

I was, by the way, in a cottage farm house further on than Yewdale and very remote, and I counted nearly 60 ancient hooks for hanging mutton hams on the beams. Never did I see quite so many! The old owners must have cured a mysterious number. There was a good deal of sheep stealing in by gone days, and it is not entirely done away with yet. A few years ago a man after rabbits found 2 sheep skins pushed out of sight down a rabbit hole. There are rascals both in town and country.

I expect this will follow you to Italy, with our kind regards and best wishes for a Merry Christmas. I don't know if your cousins are with you; otherwise I would include them. I am writing to Betty.

[P.S.]Since writing this 2 more books have come! How very acceptable. I have not had time to read more than a few pages — enough to repeat that "that there is nothing new under the sun"; and not so often plagiarism. There are sentences of description in the first chapter of *Otto* [*Otto of the Silver Hand* by Howard Pyle] that are singularly like the description of the Castle in *Sister Anne*. I suppose we each unconsciously repeated some old description. I went to Lancaster Castle one day this summer and it was much as I remembered and had tried to describe it. All old castles are much alike.

The illustrations are very good. At same time I have never complained of Katherine Sturges's. Some people say they are bad, but I thought their bizarre distortions rather suited my story.

Hard frost today and sun —

Love and thanks —

Betty Harris married Richard K. Stevens on April 25, 1931

To Betty Harris Stevens

Dec. 14. 33

(I really cannot call you "Mrs. Stevens" — with apologies to Dick!) It has been such a pleasure to see your aunt again this summer and to hear news of you. I saw her several times and we had one lovely afternoon out; though we sat at a table it might be termed a picnic. I thought her looking remarkably well and not changed a bit. Which I am thinking about seriously as I am feeling very sorry for myself. But Mrs. Perry is an example that disturbed "digestions" get over. I just got a severe chill and it has upset my 'tummy' for six weeks past.

The photograph of Nonya certainly does show her character. She looks as if she were determined to reach whatever is her mark, a fine strong child she looks; and should be, as she is like you. I do hope you and your husband will have time to come north; we shall be delighted to see you. Things don't change much here. There is a certain amount of building, but private ownership and public opinion have prevented any very bad cases of disfigurement so far. So long as ugly houses are not perched on conspicuous hills it doesn't matter.

Farming is looking up; the sheep sales have been cheerful; our lambs topped the local fair and made nearly £200 more than last year. It seems as though you are in a very unsettled way still in the states; one perplexity after another.

You ask after cross Mrs. P. Duck; she sat and she sat, and when I (at great peril) lifted her off her nest in the hay barn, she was sitting on nothing. There *had* been an egg; whether she had eaten it, or Samuel Whiskers — cannot say! But being emancipated by long seclusion + bad temper — she proceeded to die. She was of great and unknown age. The previous summer she hatched out one black chicken!! Now that is a story for Nonya when she can understand it, but she had better start

54

on *Peter Rabbit* — yet another generation of Peter's friends.

With love and best wishes for Christmas and New Year from yours affectionately —

To Henry P.

Dec. 14. 33

This comes to wish you and your Mother a Merry Christmas and Happy New Year. I had a most interesting letter from her last Christmas, about your studies and interests. I like the cutting that she enclosed; it was well written and interesting. Something to say is the first point; and the manner of saying it is the second.

I have little to say now! except that I have been poorly after a chill six weeks ago — a great waste of time in one's old age, although the doctor says lumbago is of no consequence.

Last winter my mother's illness and death interrupted my Christmas letters. She was very old, and fretful; she had lived her time.

We have had a most lovely summer and autumn, and no snow until last week in this part of the country. It is not deep but the roads are very slippery which is awkward on steep hills.

There have been rather more American visitors this summer, though they all complain of bad times. Over here things are decidedly on the mend especially in farming. Our lamb sales were about £200 better than last year's sales. But it seems as though your country has much to struggle through yet.

My kindest remembrance to your Mother. I hope some day in better times you may visit the Lakes again..

To Marian Frazer Harris Perry

Feb. 20. 34

Here have I been pitying myself all winter — and you so very much worse! To be sure a gastric ulcer will heal; but ulcerated stomach trouble is apt to recur. Were you not troubled last time you were in Italy; I wonder whether it is partly due to Italian cooking in hotels? You looked so well last summer, it is unfortunate.

My "lumbago" was the digestion; it was either a severe liver chill or gastric influenza. I had sickness and indigestion for so long that I began to think there was something wrong with me. But I got quite well, after New Year; and proceeded to fall over a board in a doorway and put my right shoulder out of joint. I can get my arm up to my head now; but I suffer a bit of pain in my forearm. Probably rheumatism. We shall all be glad when warm weather comes.

It has been open weather (not much frost and no heavy snow); but there is time yet! I was talking this morning to a farmer's wife near Keswick and she reminded me that it will be a year tomorrow since the bad blizzard when so many sheep were buried. On their farm, Middle Row, Threlkeld, they had 100 sheep in a field near the farm house. At first after the storm Mr. Corkbain saw no sheep at all and thought they had got away from the field, till he saw a sheep's head. They were all got out alive. We read of terrible cold in America. The weather is less settled today and yesterday, but more like rain than snow. Water is still very scarce in the large towns. It does not seem as though the Italian spring was much in advance. Here there are yellow crocuses and aconite in flower, and the snow drops are lovely. There are thousands in front of the windows and in the orchard and in the lane. That is why I have an untidy garden. I won't have the dear things dug up in summer; they are so much prettier growing in natural clumps, instead of being dried off and planted singly.

How sad it is about King Albert; a fine character. No doubt a quick painless death; but a shock for his family. I cannot understand this rock climbing craze. I sympathize with the local policemen and doctor! The sergeant is rather stout, and he does use language (privately and confidentially) about having to go up precipices to get down climbers with sprained ankles or worse. The Coniston doctor has views on the subject too; especially on Sunday afternoons in summer. There must be some fascination.

People can hurt themselves anywhere. The colley was shut up and gnawing the bottom of the shippon door, so I had a board nailed across, and promptly forgot all about it, and went over head first.

I enjoyed reading *The Tory Lover* [Sara Orne Jewett] while I was laid up, a most charming story. As a work of art it is less even than *The Pointed Firs*; either less mature, or perhaps it was beyond her to keep so high a level throughout a long story. But the parts that one might have thought most difficult for a woman to write are the best done, the nautical and political. Very good it is.

Post is just going — so I make a dash at the numerals from memory:

Yan tyan tethura methura pimp
Yan a pimp etc. dik! = 10
Yan a dick tyan a dyk
bumfit — 15

My husband has kept very well, and as for me, I'm still going pretty strong. I'm glad your cousins were with you. With love,

To Helen Dean Fish

May 16. 34

I have pleasant memories of the long one and the short one — though with such a bad memory for faces that you will have to tell me which is which next time you come over. Did you really mean it, when you included me in that august list? Or was your judgment coloured by personal recollections. Flattering in either case!

I entirely agree with you about English children's literature. The authors used to write down to children; now they write twaddling dull stories, or odious slangy stuff. I thought your article in *The Horn Book* was excellent.

Noel Moore says that his original Peter letter is dated Sept. 4th, 1893. *The Tailor of Gloucester* was written for his sister Freda Moore, but not in a letter, so the date is merely December 1902. At least I cannot remember any letter, and I think '1901' is a misprint in the dedication of the 1st edition. *Peter Rabbit* was printed privately for Christmas 1901, and the *Tailor* was printed privately the following Christmas. Nobody would publish poor *Peter*! I have very few copies of him in black and white. I have a fair number of the *Tailor* and I will post you one, it has several plates that were not used afterwards.

The country is lovely now, the bluebells are just coming out and the spring tints are wonderful in the woods and coppices. But it is bitterly cold again; treacherous weather.

With very kind regards to you both,

[P.S.] I was born July 28, 1866. (I keep getting mixed up in my centuries — your fault for disturbing antediluvian memories.) I don't know how to get at publication days, unless Messrs Warne knows them.

To Marian Frazer Harris Perry

Aug. 31. 34

It is a pleasure to see your writing again — though the letter means — I fear — that you are not coming north.

It is wretched weather just now, but a wet August sometimes leads to a fine autumn. I have so often wondered; when I go into Smith's Library I look around, but no, you are not there! It was my turn to write. I fear I never answered your last letter, and I had no excuse of illness. I got well again with the fine warm spring. We had good crops, lots of lambs, and now the agricultural shows are making us busy. I was at Ennerdale on Thursday, about 10 miles beyond Cockermouth. I never go in that direction without remembering how I misled dear Betty — and how well she handled that big car in narrow places. You will be glad to see her and the child again; give her my love please — also your cousins. There have been more Americans at the Lakes, but no old friends have come this way. There was a nice girl, Sarah Frazer from N. Jersey, interested in geology and rocks.

William and I took a holiday from Friday to Tuesday (!!) at the August holiday weekend, and we motored through Northumberland, following the Roman wall and road to Chollerford, (George Hotel comfortable) and next day over the Cheviots to my Scotch sister-in-law between Jedburgh and Hawick; it was a fine drive. That is the only time I have slept out of this house since 2 years. It's well I have plenty of interests here.

I will ask for those books at Smith's. I have lent the *Tory Lover* to a friend, and I am trusting to see it back! The book grows upon second reading; surely the best test of a book. It has been a pleasant season, relations coming and going; we seemed to have lived in a round of tea parties this week. One very welcomed visitor was Willie's favorite nephew who has been in the Argentine 5 years, doing well on the railway. He has gone back now, for another 5 years. There is not much opening in this country; things improve, and then there is a check again.

I'm sure old England suits you better than Italy! Though I do not doubt it a better winter climate in Italy. Mr. Heelis is well and busy too.

With kind regards from us both,

Oct. 4. 34

I have just *re* read the *Child in Old Chester* with great enjoyment after getting it back safely from a borrower; it is a sweet book and you gave it to me! Little Ellen with her hair brushed back and the plain band behind her ears; mine used to be black velvet on Sundays, and either black or brown ribbon week days. I don't think my "Betsey Thomas" (who was Scotch and named Mackenzie) would ever have allowed a pink band. I remember the bands fastened with a bit of elastic, looped over a button behind the ear; it hurt.

My Scotch nurse was a stern Calvinist. I learnt nearly all the *Lady of the Lake* by heart when I was very young, perhaps 7; and I remember crying bitterly because Ellen Douglas was an R.C. and therefore *must* have gone to hell. Children take things seriously; at least the old fashioned ones did. I have another American book that is a favorite; *Hitty*, about a doll.

It is sad that we shall not meet this time, but we will look forward to your next visit. And you are wise not to come north now, for the weather is completely broken, and sometimes bitterly cold at night after a stuffy day; probably thunder.

We are taken up with sheep fairs just now. I had a good sale at Ambleside fair, and there is another at Keswick tomorrow. I have about 700 sheep to draft out of the flocks this season. The nuisance of sheep stealing has cropped up again; at a season when so many sheep change hands lawfully, it is too easy to put a wrong lot through a distant market. It is probably a motor van, and a clever dog trained to hold sheep, without barking.

I hope the weather will be less windy when you sail; and I hope you find all well. Give my love to Betty and Nonya.

[P.S.] If you really want to send me one more book at parting — please send another of Willa Cather's? I just have *Shadows on the Rock*; it is a lovely book.

Oct. 17. 34

Thank you so much for the lovely book of Willa Cather's. The landscapes are wonderful — and the moving figures — the two priests on the fawn coloured mules.

The child-doll is called *Hitty, her first hundred years*, by Rachel Field, Macmillan and Co. Now I wish you a pleasant voyage and a happy reunion — and come again to England another year.

To Helen Dean Fish

Dec. 8. 34

I think your *Children's Almanac* is delightful, and it brings back so many favorites to my remembrance. Of course I have many of them still. I have been reading Miss Edgeworth's *Simple Susan* lately, again; with as much pleasure as ever, in a little old dumpy edition that belonged to my grandmother.

It is comical that I offered you a second copy of the pink *Tailor*. I must have felt you would appreciate it for I am not in the habit of throwing it about! So I will send a photograph instead, reprinted from an old one. It has no date, but probably I was six or seven. I know it was about that time that I was playing in the same garden when a friend of my father's, Professor Wilson, from Oxford, came in and produced a book from his pocket and discussed with my Mother whether I was old enough or whether the book was too old? which was the same thing. It had been written by another Oxford don and was attracting attention. I became immediately so absorbed with Tenniel's illustrations that I don't remember what they said about Lewis Carroll. It was not the first edition — neither was the *Water Babies*. I had Mrs. Molesworth's as they came out, with Walter Crane's pictures.

It is curious — the books that appeal to some children. I was very fond of *The Wide, Wide World* — the farm life part of it. [Elizabeth Wetherell, pen name of Susan Bogert Warner, the daughter of a prosperous New York State farmer, published in America in 1861] I did not meet with *Little Women* until much later.

There has been time for reading lately; outside work is mostly finished for the season, and the country is rainswept and misty — but always beautiful. The fells are even more impressive in mist and snow than when you and Miss Street saw them in August.

With kind regards and all good wishes to you both.

To Mrs. J. Templeman Coolidge

Dec. 12. 34

This comes to wish you and Henry P. a happy Christmas! It seems a long time since I have seen any of my old American friends — though there have been more of your countrymen in the hotels this season. I hope a sign that times are a little better. There was a pleasant girl,

Sarah Frazer, Morristown, N. Jersey, called here, interested in geology, and 2 young men I missed seeing — but no Henry P.! Someday, when he has finished his education he will come again. And not find me any younger. I have nothing to complain of; but one feels less active, and more slow in mind and memory as the years slip away..

It is very dismally wet dark weather, not seasonable and not like Christmas. Things improved in the farming world last autumn, but the later sheep fairs were not so good. We have plenty of hay which is something to be thankful for.

There is much talk in the Lake district about roads, building, rural planning and "amenity". It is well that public opinion is being roused at last; it is such a little bit of country. The latest controversy is about road widening through Rydal which might cut through Wordsworth's daffodil field. I think these very wide motor roads are no safer; and people ought not to rush through narrow valleys. This little corner of the country should be kept unchanged for people who appreciate its beauty.

We are well here, except colds in the head which one must expect in winter. With very kind regards,

To Marian Frazer Harris Perry

Dec. 12. 34

This comes to wish you a happy Christmas! It is not lively times here; heavy rainstorms; colds in the heads; very dark days in the country and fogs in the towns.

My husband has repaired the top of the "Noah's Ark" with strapping plaster! and it is dry inside, but very sloshy and muddy when I alight. Outdoor work has slackened off for the winter; but one cottage after another forwards complaints of roofs raining in, so this amateur land agent is still trotting around. I was perplexed yesterday by a request for a new window frame "before spring cleaning time". Little old panes of glass with only one small opening 12" x 5" is a stuffy state of affairs. But one of the panes has a date scratched on it 1826; it is a pity when old time things have to go. The new roofs and windows never look the same.

There was 4 inches of rain during the first week of December. The weather has been rather too mild to be seasonable; bulbs are growing; both snowdrops and tulips are pushing through the soil, and green buds on azaleas and lilac bushes.

There is a big crop of holly berries, and trouble as usual. If they are not cut for sale they are stolen and the bushes are torn, and if we sell them the dealers are so greedy they cut back the poor holly trees to bare poles. I rather hoped the birds would have cleared the berries before Christmas, but there is a glut. The trees are lovely in secluded places where they have been left alone, glowing red and shining green.

Hoping you are well and with best wishes,

[P.S.] I have missed you! I did enjoy you and your cousins the year before.

In September, 1932, at the age of fifty, Bertha Mahony married William Miller, the owner of the W. F. Whitney Company, a business which manufactured reproductions in maple of colonial furniture.

To Bertha Mahony Miller

December 13, 1934

I have just been reading again your most interesting letter of Jan 30 — never answered by me yet. I think time slips away faster and faster as one grows older — partly because this person when tired falls asleep, which is not conducive to writing letters, or any thing else. I have only done a Christmas card; the proceeds go towards maintaining 2 beds in a children's hospital.

I *do* get *The Horn Book* regularly. I thought it must be sent to me from the Bookshop? I really ought to pay for it? There is the postage too. That feeling of indebtedness was the reason I did not cash a little cheque for a drawing; but it may have been a childish way of balancing accts. I wish I could think of something worth while writing for it. It is a splendid publication; the articles and critiques are so alive — and real criticism, speaking out. Here, the review of the new crop of children's books is either indiscriminate, exaggerated praise or silence.

I think your mind is occupied with two delightful interests — books and old furniture. There is a periodical on this side, *Country Life,* which publishes views of old houses, indoors and exteriors and there have been several of Georgian houses in the states. We used to feel that rich Americans were carrying off too many treasures, but it seems as though you have Chippendale and Sheraton furniture of your own.

I think the new style furniture and architecture is hideous; it is a craze that will pass. But the old mahogany styles will always survive and be beautiful. I have a few good pieces — no complete big set of chairs, but a few very good 2's and 3's. We have got 2 chairs which were lying in a garret over my husband's office 40 years ago, rather elaborately carved Chippendale. There were usually good mahogany chairs in lawyers' offices. I have a Queen Anne style fiddle-back chair which had been painted green, in a farmhouse in Wales. The local furniture in this district was oak, rather out of fashion in the sale room now, but I collect any genuine pieces I can get hold of to put back into the farmhouses. The court cupboards with carved fronts are the most interesting as they are usually dated. It is a great shame to take them out of the old farmhouses for they really don't look well in a modern room. There are a good many in cottages belonging to the National Trust which will be preserved safely. The oldest I know is 1639. I was in a farmhouse this morning looking at some good oak panelling which the young woman had uncovered under many coats of wall paper and whitewash. The country people are learning to appreciate polished oak; they have discovered that tourists — American and British — are interested. There is a very fine old house, Yew Tree Farm, near Coniston, belonging to the Trust. We fitted up a tea room with good furniture and pictures. Unluckily the woman has been ill; it was a great success the first summer it was open.

I am "written out" for storybooks, and my eyes are tired for painting, but I can still take great and useful pleasure in old oak — and drains — and old roofs — and damp walls — oh the repairs! And the difficulty of reconciling ancient relics and modern sanitation? An old dame in one of the Trust's cottages wants new window frames because only 2 little panes open. A date, March 1826, is scratched on an old pane.

Such are the problems that occupy my declining years! I am 68; we have both had colds; it rains and rains and rains and is nearly dark. Things might be worse.

I only hope things may *not* be worse. I am one of the sceptics who refused to sign the L[eague] of Nations manifesto. Your government has not sent troops to the Saar. It is a nightmare. If the Saar vote goes against Germany and the Germans advance, it is not our handful of troops and the League's talking that can stop them; another retreat from Mons. It will be an anxious time.

If they *will* fight, let them exterminate each other and hope that England, the Colonies, and the States may survive to see — rule, really rule by power, not by preaching — a better world.

I wish you and your husband a happy Christmas, and success in two good works — providing wholesome, beautiful literature for children and continuing a fine tradition of furniture.

[P.S.] The photograph is pretty, is it not? It was taken by my father and is not copyright. I don't know what to think about it? I could have written a few words about the little girl who used to be me — the books she liked or the pets? Or would it be egotistical. I do hate anything like advertisement.

The original print is not dated. I might be 6 — 1872. I was born [in] 1866.

To Marian Frazer Harris Perry

Feb. 4th. 35

I was grieved to hear that you were laid up again with that troublesome complaint. I do hope that you are feeling better and quite recovered. Bed is the warmest place! I have returned twice this winter with heavy colds — not serious but troublesome.

We read of snow elsewhere. We have had our share of gales but not any depth of snow on the ground; it has been a green winter. The snowdrops are very pretty in the garden and the witch hazel bush is in flower. Probably there will be a frost in Spring.

How comical to think that I am responsible for providing little Timothy with a nick name. "Timmy Tiptoes" is really rather pretty for a baby name. When I commenced to read about his arrival I thought "here is a little brother for Nonya"; but her parents talk of a possible trip to Europe so that cannot be. It will be joyful to see Betty again, and meet her husband.

By the way the good Baldrys have had their golden wedding and retired from Moss Grove hotel. I am going to post you a photograph of myself aged 5 or 6. I think the ribbon was *white*, just possibly pink, certainly not blue. The elder child with the finger was a cousin, Alice Potter.

I have been enjoying *Passe Rose* [Arthur Sherburne Hardy]. Thank you for sending me such pleasant books. I have read *The Tory Lover* a third time and each time I like it better, finding new beauties. The first time I read it, the tale seemed long drawn out; it is the right way when a story improves with reading. You have sent me 3 books, 2 of Willa Cather's and *Passe Rose* that describe the sublime attributes of the church of Rome. Is it a coincidence? or are you a R.C.? or are you — like me — sufficiently detached to appreciate the beauty of holiness in that ancient faith? It is beautiful as a faith, and to read about. But the ordinary Catholics are not altogether satisfactory. There are many Irish R.C.'s in Barrow. We had one for a servant one winter. She was very funny. I must say everything she borrowed reappeared at the end of her engagement; except the cigarettes, which she certainly did not smoke herself. We concluded she gave them to the priest!! Poor Kathleen, she still comes to see me. She is — in spite of peculiarities — more attractive than the Baptists — for instance. There is a small sect of Baptists and a meeting house near Hawkshead. They have lately made a cement bath, for all the world like a sheepdipping tub, and they dipped an elderly spinster, Miss Sarah G., and she walked home in her wet clothes. It is understood that the water was warm; but the weather was chilly. She did *not* catch cold — that *is* faith! But somehow it is merely absurd. Things that Kathleen did not eat when she fasted she stored in a hat box under her bed. A shocked and spiteful Protestant fellow servant took me to look at this cache one day when Kathleen was having her day off. Items — 10 eggs, 1 2 lb. jam pot full of bacon dripping, nearly 1 lb. butter, and (I regret to say) 1 ½ tinfuls of Mr. Heelis's cigarettes; all covered up with clothes! I said firmly as Kathleen's engagement was only temporary, it was unnecessary to make trouble. I heard afterwards that she stroved and stinted herself to support an invalid sister at Barrow. Nail scissors! Pocket hankerchiefs! They all came back. What I was afraid of was the butter perhaps coming back, from under her bed, if we happened to run short.

It is well to be able to see the funny side of things.

I hope you are quite well again and I look forward to seeing you again in pleasant summer. Winter is becoming a trial as one gets older. I go to Coniston on fine days and find slates blown off.

May 31.35

I was just wondering at Jubilee time whether you had got a good seat!! and your cousins too. You Americans don't miss much. Here it was children's sports and teas and bonfires. Our village bonfire was so very big and hot that we did not see much other; just a little twinkling light on Coniston at 9.45 as a signal; and a distant light above Grasmere, besides some in the immediate vicinity. Now it is a painful drought. We hoped it would last over Jubilee, but it is getting very serious. We are getting short of grass and water, and a bad prospect for hay.

It is good of you to send me more books; they are charmingly written. The writers take more pains with juvenile literature in America. They seem to think anything is good enough for children and for the circulating library here. The ram is rather a funny sheep; but never mind; it is a new moon and rams may be different in Ireland. Both story books are very pretty and pleasant. They have solaced me with a bad cold. We have been unlucky that way. My husband had a real sharp attack of influenza 3 weeks ago. There has been a good deal up and down the villages. The country has been lovely; it is a pity fine weather should do harm. One late frost caught the young oak leaves so that many oaks looked bronzed — like copper beeches.

I shall look forward to seeing you all again. I wonder if Betty will get up north too.

With our kind regards to you and the cousins (beware of crooks!!).

To Betty Harris Stevens

June 13th 35

What a weekend to choose! It is August Bank Holiday. Thursday is August 1st. You will have to book your rooms at once. I do want to see you again and make acquaintance with your Dick. We go away only once a year from Friday to Tuesday; neither of us have slept out of the house since last August; and it is no rest to *me* as I am a bad traveller by car and always relieved to get it over. I am beginning to feel very old.

There are several hotels that can be well recommended, but I don't know much about the Ambleside hotels Queens and Salutation. A recently opened very pleasant place is 'Langdale Chase' on the shore of Windermere Lake between Windermere and Ambleside. Lowood Hotel is comfortable (rather spoilt by the noisy road). In Hawkshead 'The Old Red Lion' Mrs. Milner's, board and residence is very good cooking and very quaint. Also 'The Hotel', Far Sawrey, Mrs. Robinson, very comfortable, in the further end of the village, going on towards the ferry. The Ferry Hotel itself I don't much fancy.

In the village there are very nice clean rooms and nice sitting room at Low Greengate, Mrs. Stevens, our chauffeur's wife; it is the old post office near our garden, which I bought and renovated (for fear of worse neighbors). We have visitors bed and breakfasting there this week 16th July — as I could not get all in here. We have so little room and the domestic side is rather a struggle.

I feel unhospitable sometimes, but I get overtired and busy, dear Betty; if you want to come to stay with *us* you must sleep at the "post office"? I have a family of cousins coming tomorrow and some special London visitors, partly on business, from Wednesday till Saturday next. The cousins may stay 10 days or get into a caravan trailer on Saturday.

We are having a strenuous hay time, very good weather so far.

To Marian Frazer Harris Perry

Sept. 19th 35

I wonder whether you are still in England? or whether you have gone back to the States — or *Italy*. You are citizen of a country that has had the sense to keep out of the League of Nations.

Summer has been perfect here, following a lovely Spring. Now the weather is very wild and cold; we wonder if it is a complete break, for winter. But often there is a spell of sunshine in October. We were delighted to see Betty and her husband. We liked him very much. One cannot make much acquaintance in one afternoon, but he made a very good impression — and Betty was her own self, a little bit thinner.

I am taking a rest indoors today; there is a grisly wind and I have a bilious attack! But we have both kept very well and busy; lately the agricultural shows have been a dissipation and the sheep have taken many prizes, including a silver cup, won outright, (the 3rd time) for champion Herdwick ewe.

I never read the book you mention. *The Little French Girl* by Anne Douglas Sedgewick. I feel greedy offering to accept another! You do send me books that I like. I thought *Rain on the Roof* [Kay Lipke] was a very pleasant story, beautifully written.

67

I had a letter from the Editor of a farm newspaper. *The Farmer and Stock Breeder*, asking me to do a serial for a picture page — 4 drawings a week. I have declined. I do not think I could screen one out — though I should have liked the task if I had been younger. I felt that the later books of the *Peter Rabbit* series were being less spontaneous — an effort.

I wrote *The Fairy Caravan* and *Sister Anne* with pleasure to amuse myself; but they were different, and they had not the same appeal. Also the *Caravan* was too local for general consumption. I should think "stock breeders" further South would be very much surprised if they saw our wild and primitive methods of farming — though not many of them would have 400 lambs to sell at once!

I have had the pleasure this summer watching 2 puppies work, bred from my favorite colley. Their intelligence on the fell side is more genuine than the "trials" which have become so artificial that one old farmer compared it to putting chickens into a coop. The trial dogs are models of obedience; but useless on the fells where much of the dog's work is done out of sight of the shepherd.

Now the sun is coming out, and the apples are coming off — what a gale.

I hope if you do come north you may be favoured with better weather — bring it with you!

[P.S.] The world seems to have gone mad. Have the nations already forgotten the last war!

Dec. 15. 35

I wonder if you have gone home? or whether you are in Italy, like my American friend Miss Owen? She does not seem to find conditions too comfortable there. What a mess it all is. Your country has shown better statesmanship than this. We are well here, and at last we have had some dry weather. Only we are still grumbling for after a week's pleasant frost, we have a thin covering of slippery frozen snow. I think you were wise not to come north late on; there has been so much rain and wind.

But I hope it does not mean that you have been unwell, or disturbed in your plans. I believe it was my turn to write and I have never thanked you for the little French girl. I did not like her as well as the little Americans! I don't think the marriage would turn out well.

I have been lazy about any original work; this Peter is an old illustration used again; at least it was drawn a long time ago. But it serves as a messenger of remembrance and love to distant but not forgotten friends.

To Helen Dean Fish

Dec. 15. 35

My memory gets worse and worse! At least it comes back only in 'pictures'; (do other people have the same repeats?) Quite occasionally — often as I come over the hill into Coniston I remember the short fish and the long street at the point where you told me. But I cannot remember whether I ever answered your letter of April 29, '34 asking for dates. I am very sorry indeed if I have been careless. Unless I answer by return — I don't answer. It is too late now, so I can only hope I did so. I got out a packet of last year's American letters to look for addresses.

We are well here and I hope you and Miss Street are the same. It has been a good season on the farm, good crops and pleasant hay time. Autumn very wet, and now a slight covering of snow. Things are anxious abroad. It always seems so at Christmas. If that wretched League does not drag this country into war it will be a wonder and a mercy. The League has no real power.

With kind regards, yrs. sincerely,
Beatrix Potter

To Bertha Mahony Miller

December 15, 1935

I am a *bad* correspondent; in jerks; a long letter; then silence! Although it might not so appear, I was most interested in the Whitney Catalogue, which lies before me. It is beautiful furniture and looks as though it were splendidly made. I am interested in the stuffed furniture, pages 30-31. The British new style chairs and couches are awfully unwieldy and ugly; in part through a mistaken idea of giving a square hard-cornered shape to goods which are really soft. The treatment of 3525 and 3637¼ is particularly successful. The frills on some of the armchairs are amusing; why not?! We see enough of human female legs; it's a refreshing change to meet with flounces on a chair. 3648 is charming, and *is* that *the Culgrith printing*? There is a block cretonne printing small factory near Carlisle — some such a name as "Cummerlands" where very lovely flowers are printed. But they don't sell the chintz because it is printed exclusively for a firm in U.S.A. My sister-in-law, who lives near Penrith, got some remnants once. It was very pretty. I have been embroidering a valance for an old 4 post bed. I used some old green damask and worked on it with old gold coloured silk. I got wall paper for the room from Morris and Co. The firm still prints William Morris's handblock printed wall paper designs. They are not suitable as a background for pictures in watercolors or prints, being a decoration in themselves, but for a background to my 4 poster nothing could be better, except tapestry. The bed came originally from a farm near Warcop, Cumberland; it is a fine specimen of Jacobean carving, untouched. Morris and Co. make good reproductions.

I never saw these butterfly supports 7114. I bought a dirty, ill-used old oak table the other day. Unhappily the legs have been cut off short at the stretcher. I asked whatever had been the matter, and she said the servant lass had been short of a bit of kindling — i.e. firewood. I thought it was worth rescue at 10/. It has nice turned legs, like 7126. How I wish I could show you and Mr. Miller my things! The best oak is fixtures in old farmhouses (and it never looks so well transplanted elsewhere). For one's own use I prefer Mahogany. I *did* write something about my pets, but I never posted it. The year seems to have slipped away. The summer very fine, the autumn very wet, and now snow. The sheep and cattle are down hill for the winter. It seems strange there are so few sheep in the U.S.A. But it's hardly worth while *starting* sheep farming till people recommence to wear clothes — frills?

The news abroad is very disquieting. That wretched League. When it has dragged England into foreign wars, U.S.A. and the Colonies will have to rescue what is left of us.

With best wishes for Christmas and New Year,

To Alexander McKay

Feb. 5. 36

Thank you for the statement and remittance which I ought to have acknowledged before now. I have paid it into [the] Bank, and it will help pay some bills.

We are well and hope you are the same. It has been a very severe winter; more snow than we are accustomed to in the Lake district. Very beautiful to look at, but hard for the mountain sheep when it lasts so long.

I have not done any writing for a long time; I am alright but feeling old and lazy.

To Marian Frazer Harris Perry

March 1st. 36

I am sorry indeed to hear of so much illness. I got a card from Betty, and never thought of her being ill — though I wondered rather anxiously what had happened about you.

Bronchitis is rather a risk in such weather. Your 'Zero' sounds startling, but probably it is a drier cold than ours. I never felt so cold as that week our dear King died — a damp searching cold that went through and through. It has taken many, high and lowly, affecting those that are old or weak in heart. So many village friends and neighbours are gone, it makes me feel like one of the few old ones left. Mr. Heelis and I have kept well, but I have been indoors a good deal. The snow has come again and again — not so much down in the valley, but terribly severe for the sheep amongst the fells. They are not accustomed to eat hay; indeed it would be impossible to feed them in thousands; they come down into the woods and scrape and nibble what they can. But repeated snow storms mean weak ewes and a poor crop of lambs with many losses. So far as we know there have only been some half dozen smothered in snowdrifts on my own farms. There is a young dog, Matt, who has a wonderful sense of smell for finding sheep buried in snow. The shepherd says he has found sheep buried 6 foot deep — in time to save them. Some one — was it you? — wondered why there are comparatively few sheep in the States. I think your heavy snows may be the reason. There is a lovely flock and story in the *Pointed Firs*, but that will be further south than N.Y. and nearer the sea. Those books grow upon one; I did not appreciate *The Tory Lover* sufficiently the first time I read it.

The postman rabbit was a very successful Christmas card. I have just finished another for next year.

Dear little Jean [Nonya] must be amusing with Hunca Munca. There is a scheme to film *Peter Rabbit*. I am not very hopeful about the result. They propose to use cartoons; it seems that a succession of figures can be joggled together to give an impression of motion. I don't think the pictures would be satisfactory without the landscape backgrounds, and I doubt if the backgrounds would be satisfactory on a larger scale and without color. I think children with masks, acting the stories against a natural background would give more satisfaction. I am not troubling myself about it!

We have a queer little animal here, a small female Pekinese, a very "heathen Chinese" for mischief and naughtiness, but engaging and affectionate. The colleys don't like her; she is impertinent.

We have been listening to the new King's speech. It will take time as you say — to realize that he is not the Prince of Wales still. How clearly and firmly he spoke: it was well done. But not so touching as to listen to the kind fatherly voice that we heard last Christmas. I am told by another American listener that the funeral came through in the early morning. We did not hear it well. We thought it would be proper and right to go to Ambleside church where it was relayed, but the radio was not properly turned up — in any case I did not like that broadcaster — but to have a very loud harsh human voice breaking in when one was hearing the faint distant wailing notes of the bag pipes — he need not have told us! The guns were most impressive. Pray God we do not hear them again! It reminded me of the German guns bombarding the Cumberland coast at Eskmeals. This country should be thankful to U.S.A.

. . . Don't come over *too* early dear Mrs. Perry; it can be very cold on an English May day. We shall be glad to see Spring again.

I remain with kind regards from us both,

To Betty Harris Stevens

July 13th 36

I was so much interested to read your happy letter. What a joy it will be to Nonya and to you and to Dick when the little pink stranger comes! Will Dick please send me a line — if only one line. Tell him I got out some little knitted shoes yesterday, made by my mother when 89, and thought — shall I send one for luck — but whether *blue* for a girl? or pink for a boy? For a moment I thought of sending *both colours,* but perhaps you do not want *twins!?* So I will wait, for it is evidently too hot in U.S.A. for a baby to wear woolen boots at all.

It will be very charming to see Nonya with a baby sister. Some how I think it will be a sister — (perhaps for the inferior and degrading comparison that I bought a sister puppy for Suzee). I think an only child is a pity; it is better for the child herself to have another to share her parents' love; besides as she grows up it is happy companionship, and looking back in remembering together.

I hear from Mrs. Perry that she is not coming to England this year. I do enjoy seeing her; but somehow — better next — I don't think if I were an American I would be in a hurry to come over.

The work of ship building and guns is proceeding at a great pace now; and a connection of ours — a cousin's husband — who is on that work says there is one consolation for delay. All will be up to date. The German airship has been over this way, but I did not see it; it was flying very low. I suppose it had a look at Barrow-in-Furness. The crew tried to drop a wreath on a German soldier's grave in a cemetery in Yorkshire, but they did not exactly place it. We are struggling with a very very wet hay time. Please send along a bit of the heat wave!

With love and best wishes,

To Marian Frazer Harris Perry

July 13. 36

It is a trying task to have to dismantle a house. Eight years ago I went to London for a week (!) to clear my parents' house in South Kensington. My mother had not lived there for 11 years; and there were the accumulations of 60 odd years — perplexing, overwhelming, grimy with London soot. I had no sentimental repinnings as I had been discontented and never strong as a young person in London — but what

73

a task! and what to keep and what to sell? with a rather imperious old mother awaiting 3 van loads in Windermere. She was asking for various articles to the end of her long life; I think "caretakers" had taken toll — not me.

I have been very slow in replying to your good kind letters. I don't know what comes over me about letter answering. I am owing half a dozen to America; and as the world goes, old England must not lose any American friends.

A number of our newspapers and politicians are possessed with lunacy. How *could* we have fought Italy without sufficient ships or guns? Work is going forward feverishly now.

I am sorry not to see you this summer, but let us look forward to next year! I have had a very cheerful interesting letter from dear Betty, looking forward to an event. When she is safely over it — it will be a great happiness, and benefit to little Nonya. It is not too good for a child to be the only child and evidently a "character". She seems to be a most amusing little person. Here we have found mild but harmless amusement from 2 little Pekinese ladies. I always despised foreign dogs; but these are both spirited and affectionate, and less trouble than terriers, as they get sufficient play and exercise in the garden.

At present we are having a wet hay time, after a very dry Spring. We have had good health ourselves. Much illness amongst old neighbours in the village; and some troubles with tenants and servants but such is life!

I liked very much the article which you sent me, about the Jubilee; it was beautifully expressed and written; it conveyed the writer's deep and thoughtful impression; not the mere description of a passing show.

To Betty and Richard Stevens

Sept. 10. 36

Most hearty congratulations upon the arrival of the dear pink Baby! I expect you are home again. I have been slow to write; but not through want of sympathetic pleasure. I had been thinking very hard about you and wondering from the end of July; and directly I saw the letter I thought here's news! I am so glad you had not much trouble and I hope you are well again. Nonya will be most interested and full of funny remarks.

We are having a wet dreary season. The hay is in the barn at last and some of the corn. What is still out in the field is nearly black and spoilt. There is a good deal of grass still uncut in the district and nearly all the corn is spoilt. It is not a corn growing country; but we use the oats and oat straw for the cattle so it will be a loss of fodder next winter. Some of the small farmers will be half ruined. They are still wanting a reduction on their rents. Sheep are a better price, as the fields are deep in green aftermath — what we call fog grass — so store lambs are being bought to eat it off. I think that is the reason you have so few sheep comparatively in the States; I am told your fields are bare after the hay is carried.

I have had a good many American visitors. Two delightful girls, (niece and friend of a friend known of old). They had come over 3rd class and were tramping all over England, doing it economically. Also a young woman, a Londoner, who went out as a young girl and married. I had not seen her for twenty years. She came over to see her brother, bringing her own child. I was very relieved to find I liked "Ivy" as much as when she was a young girl, and I was interested in her girl. I suppose you have no classes in America? Anyhow Ivy's husband is in the telephones and her child goes to what would be equivalent to board school-council school here. It was the first time I had ever heard the native accent of Bronx. I am tempted to say I hope I may never hear that accent again. She was a dear child. When one got over the accent she compared favorably with the average English child of the same class; obedient, intelligent, and natural manners without forwardness. But the accent was a caution; on her father's side descended from Glasgow Scotch which is even worse. I was not edified by what Ivy told me about graft in N.Y. Your politics are beyond comprehension, but there's "something rotten in the state of Denmark". I also had two charming Boston boys whom I had seen six years ago.

But Mrs Perry is a missing visitor — and I have missed her.

With much love to Betty — and all of you,

To Marian Frazer Harris Perry

Dec. 16th 36

It is a long time since I have heard from anyone in America. I have not felt like writing; possibly American correspondents may have had the same feeling. Yet I sometimes wonder whether England is not under an obligation to Mrs. Simpson! When a man is sodden with drink he may do anything; if matters had not come to a crisis over here — there would soon have been some other intolerable situation; perhaps even more dangerous for home politics or foreign policy. King Edward by his obstinate wrong headedness proved himself utterly unsuited to reign as a constitutional sovereign. He has set the very worst example amongst fast young people. He is a good riddance of bad rubbish. No doubt a kind heart, a wonderfully good memory stored with facts and rememberance of faces; but no discretion, no self restraint, and no sense of decent shame. It is the custom to say that the war left an unfortunate impression on the younger men; certainly the Prince of Wales made no attempt to pull up. It was a pity he accepted the crown.

So we are to have a Coronation after all, which has been in some doubt recently, and I hope American friends will come over in great force!

It has been very wild weather lately — snow, gales, and floods. Indeed the seasons have been disappointing — for the only lengthy fine period was in May and June when the grass should have been growing. It was a late wet hay time and harvest. Instead of being a pleasure the hay making was wearisome, though not much was actually spoilt here. We finished late in September.

I have been at Coniston this morning; there had been a flood over the meadows when we walked with your cousins — a torrent of melting snow from the fells. The farmer had 4 sheep washed through a hedge into a river and drowned. You would not guess — seeing it in summer — what the country can be like when there is a "wash out" especially after snow. The roads have been very slippery. I suppose in the States the snow is deeper and *dry*. The repeated half thaws and half freezing spoil the pleasure of snow here; it is seldom dry for long together. Well — we shall welcome Spring!

I hope you are keeping better, and comfortably settled in your new home. Betty's baby will be a lively addition for a Christmas party. We spend it very quietly here. We are quite well, but I have been indoors a good deal, owing to the slippery roads. Our two little Pekinese dogs are amusing company.

I hope you will like this card; it's becoming difficult to invent yet another picture of Peter.

With love and best Christmas wishes,

To Bertha Mahony Miller

Dec. 18. 36

Another year slipped away, and no article for *The Horn Book*. I'm afraid I put it (the article) in the fire for rubbish! I don't seem to have a mind for writing anything, only sometimes a letter to the papers about farming or country affairs, which as often as not does not get printed.

The "times are out of joint," but strange to say, I think England may have cause to be obliged to Mrs. Simpson for bringing a scandal to a crisis — which has rid us of a most unsatisfactory king.

I have been thinking about furniture, and the very excellent, sensible designs in the catalogue. I never heard of the short and long skirt theory! The massive, square furniture has always appeared to me to be a branch of Cubism, and the Cubic rage in architecture was surely started about the time, or soon after, the finding of Tutankhamen's tomb — a sort of quasi-Egyptian style. Very fine in the East, and probably tolerable on the English south coast with hot sunshine and rolling chalk downs for background instead of the desert, but most absurdly unsuited to its surroundings when plumped down amongst the English fields and lanes, and especially amongst the Lakes mountains. There is an outsized large Cubist house near Wastwater Lake which looks altogether out of scale and too exotic, with flat roof, vast curved walls and bare terrace. Advanced, up-to-date people say we should get used to them, but I do not think flat roofs can be suitable for carrying a weight of snow. Anyhow, the District Council has refused to pass plans for a similar house near Lakeside, Windermere.

It is sad how many pretty old cottages are being condemned; slum clearance is necessary in towns, but old-fashioned cottages should be reconditioned in country districts instead of being scrapped. The Council houses which take their place are not solidly built, and yet the rents are beyond what workmen can afford comfortably. It is foolish to have the same regulations for country dwellings and for town backstreets. And even in towns — I do love Kendal — fine old houses piled up along the narrow yards, with oak floors and stairs. Fortunately, most of them are used for offices or warehouses, but too much is being pulled down in this craze for rebuilding.

I got a notice from the Bookshop. I am glad the change does not mean that it is coming to an end of its career of usefulness.

With kind regards and good wishes for 1937,

[P.S.] I do not quite understand the position of *The Horn Book*. Is it going on or not? and ought I not to pay for my copy?

To Anne Carroll Moore

Ap. 17. 37

It will be a pleasure and an interesting event to see you again! It sounds as though you and Nicholas are still going strong! I remember a dear old lady in my youth who replied to an inquiry as to how she was getting on — "Faint tho'pursuing"!! It is an up hill fight. The district is not greatly spoilt or altered since you saw it, except that the little towns grow larger. For the last three weeks my husband and I have been arguing with a new sanitary inspector who is applying a new housing act (intended for town slums) to the country cottages. You had better come and visit the district yet again while there are any left; he says half Hawkshead wants pulling down. The new type of council house is ugly and flimsy and high rented compared with our old thick walls and stone built chimnies.

It seems very shortsighted policy when the Lake district depends so much on tourists and visitors. The old Baldrys are gone from Moss Grove. I think one or both are dead. I believe Mrs. Scott is still at the Prince of Wales's.

My husband and I have escaped influenza this winter, and now we are enjoying a real showy April which is making the grass grow and helping the sheep and lambs. The ewes had a bad time after the great blizzard on March 1st but a favourable spring will help them to recover. We were lucky only to lose about 30 in the drifts. The snow was slow at melting so we had no serious floods here — though enough to condemn a pretty old cottage belonging to me at Coniston. I think our 'sanitary inspector Cooke' wants transporting into your Ohio Valley. Twice flooded for a few hours to the depth of 3 inches last winter; never during the preceding 18 months; and the old lady who tenants it has never had a doctor during 40 years.

We are going to be content with local Coronation festivities without attempting London.

Perhaps you may have the luck of a stout short — very short — elderly cousin of mine, at Silver Jubilee time. She took a soap box to a good position opposite Buckingham Palace, sat upon it till the last minute, and was hoisted up upon it by obliging neighbors in the crowd. Price of soap box 3d. But there is always the risk of soap boxes being ordered off by policemen — don't depend on my suggestion!

Telephone when you are coming.

You will be welcome,

May 4. 37

I wish you had been here this week. The country has been looking so lovely. Cherry blossoms, Whitethorn — damson all out in bloom together. The bluebells are a miss this year, little starving bells, twos and threes on a thin stalk. Either this dry weather, or, more probably, a very very full blue last year, and the bulbs are dividing this season. A thunder shower would help them. They will be out next week I think so far as my bluebell wood is concerned other woods may be later. We shall be so pleased to see you and Nicholas again; any night — there is no other visitor in prospect. I missed post owing to a few loud claps of thunder. When it had passed over, I went across the fields to the wood. It was starred with anemones but only one part was really blue.

[P.S.] The hawthorns will be very fine, buds just partly showing. I will show you this Troutbeck woods if we have time.

May 11. 37

The years have dealt more kindly with you than with me if you can face travelling on Whit Saturday!! (I begin to feel very slow and tired). But I acknowledge the attractions of Knole. You will get a train for Windermere at Oxenholme but I doubt its getting in at 5 any thing, probably very late. There are buses on to Ambleside, and late bus on to Hawkshead and Sawrey from Ambleside.

79

You had better memorize our telephone number in case you are stranded. You know what sort of place you are coming to — that's one comfort! if other elegancies are deficient. There will be enough to eat; you will make allowances for holiday time won't you.

The bluebells are very pretty still — and we have sunshine this afternoon with an east wind. I do hope it may keep fine tomorrow, after the great preparations. The weather has been showery all this week.

To Anne Carroll Moore

[May 1937]

I can send to meet the 5:15 at Windermere on Friday — an old fashioned black and green Talbot saloon and an aged chauffeur. I might be there myself; it's really better than searching the roads for you! It was wet — very — passable last weekend, but hope for a pleasant fine visit this time.
In haste to catch the post out
(yrs just received)

To Marian Frazer Harris Perry

July 6. 37

It will be such a pleasure to see you again. I missed you last year when you did not come. It does me good to see you and I have been feeling *old*! We are well but the hay is depressing. Certainly, I will keep those 3 days free.

Give my love to dear Betty and her family when you write to her. I have opened the book and nearly lost the post. Why are American books so much fresher than ours?

To Anne Carroll Moore

> Ashyburn
> Ancrum
> Roxburghshire
> Aug. 2. 37

Here we are on holiday, enjoying the first real summer hot weather! Actually the second week without rain, and the hay-making was finished at home before we left. We go back tomorrow. It has been a nice rest. This district is interesting, histories of Border warfare and old abbeys and castles — no doubt it was mean petty fighting but at least there was scope for romance and personal bravery. On Saturday we were shown through an old fortified house at Darnick, near Melrose. The owner, an elderly lady, tries to earn a living by showing the tower for 1/ and by making teas for visitors. Fancy the same family inhabiting since 1450; and the accumulation of old weapons and curious implements; like a museum, only a real dwelling where one is permitted to handle things. They showed us old carved furniture, one piece was different in pattern; they said it was by tradition *English*, and acquired in a raid. A cupboard seemed a curious and cumbrous article to steal, but undoubtedly the carving was of the same design as that of my 4 post bed! They had a 4 poster, much more elaborate than mine; said to have been slept in by Mary Queen of Scots, who poor lady seems to have slept in as many beds as Q. Elizabeth.

Kelso, Abbotsford, Jedburgh, the Eildon Hills and the Cheviots are all within driving distance. My sister-in-law has let the farm which my brother willed to her and lives very quietly with her niece. Wm. at time of writing is out fishing with the gardener. There is very little water in the river, but there are some salmon in the pools. It is a stream that flows to the Teviot. We had a call from Mary Haugh and her husband a week ago, they were in Bowness, very pleasant and interested in everything.

Mr. Zipprich had some of my original illustrations out to look through, which reminded me I never showed them to Nicholas, but I daresay you saw them before. Mrs. Fausler of N.Y. Met. Museum has been to Messrs Warne's office wishing to borrow the *Peter Rabbit* originals. They were willing to lend them and I have no objection. I don't think the *P.R.* drawings "represent a very high watermark in the history of book illustration" to quote Mrs. Fausler!! In fact I think them bad; the rabbit on the cover I have always thought a horrid monstrosity all out of drawing. But undoubtedly it was that first book *P.R.* which hit "a mark" of some sort. The much better-executed illustrations of following books of the series did not make the same hit. I was trying to talk about it with Mary Haugh, but, — as you probably discovered — I am slow at expressing what I am driving at. I was trying to ask her whether the art of live speech story telling is not the real thing? I expect *P.R.* comes nearer to word story telling than the later books, which she probably has to cut and put into her own words. I was very interested to hear her praise *Sister Anne.* I did so much enjoy your visit. You are over my head intellectually, but you appreciate old fashioned simple memories and pleasures. I am glad you and Nicholas had a pleasant passage back to N.Y. My love to you both,

To Marian Frazer Harris Perry

Dec. 14. 37

It would be uncivil to commence a Christmas letter with an expression of satisfaction that an *American* gun boat has been sunk. It is maddening to think what this country has endured from the Japanese. When I was young there used to be what was called a 'naval demonstration' if any other country was impertinent; if our China squadron "demonstrated" at Tokyo — presumably the Italians would attack the Suez canal. It is to be hoped that the United States will realize what sort of neighbors the Japanese are likely to become in the Pacific. And to think that the horrid little men learnt so much of their mechanical skill at Barrow! A few years ago they used to be a common sight at weekend, strolling in two and threes, enjoying the beauty of the Lakes landscapes. Which may be a little bit like Japan. At present we are buried in a heavy fall of snow; there have been several falls, and it has been 18 inches deep on the exposed places since Sunday and very little softening yet, which makes it bad for the sheep. They can stand hunger better at the beginning of winter than in March, but I am afraid there will be losses.

I am thinking of Cornelia Meig's description of a great snow storm in *The Covered Bridge,* where the sheep were housed in a barn. It would be as impossible to house our little half wild sheep as to confine wild rabbits. Forty of the older less hardy Sawrey sheep have been brought home from the moor today, they don't seem particularly hungry; at least they are not keen to eat hay.

It has been such a lovely autumn, mild and sunny right into November — the winter weather came all of a sudden. We have been in good health — But considerably disturbed by the doings of a sanitary inspector under the New Housing Act. It is aimed at town slums, but the Council abuses its powers to attack country cottages and villages. The inspector says half of Hawkshead needs pulling down; he told someone "all this talk about preservation is piffle!!" There has been such an outcry that it is hoped the Council will not touch the little squares and archways. Some houses in back lanes are admittedly bad, and 11 cottage owners have been plastering and white washing to smarten things up before the inspector calls. We are wondering whether he will come to this cottage, the low rooms and flagged floor in the kitchen would be contrary to rules.

I hope you and your friend had a pleasant journey home. I enjoyed seeing you again — and looking so well — you have not changed a bit since the first visit! I begin to feel old and stiff — I have stopped indoors since the snow, except just feeding birds in the garden.

Do you remember I told you about some furniture and china at Belmont Hall near Hawkshead? Miss Owen could not make up her mind to sell and disperse it — she went back to Rome in very poor health, and the place remains locked up. Romantic, but damp! She burnt a lot of clothes and things in the yard before leaving. You have had the experience of dismantling a house, things do accumulate. She brought a good deal from N.Y. forty years ago. I have not any rabbit card this year and I can't get out to shop! With love and good wishes,

To Anne Carroll Moore

Dec. 18th 37

What delightful books! [*And To Think That I Saw It On Mulberry Street*, by Dr. Seuss, and *Christmas Carols*, by Grace Castagnetta and Hendrik Willem van Loon]. The magistrate's clerk does not often unbend to so much amusement. Police on motor bykes are irresistable. — the old man hitched behind — he did laugh! Yesterday at Grasmere — returning from a funeral in deep snow — the Grasmere constable stopped his legal adviser. He wanted to know how long he was required by law to keep a turkey alive (at Christmastide!)? The bird had been found walking northward in the snow up Dunmail Raise, and no one claimed it; an incident almost worthy of *Mulberry Street* which I think is the cleverest book I have met with for many years. The swing and movement of the pictures, and the natural truthful simplicity of the untruthfulness. I think my own success was largely due to straight forward lying — spontaneous natural bare faced! Too many story books for children are condescending self-conscious invention — and then some trivial insight, some small incorrect detail gives the show away. Dr. Seuss does it thoroughly! The *Carol* book is charming, only I do not like the scratchiness of the cover design and *one* or two other full pages. The landscapes are very beautiful and full of feeling. But I wish the artist had not put in the star with the solid tail in the "First Nowell" . It is like an aeroplane; which is an emissary of the devil.

"Give peace in our time O Lord!" We are so often on the edge of the abyss. I love to hear the carol singing on a frosty still winter night. But we are sadly wanting a thaw; it is so cruel for the poor sheep — there was a very heavy fall last Sunday, and it has frozen on the surface. We have plenty of hay but the sheep are so little accustomed to eat it that they prefer to wander about scraping holes in search of withered grass. There will be many losses if there is not a thaw soon. It has been a lovely summer and autumn, warm and sunny right into middle November; then suddenly a killing frost. We have both kept well. I don't know how to excuse my neglect in never having written to you, when I look back to the true pleasure that your visit gave us both. I seemed to get to know *you* better, beyond your fine work which one realized before — dear Anne Caraway [Anne Carroll Moore's nom de plume] and Nicholas!

It has not been a very cheerful season, so many old friends and neighbours dead or gone from the district; and one or two big worries. The latest seems successfully conquered — a most horrid stupid attack upon the old village of Hawkshead and old cottages in general by an ignorant sanitary inspector, who announced that "all this talk about preservation is piffle!!" The Council takes proceedings under a new housing act which was intended for clearance of town slums. The Ambleside and Grasmere Council and their surveyor have been perfectly reasonable, only attacking abuses and really unsanitary conditions — but we have the misfortune to be local-governed from Ulverston, which is an industrial center. The Ulverston Council have been giving their inspector a free hand; which ended in causing the death of a poor old widow, who lived in her own *good* dry house near Hawkshead.

Without any previous warning about defects requiring repair, he served a notice that the Council being satisfied the house is unfit for human habitation and cannot at a reasonable cost be rendered so fit etc. She broke her heart over it and was found dead in bed. Which caused an uproar, as he had been in quantities of houses, saying they should be cleared away. The matter got into the newspapers, and the Council is singing very small indeed. I hope it lasts !!

Very kind remembrance and good wishes from William and me to you and Nicholas —

Yrs. affectionately,
"Beatrix Potter"

To Marian Frazer Harris Perry

Oct. 4 38

I have been very neglectful about writing letters this unpleasant summer — and now one has a feeling of stupefaction. Anything — "nearly" anything — may be better than war. It is not an honourable fear — and doubtful whether it has any permanency.

Can you hear Hitler over the wireless as far as America? Did you ever hear such a brutal, raving lunatic. I could not understand a word of his clipped rapid German; but the ranting note and the smiling face in the telegraphed photographs are not sane. If Mr. Chamberlain believes in his promises he must be an incurable optimist. We did not take gas masks very seriously in this remote district; which was just as well for our peace of mind as they were supplied wrong size — so few small and medium compared with the large size that the police sensibly decided it would be best to withdraw them. It is the Air that has let us down — the Navy was ready. I wonder whether a new and more solid frame of mind will emerge from this slap-in-the-face; there ought to be conscription. Czechoslovakia would have been wiped out in any case; but it is a set back for England.

The season has been wet and dismal, not to be called "summer". The hay was a wearying long task; it was finished on the same day as our small harvest, Sept. 19th. The corn was got well. There is still a good deal out in the north; but taking one place with another there are heavy crops. We burnt some of the last of the hay; the barns were full and it seemed little worth, after repeated wettings. This last weekend there has been a wild gale.

The sheep sales are coming on; up to date they are bad, prices 5/ per sheep down from last year. Everything is in an upset way.

That is a most curious book you have sent me, so "alive" [*The Yearling*, by Marjorie Kinnan Rawlings] — I find myself trying to make out how the illusion of reality is done? I liked it extremely until I came to the rattlesnake which gave me creeps and horrors! The end chapters are too horrid.

My brother years ago had a very bad accident with a viper; he sucked the bite and the poison got into his throat and inside him. I wonder if it is a superstition, or true, that newly killed flesh will draw poison? I have heard or read it before, but it scarcely seems explainable. One of our little peke dogs got bitten on the nose this spring, and was very ill; we dosed her with whiskey and carbonate of soda. The actual bite did not swell; but the swelling and pain went down the gland of the neck and paralyzed the hind legs. She got quite well again within a week. They are good company, but sad pickles, always hunting. Tzu zee had killed 2 large rats successfully, so she must tackle a snake.

I have not been at all well lately. I got a chill, and the weather has not been helpful. My husband has been over worked; old friends and neighbours dying, and their affairs to wind up. There are these black depressing seasons! I hope we are properly thankful that there is no war. For which we may thank the unhappy Czechs.

Perhaps a better, more wise world may emerge. I have not much faith in Mr. Chamberlain, and if we are ever in the "same mess" as the Czechs it would be little use to wait for U.S.A.!! Everyone for themselves — and under ground in tunnels! Thanking you for the book.

[P.S.] My old American friend went back to Rome; she feels safe with dear Duce. We all think the mobilization of our Navy stirred Mussolini to intervene.

P.S. I have been reading your letter again — of June ! The book did not come quite so long ago as *that*; your cousins had sensibly read it first. It is a curiously graphic picture of Florida swamp life.

86

I never heard of "trench mouth" — Shingles does go in epidemics in this way — that it so often coincides with chicken pox — too often to be a coincidence. Thus I had chicken pox being nearly 60 when William had shingles; but which of us started the infection or where caught from cannot say — I hope Dick got clear of it. Shingles leaves ticklings which can be mildly troublesome for years.

It was well that your kind thought for your friend kept you out of Europe this summer. Surely things must settle one way or another.

The best chance would be realization by the German people. I do not believe they could have won a war. But I am afraid they will be strengthened by the acquisition of Bohemia. And this country is kept in the dark too. We are completely perplexed about Russia. Not an agreeable idea to have to line up with Russia. But the silence seems strange; unless it is completely rotten.

Was it you who sent me *The Country of the Pointed Firs!* I have been reading it with great pleasure. I shall never go over the sea; but I think I would like the New England States.

To Anne Carroll Moore

Nov. 17th. 38

Thank you for your card, and Nicholas's invitation — How I have thought of writing to you and put off — uncheerfully! It has been rather a miserable season; and now this crisis and humiliation by way of climax. We do not like Mr. Chamberlain. He could do no other than give in at Munich — things were in such a helpless muddle; whose fault?? and there was not a clear case for the Sudetan question or for the Czechs. The serious thing is his want of any proper sense of responsibility *now*, which has simply thrown the advising of necessary defense measures into the hands of [the] Labour party and some "War mongers". The unpreparedness and muddle were incredible, and panic in the towns — As one police sergeant says — the authorities frightened the civil population, without doing anything to help them. We did *not* have any refugees here; but before another crisis we hope to get something arranged.

No one would object at a time of crisis; but imagine having Barrow low class Irish — perhaps 6 or 8 — quartered in one's house for months! The proper way is to arrange hotel accomodations. There has been a

sound of heavy guns all afternoon. Either our own testing at Eskmeals
— or else one of the Spanish ships that takes one into Whitehaven. To
think that in one's old age one must hear that sound again! The seasons have been all wrong; March was warm and lovely, and the blue
bells came out early. The summer was rain — rain — rain. We did not
finish hay till Sept. 19th. There is plenty of it, but not very good. My
husband is well — I am not! I have had colds and sciatica and chills
one on top of another — I went away for ten days in October to stay
with a friend near Liverpool—which is a wonder for me, as I am such
a stay-at-home! The change did me good, but not yet quite right. Liverpool was interesting — but not exactly cheerful. My friend's son had
just come back from China, a second engineer on a liner. His boat had
been driven out of her course in a typhoon and got inside territorial
waters near Tokyo. A Japanese gun boat held them up and cross examined them with such impudence that they began to think they
would be interned. The Union Jack and the Stars and Stripes don't
count for much now in the East.

The weather is mild and damp — the autumn leaves are falling fast.
I very much enjoyed making acquaintance with your friend Priscilla
Edie, very much — I enjoyed her call — thoughtful — "quietly" strong
and sensible. She was fascinating. I have found a little pipe I would like
to present to our dear friend Nicholas — I remembered several things
after you and he had gone! I hope you are in very good health. You
have the satisfaction of being rather further away from Hitler than we
are!

With our kind regards,

[P.S.] Please do not think me "snobbish" about possible refugees — The
police fear it may be like the Belgians last time — i.e. the responsible
better sort of householders would stick to their homes through thick
and thin, but 'n'er-do-wells' and flotsam would bolt and take up quarters as entitled. The Ambleside residents were warned that they would
be required to board 2,000 from Newcastle if war broke out. I have
been used to lend sites for Girl Guide camps of town children, and
would gladly organize *with the police*; but the authorities are hopeless!
from Mr. N.C. downwards!!

To Bertha Mahony Miller

Dec. 11. 38

All greetings of good cheer to you and your husband — who have the luck to live beyond the Atlantic! How goes the furniture? In turning over the leaves of a bookseller's catalogue, my eye caught this advertisement of a secondhand book, and I wonder if it is interesting. The pleasure of collecting is in abeyance here, under the cloud that overshadows life. Personally we are in no danger from aeroplanes amongst the mists and rocky valleys, but as regards good furniture and china and the comforts of home, we would in case of war be swarmed over by refugees from Barrow. The shipyards and docks are only fifteen miles away. No one would grudge asylum in a raid; but the dockers' families are rough, mostly Irish Catholics, and the prospect of possible billeting at the rate of two per room (kitchen and bathroom counted) and to sleep on floors for an indefinite period is startling! Still that's nothing compared with the peril to this country. Unless America backs us up, we are done. It is fatal to give way to bullies in the first instance. If the navies of U.S.A. and Great Britain had been allowed to put down the Japanese at the time of the Panay incident, there would have been no European crisis. You cannot imagine what the "crisis" was like. I felt ashamed, and yet when one looks at the vast size of our open, defenceless towns, will they — *can* they? — ever face modern bombardment? The trenches dug in London were standing in water — wet graves in cold weather.

It has been a miserably wet season, no real summer, and such constant rain. We may be thankful it is not snow or we would be buried deep. My husband is well — only getting wet and sneezing. I had a long bout of lumbago and sciatica, so will just have to be careful of the damp, and long for spring and happier times. Enforced leisure indoors does not reawaken literary inspiration. I'm sorry Miss Mahony. The wells of fancy have run dry! I can think of nothing but forebodings. Farm prices are so low that the farmers are in revolt. It sounds unpatriotic, but they cannot pay the standard wages and carry on without going bankrupt. Fancy selling a live sheep for 5/3.

There was an interesting sale of old family goods at a house near here, a house furnished throughout with Sheraton Mahogany and containing some older oak and silver. A two-handled cup 1705 made £110. And a Queen Anne cabinet £60. It seemed a pity to see old silver with the family crest sold to dealers and dispersed, but young people think of nothing but motor cars and aeroplanes now. And if our "antiques" go to America — perhaps they will be safer there!

There have been some American visitors this summer — Anne Carroll Moore in June, and later in August that nice boy Henry P. Coolidge — grown up now. He looked over my old oak with renewed interest. I did not buy any at the Green odd sale. There were two Charles II chairs, cane seats. I fingered these a long time. A dealer friend said they were genuine, but I could not *quite* believe in the cresting, though I could not feel any new joining on, so I did not bid. They were too perfect to be true. I have a pair bought from a trades-man's humble sale, but both of the backs are frankly repaired. I fancy those very tall-backed Charles II chairs had a failing of getting tipped backwards.

I am not often near any good-class shops, but I am pleased to notice from illustrations in better class newspapers that the hideous Cubic furniture is losing ground. So far the reaction is mainly to Empire; but Chippendale models and reproductions are coming back also. I don't admire tubular metal chairs, but there is more sense and reason for them than for the bulking square monstrosities.

I liked your catalogue extremely — flounces and all. There used to be a legend that American pianos wore frilled trousers to conceal their legs, excessive propriety! My old American friend dispursed her N.Y. family furniture before she went back to Rome last August, at least she arranged the sale. It was sold at the date of the crisis, very badly. In any case, I fear she would have met with disappointment. The mahogany was scarcely old enough, about 1840. She withdrew the silver; it is at the bank in Ambleside. She was in Rome during the crisis, and wrote provoking letters. She said the U.S.A. Consul advised her to return to America, but she felt so safe with the dear Duce she would not think of leaving! Especially as she hates Roosevelt. No doubt Mussolini has done fine things for Italy, in Italy. But these dictators are ill neighbors; and Mr. Chamberlain is no match for them. He did his best, but he has been made a fool of, and the unpreparedness is unforgivable. All except the Navy. Thanks to Mr. Baldwin the fleet is alright now — but cannot be used, for fear of bringing the aeroplanes upon our open towns. Even the electricity is *one* vast unprotected overhead grid; all vulnerable.

To Betty and Richard Stevens

Dec. 11. 38

I won't say "morituri te salutant". We are not in personal danger here amongst the misty hills and valleys, but the outlook is pretty bad for this country. You are lucky to be across the Atlantic. You cannot imagine what the crisis was like. Utter confusion, unpreparedness and panic in the large towns. I do not see how the enormous towns *can* be protected against bombardment. A friend who has been in London says the trenches are standing water. It would be a case of choosing between shrapnel splinters and pneumonia if it became necessary to use them in winter. It is a bad mistake to give way to bullies in the first instance. If the Americans and British Navies had been allowed to give a lesson to the Japs at the date of the Panay incident, there would have been no European crisis.

It is very wearing; one incident follows another; and what an artificial feverish "work" — a necessity to arm, but what is to be the end? and what reaction of unemployment if and when the armament ceases? It is a horrid world, and makes one feel old and tired.

Also it never stops raining; the last settled fine weather was in May. We are pretty well, only W. gets wet and sneezes, and I am afraid to get wet because I have had lumbago and sciatica. So we will be glad to get through winter.

Is Dick quite well of the shingles? I don't know 'trench mouth' — it sounds horrid! W. had shingles once rather severely, and if he gets a cold — like a chill through wet feet — he complains of still feeling tickles in the middle of his back, although it must be ten years or more. So I hope Dick being younger manages a thorough cure. Shingles is sometimes coincident with cases of chicken pox, though it is difficult to see how there can be any connection.

Nonya will be getting a great girl? And the 'new baby' has turned 2 years. How pretty they will be playing together. I daresay I will be hearing about them from Mrs. Perry — and I hope to have a letter from you or Dick, dear Betty. I am afraid I never wrote last Christmas. I am in good time this year.

Do you remember meeting the big car in the narrow road near Buttermere? There has been a controversy about making a big wide new road, but the Buttermere folk have succeeded in opposition; there are just to be some wide passing places at intervals, and improvement of corners. The district has not changed much; the town of Keswick has grown much larger; but the shores of the lakes are still beautiful and unspoilt. Another place where I think of you is at Grasmere where you bathed.

[P.S.] Why oh why such dislike of Roosevelt?! Not that I know or care! but I hope if he were beaten it would not mean that the States would be still more standoffish? If we are doomed to be destroyed by the Fascists — your western cities will be in danger from Japan.

To Marian Frazer Harris Perry

Dec. 13. 38

I am posting in good time, to wish you a Merry Christmas. Things are gloomy here; and full of foreboding. The best hope is that the Germans themselves will become tired of Hitler. Though the pinch of hunger will be lightened for them by his latest "peaceful" acquisitions in Rumanian and Lithuanian wheatlands. There seems no limit yet to what he will ask for, and what Chamberlain will agree to. No one wants war; but this country has been made a fool of.

I sometimes wonder if our immense defenceless towns would ever stand up to modern bombing. It is said that the trenches dug in London are standing half full of water. What is the use of piling up armaments if the government and the unhappy civilian populations can be bullied? Perhaps to provide weapons for Germany to seize, like the fortifications in Czechoslovakia!

We have rain — rain — rain — luckily no snow in the lowlands or we would be deeply buried — never was such a year in oldest memory!

It is very raw, and I have to be careful. My husband gets wet and sneezes, but so far we have not had bad colds. I have sent a card for Nonya to Betty. I hope to be hearing from Betty, about the children, and I hope Dick alright — "trench mouth" sounds horrid!

[P.S.] My critical verdict on *The Yearling* — splendid but too painful for satisfaction.

March 7th. 39

What a very charming book you have sent to me this time! [Elizabeth Coatsworth's *Here I Stay*] It appeals to me. The strength and beauty of the girl's character — the poetry of the great lonely spaces and woods, and the dependent domestic animals. The writer has described the helpless distress of being unable to feed them in a great snow. Fodder is always obtainable — at a price — in this country, but our hardy sheep which have never been accustomed to hay are hungered in long spells of snow; it is pitiful to hear them bleating. They don't seem to care for hay, and won't touch any that has been thrown down and trampled, not even when the black cattle are being fed in the snow and show them an example. There have been repeated falls this winter, but alternating with thaws and heavy rain — its been a wretched season. We have all had influenza, to great inconvenience, although not serious. I was indoors 5 weeks, but it was partly owing to the weather and the illness of my maid. A waste of time! Indeed it is only a time to struggle through. I am afraid there are still idle thoughtless people who can live giddy lives and enjoy the racket. No sensible person can feel otherwise than anxious. There has been distinctly less acute anxiety since Chamberlain spoke out about siding with France. But the lull is not cheerful. If it is not coming — what an awful waste of money and energy! though the only security is to prepare. The town dwellers are now in less fright and objecting to having steel shelters dumped on their door step. They have this much excuse — they are told to plant the shelters 3 foot deep into the ground and to heap the dug out earth on the roof — which is a problem in a small back yard, floored with *concrete*; I think the shelters are much more sensible than the first orders about a gas proof room in every house. The modern brick houses in towns would collapse on top of their owners. We are doing nothing here in that line, only very slowly organizing.

I don't know what to say about your projected tour. If I were you, I would wait. This tension cannot go on — year on end. I read your enclosed cutting from 'Walter Lippman' with interest. I agree with his deduction, i.e. about Hitler hesitating to attack. The risk is — whether Hitler can *control* indefinitely long the powers of evil which he has inspired. Take Japan for instance — probably it would *not* suit Hitler to have war break out in the Far East — but the Japanese are such an arrogant fearfully cruel people that they — being encouraged to have swelled heads — may at any moment commit some atrocity which will almost oblige America and England to punish them. Would that not be the beginning of a conflagration? Yet too much wrong has been conceded already. It is a pity your Roosevelt is so impulsive to domestic politics; if he were steadier and more trusted at home — he would have still more weight in the world. Unless America seriously prepares — she will someday be at the mercy of Japan, as Australia is now — except for our overworked British Navy.

My old friend Miss Owen has died in Rome — unashamed old Fascist — in spite of the wise good Pope. She had still some furniture and books left at Belmont Hall. Such a search and inquiry for her latest will. I thought the R.C.'s would have had it; but her executor turns out to be the Hanover Central Bank in N.Y. I suppose I shall hear in course of time who is entitled to deal with the remaining things — not me — if a letter "giving" them to another friend holds good. They are getting dreadfully mildewed, but of no great value; unless there is anything of interest in a locked room.

My husband joins in kindest regards — we *would* like to see you again; and in safer times.

The Woman's Hospital
Liverpool

March 30. 39

You may be surprised to see this address. I was in last Nov. for what seemed a trivial matter. There was some disquieting symptoms of bleeding a fortnight ago, so I came again and the surgeon is somewhat serious. I don't suppose it will be worse anything than "curetting", but anything in the womb is apt to be the beginning of the end. I am in no pain or discomfit, but awfully worried about my husband. You might have noticed, I am the stronger minded of the pair, also the money is mine; death duties would make it awkward for him and the servants. He belongs to a family who have the privilege of dying suddenly — in their sleep. I have always hoped to survive! At all costs I hope he will remarry happily and sensibly. I have felt very tired and aged the last two years. Maybe the surgeon will put me right — but he cannot put me young again. I think you stop on the safe side of the Atlantic. You see the feeling of confidence was only a ruse. Now the Italians are doing "says the spider to the fly" to France this time, and

perhaps France also has made a fool of our Chamberlain and his umbrella (which he lost in Rome). It is a weary world. I have done my bit
— here's fame!! The surgeon says he backed a horse called "Benjamin
Bunny" and it only got half way round the race course.

What do you think I am reading? *Uncle Tom's Cabin*. I had not read
it to myself. I remember my nurse reading it to me when I was a small
child — Eliza springing across the ice on the Ohio River. Hospital is
very comfortable; ward sister is such a nice sensible woman. Give my
love to Betty and Dick and 3 of a family, and with love to you dear
Mrs. Perry, I remain,

[P.S.] The surgeon has just been in again. He does not anticipate a
severe operation, but it is not a pleasant prospect to envisage any thing
wrong at all. What a pretty country it is at the Lakes, is it not? Hitler
cannot spoil the fells; the rocks and fern and lakes and waterfalls will
outlast us all. I can see the tower of [the] unfinished cathedral from the
hospital windows. It seems a waste of money, apart from air raids. And
councils still pass plans for great institution buildings and block[s] of
lofty flats — it all seems so inconsequent and unreal. Why don't they
have conscription if in earnest to defend?

I hope to see you again in better times, but I trust not as an invalid!
I would rather go to rest. I am a very good patient and cheerful, in spite
of this rather morbid letter. I want to say how much pleasure I have
had from knowing you and other delightful New Englanders.

*The book sent by Priscilla Edie, a librarian at the New York Public
Library, was* The Flop-Eared Hound *by Ellis Credle which was illustrated by photographs.* The Five Chinese Brothers *was written by Claire
Huchet Bishop and illustrated by Kurt Wiese.* Mei-Li *was both written
and illustrated by Thomas Handforth.*

To Anne Carroll Moore

Women's Hospital
Liverpool

March 30. 39

I cannot remember writing to thank you for those charming books at
Christmas. They were an interest to me when I was in bed with flu.

Also a lovely one, *The Flop-Eared Hound*, sent to me by that nice Priscilla Edie. Will you thank her for me? I haven't her address here. My husband was most amused with the Chinese brothers, most laughable. And *Snow White* very pleasing, put as it ought to be. *Mei-Li* makes one sad. Remembering the horrors in China and elsewhere one ought to appreciate being ill in a comfortable bed. This is my second visit — last November — which was thought trivial, but there came to be more serious trouble. I am an old woman and tired. I am exceedingly sorry for my husband. You may have noticed I am the stronger half of the pair — moreover the money is mine; and death duties are so heavy that my death before his would be awkward. I do not anticipate anything worse than curetting, but I suppose it may be "the writing on the wall". What a state the world is in. I should like to see the end of Hitler — but then it might be "the end of us". I sometimes wonder whether France and England have the manpower that can conquer or whether we are making munitions for him like the Greeks. Things seem very slow to get organized. I have come here without a gas mask! It has been a very trying winter — wet and gloomy weather — and anxious news abroad.

Now I am sitting up in bed in no pain or discomfit and joking with the "probationers," a set of little monkeys. I am also doing a bit of the valance embroidered on the 4 post bed at Hill Top. I took you to Tom Kitten's house, did I not? I dare say finishing the curtains will be nice amusement if I cannot go about much. As to finishing any more stories — I doubt? For sometime I have resolutely refused to try to do any more for publication but there are some wanderings further of the *Caravan* that it's a pity, they were floating ideas not written words. I wrote the easier stories and perhaps they were more than enough long winded, but there were several rather pretty that never got hatched.

I have always felt that the New Englanders understood and liked an aspect of my writings which is not appreciated by the British shop keeper, though very possibly children the world over appreciate it, without consciously understanding that there is more in the books than mere funniness. They circulate anyhow; more than 150 thousand sold last year. Astronomical figures! How ever will the nations pay their debts?

I have had very great pleasure from contact and friendship with the Americans — so good luck to you and Nicholas and good-bye if we don't happen to meet again. Keep on the safe side of the Atlantic. Remember me to all friends.

[P.S.] I was so sorry after you left us I had forgotten to ask if you would like to look through the original illustrations again.

Private Ward
Women's Hospital
Liverpool

Ap. 13. 39

Present my compliments to Nicholas and warn him never to indulge in worries. I have survived, and feel supremely silly. The surgeon says I shall be cured, which remains to be seen. At all events, it never can happen again, "a pretty complete removal at an unusually advanced age."

I do not know when I shall be allowed to go out and home. I am comfortable here and in no hurry — only for some anxious thoughts of the bridges and bottle necks of the main road north. How very anxious the news continues to be — one crisis after another, and piling up of armaments — it cannot go on indefinitely. My husband stopped here in Liverpool over Easter and he will come for the day next Sunday. Easter was so warm and sunny, but I am not sorry to see a wet April shower for it will be getting dry for the lambs at home. I have had lots of flowers posted to me and a friend in Liverpool has lent me some books.

To think that I thought I had wound up and arranged everything — even to inquiring whether there is a crematorium in Liverpool (which is inconvenient in the Lake district) and now it is all at large again. As to whether I am thankful I refuse to make any observation before seeing how it lasts —

To Marian Frazer Harris Perry

> Women's Hospital
> Catherine Street
> Liverpool
> Ap. 13. 39

No one could be more surprised than I am — to be writing to you again! I feel rather foolish. I am not decided whether I also feel thankful — it depends on the future. Hospital is very comfortable and I devour — nearly — all food offered, and wish I could get up and cook some of it. Easter has been lovely weather, so warm and sunny; and today's rain will do no harm. I hear the lambs are coming at home — faster than the grass comes. Friends have sent lots of flowers. My husband has gone home. But he is coming for the day on Sunday.

I cannot learn when I shall be let out; there is no inducement to hurry back before feeling independently strong enough. But shall be glad to get past the bridges at Preston and Lancaster if things get any worse! A town like Liverpool will be defended; but some people think the north road would be very dangerous in the event of war. The Irish bombings are very silly; little damage, but troublesome to the police. My night nurse going home with a suspicious satchel in the early morning finds herself observed by a flutterment of policemen, rounding up street and squares.

Now I have not told you whether I am cured for I do not know. The surgeon says I am. But then he told me last November that I was a particularly healthy old woman? Four times on the table in 5 months?? A thorough clearance at all events; and a good patient "with plenty of kick." Any further relapse is unlikely. I was very sick and burst the stitches which delayed things a little.
With love,

> July 3. 39

I agree with your feeling about the newspapers. It is a nightmare. To think of that lunatic — that homocidal monster "resting" at Berchtesgaden. There is no doubt he intends to take Danzig.

Whether his cleverness and Mr. Chamberlain's "caution" will enable the Poles to be snuffed out without a general conflagration remains to be seen. The only cheering factor is the visit of our Admiral to Tientsin. This country cannot police the world, and also keep up a fleet in home waters capable of facing Germany. I cannot understand Mr. Chamberlain. Poland seems more difficult to help than Czecholsovakia. It is an advantage that Italy is likely to be involved; it is vulnerable — but imagine having to bombard Naples? War is no longer a gentleman's game — if it ever was.

I think you are wise not to come over at present — if it comes you would be one more mouth to feed! I have laid in a hoard of dog biscuits for our two little dogs; they turn up their snub noses at biscuit, while they can get scraps of meat, or rabbit. We have begun hay time — just the day before the long drought broke. The rain is welcome, as the one small field which was mown was very thin and poor — the grass is growing now.

One must just rub along and see what comes. The price of wool remains low. Government are buying wool; but softer higher grade than our mountain fleeces.

I can go about much as usual now, only I get rather tired, especially with shaking in the car. It does not do me any harm, but I feel as if I wanted to hang on to something whenever there is a jolt. I went to the Troutbeck sheep farm this morning and watched the men clipping, and afterwards herd the cattle, driven into the "West fold", a fine sight, about 30 black cows with their calves at foot, and a magnificent white bull. He is a lovely beast and so far he is very quiet. There are one or two odd mistakes in that very charming book *Here I Stay*. A mare suffers least of any domestic mother; she just lies down and up again which has given rise to the saying that it is unlucky to see a foal born — i.e. something wrong if there is time to see the birth. The mare does not "sweat with pain", and Margaret could have driven her and the new-born foal back to the barn as soon as the latter had stretched its legs; they are most precocious. Moreover "Lady" would not have gone to the top of a hill; no such luck. It is well known fact that if a mare can get into water she will do so and risk drowning her off spring, goodness knows why.

Furthermore — the lamb Whitey was an unconscionable time of growing up! But it is a most sweet story.

I suppose we will get through the future somehow — we always have.

Aug. 24. 39

With a worse crisis than last September's — one does not know what to think? It is — at best — very wearisome. Neighbors busy stitching black stuff for blinds. I have my dark curtains, rather moth eaten, from last war. I suppose it's the same all over. The black-outs have been held late, after people have put their lights out; to save inconvenience. It's difficult to strike a mean. It seems like playing at being ready for war; and neither the Germans nor *us* know whether we are serious. I dislike Chamberlain more and more. He has been saying this afternoon that he has an "unpleasant surprise"; he has had too many of them — no fore-sight — no leadership. If he has an idea of autocratically directing the forces it might lose us the war. Impenetrable self-satisfaction.

It is well you did not take passage to Europe. Apart from this latest development it would not have been pleasant. A young woman from this district who has been on a trip to Italy says she had to undress at the frontier coming out of Italy, but you being an American citizen might have received more consideration.

We have had ten days of real hot weather and got in the hay and cut the harvest. Life is perplexing. Whether to lay in much stores or not? I have got a lot of sugar. I personally missed butter and sugar worst, last war. We seemed to be kept very short in spite of ration cards. And I have got a store of biscuits for my 2 little dogs. They have been a great pleasure and amusement to me since my illness. I am feeling much stronger now, able to get about and get through some of the arrears of things that have not been attended to on the farms. Farms are very bad to let. Everything seems to be listless and in a muddle; except of course ammunition works and camps.

What an uncheerful letter! Perhaps it will all fizzle down again. But at best it is wearisome and costly.

[P.S.] My husband is well and wisely declines to bother himself. Just plods on, with too much to do all day, and bowls of fine evenings. Kindest regards from us,

To Mrs. Charles Hopkinson

Nov. 3. 39

We both of us remember you well! You were so like Wm's youngest sister. And your husband sketched opposite on the croft — and more and more daughters. I hope the rest has recovered you as much as an operation did me! I was out of health for a time but now I feel active and well at 73. And I hope to see the end of Hitler, — surely he has wrought his own doom; though the endless mischief which he has sown will take a very long time to end, or stop.

I wonder if your daughter and her husband are in Geneva. But one place is like another — unless folks have the advantage of the Atlantic between.

We are very busy, though not involved with any near relations or servants in the war this time. So far there is no shortage at all — though butter will be a perplexity. I don't know who will stop us eating our own but I suppose conscience will prick. There are no evacuees in this village. We see a good deal of activity overhead being near the coast, but so far no raids have come so far as the west coast, and every one runs out when we hear a plane.

With kind regards,

[P.S.] I don't draw pictures now. I am 73.

To Marian Frazer Harris Perry

Nov. 26 39

I have posted you *The Country Child*. I think I prefer "Susan" to "Lucy" who I hope followed "Delia" to school, and forgot some of her fancies, which were more highly strung than the open air fears of *The Country Child*. I do not remember ever fearing trees; but I did not — like little Susan — have long dark walks from school all alone.

The Welsh background of *Dew on the Grass* [Eiluned Lewis] is very life like, and the contact with the Welsh servants. I had an old uncle — a typical Manchester merchant, who had a country house near Denbigh, where I often went to stay. The servants were charming. But "Taffy was a Welshman, etc.". My cousin said she could not keep pillow cases. In those days we wore chemises!

I like the chapter about the shooting picnic and the dog cart especially. Shall we get back to pony carts? We have just — and — so managed on our petrol ration so far.

The weather is very wild and broken, and work is drawing in for the winter; one can take it easier.

The mines menace is disquieting; some way of dealing with them must be found. It must be very nerve racky. My friend's engineer son arrived safely from the far east — many weeks late — in a convoy; they had bumped two mines in the Channel which did *not* explode. Also one ship had rammed another ship in the convoy. They arrived safely. Nothing is rationed yet except petrol. I remain with kind regards and thanks for the book.

To Betty Harris Stevens

Dec. 15. 39

This is a reprinted card so Nonya *may* have had it already, but it is appropriate as there are now 3 little bunnies. Your aunt wrote that there was another baby and you and Dick as young as ever.

We feel old here, but fairly well. It is a worrying time — when will it end? With love to you all.

To Marian Frazer Harris Perry

Jan. 5. 40

I certainly did write to thank you for the book. Perhaps I may have misdirected the letter, like one I wrote to a friend in Auckland, New Zealand, and forgot to add N.Z. It reached her eventually, via Bishop Auckland in County Durham! The American mail has been coming in gradually instead of with the usual and remarkable concentration upon Christmas Eve. Your Christmas photograph card of the nativity is very sweet and touching. I told you I liked the book, all except the little girl; she was a real type of child, fanciful, imaginative — a little morbid — it would do her good to go to school! The Welsh background was vividly real. I had an old Manchester uncle who had a country house in Wales, where I often visited; the Welsh folks in the book are exactly true to life. One peculiarity, not recounted; my uncle's maid servants were charming, smiling pretty Welsh women, quite devoted to their old master. But my cousin told me it was impossible to keep track of pillow cases; they "borrowed" them to make underlinen.

You must feel glad that you did not come to Europe. There is no shortage what-ever, only dislocation of some supplies, especially butter and bacon; which it is expected will be rectified by rationing and sending to localities. Here we are perplexed about the surplus. If we may only supply ¼ lb. we shall have tiresome and varying surpluses. This is a stock raising farm where we breed and rear young cows, selling them when they are at their best; so one week there may be 2 newly calved cows and a lot more butter, and a sudden drop when the cows have gone to market — rather complicated to explain to the food controller at Ulverston. It is a worrying time for farmers, so many forms to fill in, and regulations and orders. The weather has been cold over Christmas and New Year; pleasant for young people who can keep warm and go skating. There is very little snow and a good deal of sunshine. Indoors we have had rather a depressing time; my husband has been in bed for the second time this winter, and I have got sciatica — which won't go till a thaw comes. Wm. got a chill. He has been over-worked and worried. There are colds going about, not amounting to influenza, but tiresome to shake off. We shall be glad when Spring comes.

The war looks like taking a long time, it has spread so much. Nearly all the evacuated children have gone home to the towns. The German raids have been so unsuccessful that people do not take them seriously — in fact by what one hears the public run *out* to watch instead of taking shelter, when there is an air fight near the coast. We have seen nothing here, except the usual patrols. Income tax is making a hole in the January dividends, but it cannot be helped!

I hope we may meet again in happier times. In the mean time it is pleasant to know and feel that there are real friends in U.S.A. who appreciate and sympathize with Old World troubles. I am so very glad to see there is a movement to help the Finns. That is a way of helping, if the States can send arms and Red Cross money. With our kindest regards,

Anne Carroll Moore sent Beatrix Potter a newly published volume, My
Roads to Childhood (Doubleday, 1939), *containing selections of review-
essays of outstanding books from her previously published* Roads to
Childhood (Doubleday, 1920), New Roads to Childhood (Doubleday,
1923), *and* Crossroads to Childhood (Doubleday, 1926), *together with
a new introduction, a list of representative children's books published
between 1926 and 1938, and an essay on trends and developments in
children's books during those years.*

To Anne Carroll Moore

Jan. 17th 40

It was such a pleasure — belated and unexpected — to receive your
book — Jan. 15th — the American mails have come in late and in de-
tachments. All my friends have remembered and sent greetings. Yours,
Roads are most interesting — both as regards your wonderful and successful work and as regards the cross roads leading back. I can see you
— a little girl — driving (no you say 'riding') in the buggy with your
father driving Pocahontas — and reading cookbooks, old and new —
with Charlotte, the Swedish maid!

Alas for Scandinavia and Finland! Also for good King Wencelas. I
have been reading again the book of carols which you sent to me
two years ago. How beautiful they are — and to think it has come to
this in 1940.

It is very interesting to read about the beginnings — like *St. Nicholas.*
I had it to read but not in the earliest days. I had the *Silver Skates* in
the book form, which I have unfortunately lost. I have most of Mrs.
Ewing's and Mrs. Molesworth's books — my old copies carefully kept.
They were as good as the American books for "middle aged children";
but less humorous; they had no successors for a very long time, if at
all. I have been rereading *Huckleberry Finn.* I don't think Mr. de la
Mare's or Milne's are the same sort of thing nor Kenneth Graham. [The]
Swallows and Amazons series is more like. I am sorry I never met the
author; he used to live near Windermere, but he has left the district.

We have been rather poorly over New Year, both of us! It is unusual
for my husband to take a week in bed. We could not have been very
cheerful in any case. The weather has been sunny, but intensely cold,
pleasant for skaters but too cold for old people. Let us hope for peace

before another New Year. But whether or no we will just stick it! There is plenty to eat and good fires. Of the making of many books there is no end. I have not finished reading *Roads* yet, but what multitudes you have read and digested!

With our kindest regards,

May 25. 40

The blue bells are very lovely and the hawthorn blossom like snow on the green hedges and the cuckoo calling; a world of beauty that will survive — and Freedom will survive, whatever happens to us. It is very pleasant to see green grass again. You have more severe winters in America, so I won't expatiate upon drifts and zero. No one remembers such a frost; it has cut down my old established bushes — the climbing rose on this cottage, hedges of privet and laurel, and a wisteria 100 years old. In spite of which there has been a flowery spring and a good lambing time. We cannot house our vast flocks of little mountain sheep, and they are not fond of hay, they nibble amongst rocky slopes and coppice woods; very few died in winter and they have done well for their lambs, though they still look thin themselves. We are all very busy on the farms and in the gardens. I cannot work like last war time, when I fed the calves and pigs and poultry; but I can get about and look after things, which is more than I expected. We both had influenza; Wm. recovered quickly, but I stopped in bed during the cold weather. The war has made little difference to living; there has been no scarcity yet — except paper, which we collect and save; and there is a great demand for timber, but mainly fir trees which do not cause any regrettable gap in the landscape. The larch and spruce — what you call hemlock — are quick growing, and intended for commercial felling. Of course it would be idle to conceal that we are very anxious — personally in old age — it does not matter much to us, and we will 'stick it out' what ever happens. The risk to this country is what has happened elsewhere — the alien population. You will have the same trouble in U.S.A. when you are in the same plight. The horrors of another — and more horrid — war make me selfishly thankful to have no young ones — both sides of the family seem to be dying out. I suppose there are scattered un-kept-up-with second cousins. The only ones I am concerned about are two young girls Rosemary and Jean Duke, the elder training for agricultural diploma, the younger a school girl. Their duty is to this

country; but if there proves to be *no* future, I tell their mother she must send them to Canada, possibly via U.S.A. Rosemary is a level-headed young person; being at school in Brussels Sept. 38 — she came away in a troop train. Their mother, my cousin, or niece cousin, is married to a Naval officer. There is thunder — rain this evening, it is refreshing the garden; at present a between time, only clematis and iris in flower. The daffodils have been wonderful. The rhododendrons at the other side of the road at Hill Top are a blaze of color.
With kind regards from both of us,

To Betty and Richard Stevens

May 25. 40

I have your pleasant message before me as I write, and a little snap of Nonya and her brother, taken in August 38. She looks a little pickle! Quite respectably clothed. I remember a lovely Aphrodite — or was it Milton's "Sleek Panope" — dripping from the wave and water lilies of Grasmere Lake. The pleasant peaceful days. Do you remember wriggling a large car past a large bus on a very narrow twisty lane near Buttermere? Your aunt had a confiding faith in your skill as a chauffeurese which emboldened me to keep my seat. The bluebells are lovely in the woods, and the hawthorn hedges sprinkled white like snow; the beauty of the countryside that will survive. I am glad your little folks are across the Atlantic. I see in the paper that one of your ships appropriately named Roosevelt is coming to take off Americans. Times are extremely anxious; there are such swarms of foreigners in this country. We have been too easy; like the Dutch.

I suppose your immigration laws permit "foreigners" i.e. English to land in U.S.A. provided they are self supporting? I am far too old to dream of bolting what ever happens. I am thinking of two young girls, children of a favorite cousin (I have scarcely any young relatives). The elder is training for an agricultural diploma with intentions to go to S. Africa, at present off the map; the younger is a school girl. I was telling their mother if the worst came to the worst she should get them over to Canada or U.S.A. Of course their first duty is to their country; there will be work for women in English Agriculture if we survive.

Their names are Rosemary and Jean Duke, their father Lieut. Commander Duke is a naval officer. Rosemary is a self possessed level headed girl; got away from Brussels in Sept. 38 in a troop train. And doubtless any "evacuating" would be done through consuls and officially — but if they have to go — I would give them the names of some of my good friends in U.S.A. in case they required advice. Their mother has money and expectations. At present we are solvent in spite of taxes! I have been selling pit wood — what you call "hemlock"; and wool is a better trade.

It has been a very severe winter, unusual snow and protracted frost. We both had flu. My husband picked up quickly, but I stopped in bed through the cold weather — of course getting up, but mostly like Mrs. John Dormouse — 'very snug'. I got over a severe operation, but I am rather crippled, though still smiling and very busy. Tell Nonya how many baa lambs I have on the sheep farm, 999, and the shepherd thinks there are a dozen more not counted and marked. It is surprising how well the flock got through the severe winter. Thank you Dick for the letter and pamphlet which was very interesting and instructive. Love to all — there are 2 + 3 now are there not — or is it 4? Good luck!

To Marian Frazer Harris Perry

May 25. 40

Times are extremely anxious. I do not fear a siege, defended by our navy and air force. But this country is like all the other victims; swarming with foreigners. Now I am using your name without leave or excuse — do you mind? I wrote to Betty yesterday, probably both letters will go by same mail. I receive a royalty on my books sold in U.S.A. (except of course private editions). As all the royalty payments for last season were paid *last month* by the London branch of F. Warne & Co. there won't be any further payment till next spring. If things are very bad and grow worse in this country, I want to nominate a friend in America to receive and hold the New York money for me — either you or Betty Stevens?

It would be wrong and not permissible to send money from this country to U.S.A., but it is not wrong to leave it in America where it was earned. It would not be a very big sum, the payment is at a lower rate on the N.Y. copies. I don't care to leave it in the hands of the N.Y. firm. I am not intending to bolt! What ever happens! I am thinking of two school girls, a cousin's daughters. I have explained about them in a

letter to Betty. I am *not* saying that their parents *will* adopt my suggestion that they might finish their education in U.S.A.? It just strikes me
it might be well to have a nest-egg, in case they had to be shipped off.
It is unbelievable. It is the unbelief in the possibility of catastrophe
that has proved the snare in other lands.

In the meantime Spring is lovely, the woods all a carpet of blue bells,
the hawthorn bushes, the vivid green — and facing me a bank of
rhododendrons in dazzling colour. They and azaleas and daffodils have
had a full show of blossom. I am getting about and feeling much
stronger — and my husband is well — not cheerful — how can we be?
Every one is hard at work. It's well you did not travel.

[P.S.] The Dukes are comfortably off, and the elder girl Rosemary is
sensible and capable; she was at school in Brussels, and is now at
Swanley Agricultural College. I wish their parents would send them
away, since they are not quite old enough for war work at home.

To Anne Carroll Moore

June 5. 40

We are living through an anxious time. Last week was horrible. Then
there was a reaction of relief and pride when the B.E.F. got out of
Flanders. Now there is another reaction of anxiety when we reflect
upon the loss of guns and transport vehicles. I have hardly patience to
write a letter to U.S.A. I know the New Englanders would have helped
old England if their hands had not been tied politically. It's suicidal
blindness — to put it no higher — look at Denmark which submitted
peaceably after strict neutrality — five million poultry killed off and
sent to Germany. When he has eaten up Europe — hunger as well as
greed will tempt him to seize food countries in South America. Surely
U.S.A. might have sent us aeroplanes and guns without becoming publicly involved in European war. It is difficult to realize there is a war
on. The country has been so beautiful and peaceful and there is little
change, except that people with fixed incomes find a rise in prices,
although it is nothing serious; and nothing short except paper = wood
pulp. A lot of wood is being cut in this district for pit prop wood, to
replace Scandinavian supplies — but so far it has not affected the
landscape; there are trees and to spare yet. It's different to the last war
— seems less to do individually — partly of course because we have

grown old. This is a war of young people in uniform — and more and more a war of mechanics and chemistry. Last war we were drying foxglove leaves, etc. for the druggists; now no demand; so much is synthetic in production.

We are very busy on the farms — and longing for rain. It was a lovely green April, plenty of grass for the sheep, and a good lambing time in spite of the privations of frost and snow. A spring of flowers. The hawthorn hedges and the big thorn bushes on the fell sides have been like drifts and patches of snow; and the blue bells a sheet of blue. It is un-believable that such a lovely peaceful land should be in shadow. We have become quite fond of planes; there is a patrol sailing over as I write. There has been some marvelous colonial flying, fancy a thing like a gigantic flying fish skimming over the meadows; the sheep and cattle take no notice. I wonder the Americans cannot lend planes to guard *us* so that more of ours could go to Europe? All the local men have got back from Flanders; one badly smashed and another lost an arm, but might have been much worse. There is beginning to be rather a shortage of water; but I hope this heat will cause thunder soon. The therm. was 118 in the sun yesterday and 80° in the shade. Mr Heelis is well and I am able to get about, though rather crippled since my severe operation of April last year. I have to wear a belt which is never really comfortable. So far there is plenty of petrol and I am able to superintend the farms and wood cutting. Also doing all possible repairs while it is possible to do them. The books — *Peter R.* I mean — had a good season, and they tell me they have a good stock of paper — also duplicate engraved plates at the N.Y. branch businesss — a possible plank in ship wreck!! Though Wm. and I are a great deal too old and slow to think of bolting. Some people are discussing sending children over the Atlantic. If any of my relations or friends go I will tell them to look in at the N.Y. children's library — a cousin has been considering about her daughters, Rosemary and Jean Duke, but on the whole thinks they ought to remain and work. The difficulty about evacuation is to decide in advance. It's either an expensive irritating fiasco like last Sept. — or else it's left till it is too late. If there were not such swarms of foreigners in this country, I should be completely confident about the outcome. Freedom and justice will win in the long run, but there may be a lot more misery first — and American help is not going to be in time to turn the scale before August.
Good bye,

To Marian Frazer Harris Perry

June 13. 40

Since I wrote to you, by air mail, we have gone through alternations of relief and depression. Deep thankfulness and relief that the B.E.F. got out of Flanders so well — but a reaction at the thought of the material lost. They have pluck to want to go back — but where are the guns and transport? People are rather bitter about U.S.A. The tardy help will not be in time to save France; it may be too late for us. Aeroplanes were wanted, more than men or participation in active war.

We see many here, but it is not safe to leave this coast undefended and send them abroad. There is wonderful flying. One has just passed over head at a terrific pace. There are no refugees here yet; perhaps there may not be any. Children are being moved out of London this week. The trouble about evacuating is to know what to decide before hand; either it is a fiasco like last Sept. or it is left till it is a disaster. My cousin's husband thinks the daughters ought to remain in England; they will not be sent in advance anyway. If we go under it will be a dreary prospect for the young to remain; especially girls. It does not much signify to the old, except that it is a wretched muddle. I think I am sustained by a sort of stunned curiosity to see what happens? It is unthinkable. All so normal and as usual (except a bad drought which is spoiling crops) but it's just this normal serenity that has been our undoing up to date.

I turned out some newspapers of the date Sept. 38 crisis — what stuff! Mr. Chamberlain and his umbrella; and a new era of peace! Do you remember the words of the Bishop of Warsaw warning England and France that they would live to repent? We were still worse unprepared then in the air; but it is said that these monster tanks have been made in W. Skoda works in Cz.Slov. I am very cripply, on a stick. Any dream of ending as a comfortable petted semi-invalid is vanished! But it never could have been in any case. I will hobble about till it is ended. We have the little dogs still. You will remember the girls' names, Rosemary and Jean Duke; but I scarcely think they will be sent over. I remain with our kind regards.

To Alexander McKay

June 17th 40

I do not think any royalty is due to me for a while, as I received 50 dollars 98 in March. I should be obliged if you will send future payments to my friend Mrs. Betty Stevens, Spring Lane, Roxburgh, Phil., wife of Richard K. Stevens, 1907 Packard Building, Phil.

I formally authorize you to do so, until further instructions from me, the signature to be receipt and discharges. She and her aunt Mrs. Perry of Germantown are old friends, and I recommend to their notice some young relatives who may possibly go out — though at present the inclination is to sit tight! and keep smiling!

With kind regards,

PW 18 CABLE = HAWKSHEAD MR 30 JUNE 24
HLT PERRY =
    ALDANPARK MANOR GERMANTOWN (PENN) =

PLEASE CABLE DUKE HEXHEM ENGLAND UNDERTAKING
MAINTAIN JEAN DUKE AGED SIXTEEN ROBERT TWEEDIE
ELEVEN DAVID TWEEDIE FOUR FOR DURATION OF WAR
REQUIRED FOR PASSPORT =
    HEELIS

HEXHEM HEELIS

To Anne Carroll Moore

June 25. 40

Suppose 3 children arrived in N.Y. can you tell me the address of a safe hotel or lodging they could, if necessary, stay a night before traveling to Philadelphia? They could only take £10 each out of England. At present it seems almost impossible to arrange passage and passport, but there is hope of some official scheme in a fortnight or three weeks. The eldest Jean Duke is the daughter of a cousin (younger generation than me. I look upon the Mother as my 'niece') — the father is a naval officer Lieut. Commander Duke. She is 16, very capable. The two little boys named 'Tweedie' are the children of a great friend of Kenneth Duke's, another officer. They are 11 and 4½. To think that *England* has to send her children to the charity of strangers. When I say 'charity' I mean in the sense of kindness and trouble; of course money will be sent when possible so to do. I can get an advance from F. Warne & Co., N.Y. branch, but not a big one; by ill luck my year's royalty was paid last month, or I might have diverted it. I think I can get help on the business side from friends in Philadelphia. I have had a most kind letter already from Mrs. Perry. I do not suggest meeting the boat, because amongst unknown faces it is more risk than taking a taxi to a known address.

The events of this last month have been stupefying. We are cheerful but surprised and things are so little different here — it's scarcely to be realized that there is war, the woods and mountains are the same. The meadows are much too dry, we want rain. The two officers seem to know no one in U.S.A. or Canada. They are in the ordnance department and live near NE coast. He has another girl who will remain, old enough to work, but it's an unwholesome atmosphere for 16, apart from bombs — a year or two at school across the Atlantic would be best for her. Good bye, if so be! but I hope to see the end of Hitler.

night letter 6/28/40

DUKE
HEXHEM ENGLAND

WILL ACT AS SPONSOR FOR TWO ELDEST CHILDREN
UNDERSTAND YOUNGEST CANNOT COME WITHOUT PARENTS
PLEASE GET IN TOUCH WITH AMERICAN CONSUL LIVERPOOL
TO WHOM NECESSARY CABLEGRAMS ARE BEING SENT
                              PERRY

Beginning with the June 29, 1940, letter to Mrs. Perry, all Beatrix Potter's letters were examined by the censors and often had words or phrases cut out. The letters were written on scrap paper. She used unlined exercise book pages, the backs of old duplicated forms from the Wool Control Board, sheets from a bank book, and even the unused parts of letters from the War Agricultural Committee. Some letters were duplicated and mailed several days apart, in event of loss.

To Marian Frazer Harris Perry

June 29. 40

The world gets more and more involved. Now Russia is moving; and Japan threatening to begin. Russia could stop Hitler if she took the oil wells and the Danube ports with that intention, but nobody knows which side of the fence? There are various accounts of bombing, some people find it "quite thrilling," and others complain of noise. (I have just been out to look at a plane, it is only our usual patrol). There is an evacuee family from Suffolk. They say the noise night after night was wearisome, although the damage is insignificant. We only have [censored] so far. It is not a season for bringing crowds from towns; there is such a scarcity of water; the fire engine has been pumping water out of the lake to supply Hawkshead tank, but it's only a makeshift.

It seems hopeless to try to send children to U.S.A. — or indeed any where — until the official scheme is functioning; and the age limit being 16 will cut Jean Duke out of the scheme for young children. Though one would think "helpers" will be needed if a crowd of little ones are shipped off. It is confusing every way. I know some people who are trying to send a little boy to his American grandmother in N.Y. who would meet him and maintain him, but they have so far failed to get a passage.

I make my apology to the great American republic!! *We* have done precious little good by meddling in Europe! Who ever wins the election for President, I think the American Navy will be forced to come in, sooner or later. Nobody wants the Army, to be perfectly candid. We have enough men for defence if we had more arms. Even our old sporting guns here are called up. I do hope I have not given a lot of trouble making inquiries. I am afraid it is beyond arranging. I am upset and perplexed to find Mr. Duke so anxious — he did not mind the Battle of Jutland — but he and his friend were younger then; and not overworked as they are now in the ordnance department. When officers were put on half-pay after the War, he had the luck — or the merit — to be kept on as inspector of guns and armament in a northern district; at present Elswick on the N.E. Coast and Barrow, near here. He has gone very thin and tired and worried. He calls here on his way to Barrow and has always been so hearty until recently. No doubt — apart from difficulties — it's far better to move children right way across the ocean.

Our friends from Suffolk may find themselves "out of the frying pan into the fire" but they seem very placid. Two bombs dropped in their Suffolk fields without going off, a neighbour's roof went another night, but no one was hurt. We have [censored] now, but [censored] is plentiful. I get very tired, but we are both well and busy. The Parkers are in Tom Kitten's "house". They are dear little children, but I felt it would tire me out in this house, so we have sent our spare beds across to Hill Top.

If any more evacs arrive they will have to sleep on the floor. Or of course if Barrow is invaded we will have the barns full and all. Though I do hope and believe the English will not run away like the Belgians and French. All the returned soldiers say the roads were blocked with refugees. The German tanks simply drove over them. It's a war which puts *decent* fighters at a disadvantage. No doubt if he cannot win any other way he will use gas.

If it is ever possible to send a registered parcel to America I think that fine Brussels lace of my mother's would be better sold. I wondered about giving it to the Red Cross, but I did not do so. But perhaps the Customs would take too large a toll? Stephanie talked of sending some diamonds with the girl, but I think it would be risky. I wrote to Dick also, in case you might not get the letter, and to say how apologetic I felt in giving trouble. I remain yours affectionately and grateful for sympathy,

To Anne Carroll Moore

July 11. 40

I received your cable — more than kind — last night, and by morning's post a letter from Kenneth Duke saying definitely that Jean cannot go. Her sister Rosemary was already out of the scheme. The passport and passage difficulties were adjusted (subject to waiting for a ship) but the authorities will not grant a permit for any one between the ages of 16 and 60 to leave the country. There are certain exceptions but Jean does not come under them — neither going out to join a husband or father stationed abroad, nor on public work etc. Well — she must take her chance, like others, but a year or two at school in the States would have been an enlarging experience, and taken her away from unsettled surroundings.

I am most grateful for offers of help — so are her father and mother — and several people have gone to expense of cables which most certainly shall be repaid as soon as I can instruct the American branch of F. Warne & Co. — no possibility of sending cheque or money orders from here! It is still difficult to realize that we are at war. Rain has come at last and refreshed to parched grass, and stopped our hay making. By the time we start again in fine weather there may be something to cut. I hear that the crops are good further south. We have had no raids here. People have been coming from the east coast, complaining of the disturbing noise at nights, but very little concerned about the actual bombs — which usually fall in fields, and some times do not explode. It's very unpleasant for houses that are hit, but nothing like the number of deaths that are caused by road accidents. As for invasion — we don't know what to think — there are plenty of men in readiness and barricades going up at cross roads and corners. Now I have enjoyed *Roads to Childhood* read again, and I intend to reread *The Tory Lover*. I wonder — I should not be surprised if the attack comes on the West Coast — a much less gallant and courteous foe than Paul Jones. I shall not run far, that's certain!

Wm. I am sure sends kind regards — he has rushed off to an Agricultural Committee. I think he is more suited for that work than for patrolling roads at nights with a "tin hat." Who could have imagined such times? With very many thanks,

To Marian Frazer Harris Perry

July 24. 40

I received your letter of July 5 on the 22nd. Its kindness and understanding overwhelmed me. I am disturbed about the date — July 5th — surely by that date you would — in normal times — have heard that *none* of the children are coming? I am wondering whether the congestion of cablegrams does not cause them to be slower in transit than the airmail letters? The little boys were first crossed off. Then Jean Duke was refused a permit, after passport and passage difficulties appeared to have been surmounted. Her father looked in here while on his round of inspection last week; he said it seemed a last moment disappointment after putting everyone (including you) to much trouble. He said he felt one relief; he had begun to wonder whether there might be some difficulty in getting her back, to England, if "duration" proved to be a lengthy exile; he had not contemplated more than a year — or two — at most, but we all think it will be a long time before the war is over. There is a great change of feeling — a complete recovery of confidence compared to that black ten days. And the delay has been invaluable. I may not tell you how martial we feel even here! The other day turning a corner I suddenly met a company of soldiers practising route marching in gas masks. They did not look human — more like antediluvian tapirs or short nosed elephants! We are quite cheerful, and the country is full of troops — and more and more of the Kendal boys are heard of; the local regiment was in the rear guard at Dunkirk. Some were killed; some taken prisoner; one has been heard of alive and unhurt in Morocco. The troops got mixed up and landed at random, north and south. It was just like what General Smuts said in his fine speech, a triumph of strategy and endurance; an army that could fight its way back safely is not beaten. Very few appear to have been killed. The guns and other stores were the worst loss.

There have been no air raids within hearing distance yet. Occasionally stray planes go over at night which are thought to sound like Germans; and it is very likely we may get raids yet on this coast, perhaps from Ireland; but they do very little harm; the death rate is less than the toll of the roads. People *will not* take cover. I was in a cottage yesterday when a plane flew very low and every child ran out to watch it; it was obviously a Spitfire, but it would have been all the same had it been a Heinkel. A farm house was hit further north, but no one hurt. The Germans got the nearest doing serious damage in their first attempts; they have flown higher and higher ever since, except when they dive bomb. People who come from towns complain of being kept awake by our own sirens. So long as they are not hit — it's a case of "familiarity breeding contempt." An old gentleman from this part who went away to live in the South has met with a strange fate. He was playing golf at a s. coast watering place and stumbled upon a live bomb which blew him into bits. He was a great invalid, and he did not suffer; it must have been a shock for his fellow golfers.

We have very unsettled weather. We make hay (and drill) between showers; not both at the same time. The authorities are reasonable in apportioning the men's time between soldiering and farming.

I hope Ken and Stephanie have thanked you properly. We never can thank you enough for your willingness to do so much. Steph is not much of a letter writer, but I know how grateful she is — it was a *very* black time while it lasted. Thank goodness we are on our own now, with our backs to a strong wall and the sea in front. It may be hard and cruel, but we can and must hold out. I am still keeping in better health, and able to get through a fair assortment of work. Wm. goes on the patrol one night a week; they let him off at 11, which he can do comfortably without knocking up; he is the oldest on the job. He has a "tin hat", which he refuses to wear — until Hitler comes! He's a long time about it. Now I don't know how to thank you. I do appreciate your letter. Mr. Duke cabled to you directly he knew the permit could not be granted. I suppose it must have been after July 5. Time seems to fly away.

To Bertha Mahony Miller

July 30. 40

I received your letter on (the) 29th — only twelve days — censored and examined, but all there — and I can assure you it is appreciated. We went through a very black time during the Belgian betrayal and the incredible collapse of France. Lately there has been a revival of confidence, and it has been helped by the awakened sympathy of the States. I have never for a moment doubted the good feeling — the real distress that my New England friends were experiencing through their desire to help England. We just felt that your Congress was rather slow to grasp the seriousness of the pressure? And it was aggravating to think how nearly the Germans were checked. Our men say they were "all out" — boy troops, exhausted and dazed, some say drugged; masses of troops and our guns firing into them until our guns were red hot. The Germans must have had terrific losses. The French population in panic blocked the roads. We are informed that if we bolt *we* will be shot!! But we are very cheerful up to date, and the island is full of troops. Nearly all the locals are back; one young man wrote that he was safe and well in Morocco. French soldiers got ashore in Lancashire fishing boats, all regiments mixed up, but all anxious to have another slap at "Gerry." We are well protected. There have been odd German planes over in the dark but no bombs dropped yet within earshot. I had a letter from a former servant who lives in a cottage belonging to me near the coast;

it is such a good sample of the general attitude that I will copy it. Our old stone houses can stand up to anything but a direct hit.

Copy of Jennie Mackereth's letter: "The 'A town' bombs were the worst noise here and we slept in our clothes as they were over every night after and hovered over here until the Saturday when they dropped a salvo of bombs over 'B town.' It is bad, but Isabel has been to see it and says nothing to what it might have been (!!8 bombs on a small town!!) He dropped some at each end of the town. He came again on the Sunday night but dropped no bombs. We have got the planes who did the damage. We are going under the stone stairs if an air raid comes. We had not time in the last one. I will send you some biscuits along with the rent. We would like to see you, but please do not come now; there are barricades."

Jennie's sweet biscuits are a favourite recipe — not a case of famine. Prudent Jennie! The usual habit is to run out of doors in hopes of seeing a "dog fight." The Germans must be losing a great many. By the same post I had a letter from another spot — 3 down — and none of them in the news. We see some wonderful flying by our own patrols.

One thing is certain, *I* shall not run far. I will retire into the nearest wood, the cellar of course for bombs; but it is one in a million risk. If there is invasion, I am afraid villages near the landings will be burnt. I look wistfully at my fine old furniture. I have a wonderful old bedstead too heavy to move in a hurry. Nevertheless I went to a sale at Coniston the other day and bought 3 chests and a coffin stool. The old man's father had been clergyman and collected oak, in fact, several pieces were suspect of having been cleared out of Torver Church in the last century; two of my chests are plain and long, like deed boxes. They might come in convenient in the wood for holding things, dry and solid.

There was no one bidding at the oak except myself and Mr. Telford, the Grasmere dealer. He has an American wife and has been used to do very well with tourists. I thought it a good sign that he was after bargains still. And he got some. He got an oak tallboy for 53/shillings. It required some doing up, a leg loose, but it had all the original brass handles. He will sell it for fifteen to eighteen pounds — when the Americans come again to old England! I do love old furniture and old china — especially earthenware. I got a Bristol punch bowl, early 18th century, in the sale. It has written in the bottom, "Fill every man his glass." 4/6 with 7 assorted articles, some useful. It has been repaired, but it gives me pleasure; decorated in the Chinese style, in cobalt and manganese.

If it were not giving you much trouble, I should much like either of those books about Colonial furniture. I have never seen one. It is a coincidence — that only last week, I came across the catalogue of Whitney furniture and enjoyed it again. I wonder if they are *exact* replicas? I never like "in the style of Chippendale" as reproduced over here. Sometimes the chairs are so good that it takes an expert to recognize, but then — that is suggestive of fraud. Others are bad copies or poor surfaces. The Whitney furniture looks just right. To me it seems to have *originality* as well as imitative perfection. It is all restful and charming and pleasant to live with. The furniture that Miss Owen brought from N. York to Hawkshead was more elaborate. Poor old thing. What a muddle she made with her will! She left no relations, died in Rome, and her executors are the Bank of Hanover, N.Y. They have at least proved her will in the States; now they must prove it in this country. And after all, the result will be further muddles as she left the residue to the Italian Church, enemy aliens. There is very little in Belmont Hall. I have been expecting the house to be taken for billeting — in spite of the poor sanitary conditions and water supply. So rightly or wrongly I took upon myself to tidy and sort the litter of books, letters, and broken things. I found a pedigree of her mother's family, traced back to "Simon Sackett 1602-1635, colonist, is understood to have been a native of Isle of Ely." Some of the furniture which she was so fond of had belonged to the Sacketts. I bought a little at her sale in Windermere, but she had sent a good deal to London, where it was disposed of without history, or reserve. The little that remains in Belmont Hall seems likely to moulder away. There are cabin trunks packed with clothes. I feel as though it would be kinder to burn them, with moths and mildew.

I wonder if I can find anything suitable for *The Horn Book*. I will look. I have already found a very succinct dry note (copy) to Miss Bertha Mahony in 1925 and Henry P.'s article; and I have another which I shall presently find. Did not Miss Moore write something? Or am I thinking of a book of her own which mentioned Sawrey? You tell me you find it difficult sometimes to concentrate so you took refuge in

Pig Robinson!! Well, he sailed away and away and found peace; but we will struggle on and find peace — some day — at home. I am very stiff and older since I had a bad operation, but able to get about still. My husband is well, he has a "tin" hat! What a time Hitler is of coming. The longer he waits — the more barricades and shelters.

 With very kind regards,

 In the summer of 1939, Bertha Mahony Miller read The Fairy Caravan *aloud to her granddaughter, Nancy Dean, who was then aged seven. Some time after the reading, Nancy expressed her pleasure by patting the book and saying, "Oh, lovely* Fairy Caravan, *if only there were ten of you." Mrs. Miller described the incident in a letter to Beatrix Potter and also included an account of the reading in her article, "Beatrix Potter and Her Nursery Classics,"* The Horn Book, *May 1941.*

To Nancy Dean

July 30. 40

 So you would like news of *The Fairy Caravan*? Where is it camping or whither is it wandering? I wonder if I can tell you! When we grow old and wear spectacles, our eyes are not bright, like children's eyes, nor our ears so quick, to see and hear the fairies. Just a glimpse I catch sometimes through the trees, and I hear a tinkling, tinkle, tinkling of little pots and pans and cans. I seemed to know last week that they were in Clogger Meadow. I saw something white through the trees; I looked hard — and alas it was a cow! Two wood cutters were working in the wood. Until the underwood of nut bushes grows up again, Sandy and Pony William will not stay more than a night or two in the lovely green meadow that lies hidden amongst woods. And they did not go to Cherry Tree Camp where I *know* they have always camped in May, when the cherry blossom and hawthorns are in flower. And now in August the Girl Guides cannot camp there either because there is a foot path leading to another sort of camp.

 So the Guides are camping in a little larch wood near our cottage, and their tents are dyed green. Where can the circus have wandered to? I believe I know!

 Right away amongst the fells — the green and blue hills above my sheep farm in Troutbeck. Such a lonely place, miles along a lovely green road. That was where I first saw the mark of little horse shoes. There is an old barn there that we call High Buildings. It is never used except sometimes by the shepherds, and when I was younger and used to take long walks, I used to eat my bread and cheese at High Buildings, or shelter from the rain. That was where the Caravan sheltered in a very wild rainstorm, and Xarifa made acquaintance with the melancholy Mouse. There was a story about that place and that very wet night, but it was so silly I really could not print it. Besides it might have offended my friend Joseph, who is not really a mouse. He is a shepherd. Every spring Joseph Moscrop has come to help with the lambs; for 14 springs he has come from Scotland with his dogs and fed the weak lambs and the twins with his milk bottle. And in very cold springs Joseph has a little gin in a little bottle, and last March Joseph told me "the cork had coom oot in his pocket." There was a smell of gin, but Joseph is a total abstainer — what Americans call "dry". He does not like being laughed at, especially on Sundays. He is wonderful with lambs and dogs; we all love Joseph. I do not think he would approve of me calling a mouse "Joseph Mouse-trap." Perhaps the censor would not tell him? If I copied out that very silly story? There was one about Cherry Tree Camp — but it was long and tiresome.

Good night Nancy, I am going to bed.

Yours affectionately,
Beatrix Potter

To Marian Frazer Harris Perry

Aug. 14. 40

In case letters may go astray — I am writing yet again to thank you and Betty for all your intended kindness, and for what you had already done in thinking out and planning for the children if they had come. Labour not quite in vain for it will be accounted to you for righteousness of intention and sympathy. We were needing sympathy and encouragement last June. The air battles are going so strongly in our favour that it lessens the risk of invasion; there may be painful episodes, but he [Hitler] cannot hold his communications in face of such marvellous skill in the air. Stray bombers break through; there were 2 bombs dropped last week on a farm near the N.W. coast; they fell in a field and did no damage; in fact the farmer said a large stone, or pitting piece of rock, had been blasted usefully in his mowing field.

We have finished hay, and we are waiting for fine weather to commence harvest. Corn has been carried successfully further south. Everyone is planning to plough more for next season. This last week the south wind has been blowing in wet mist from the sea. There is a fair crop of fruit, and sugar is available for preserving. Eggs and poultry are the shortest stock, as hen feed has been scarce and expensive, so poultry farmers have reduced their flocks of hens. My next door neighbour and I have started rabbit keeping; "Matilda Bunny" is making a hay nest. I don't know whether Miss Mills will have much appetite for rabbit pie. I am thinking about our little dogs; with potatoes and rabbits produced in the garden, our 2 pekes won't encroach on public rationings. The little dogs were a great entertainment to me last winter when I was confined to the house.

Every one is listening to the wireless, 3 or 4 times a day — waste of time but exciting. We cannot expect to get through without reverses; so far it goes well. This is a military area. We feel well protected. I do feel grateful to you about Jean. The elder girl was here last week with her father. At least he slept one night on his round of gun inspection. He is very grateful for all you intended. The girl, elder, Rosemary, provoked me. It is one of the misfortunes of war that it affects unfavourably young people — no doubt both sexes, but the boys have stronger heads! and grow into men. It's particularly bad for girls. They get so excited — rushed about — and 'values' all wrong; however, she has been prevailed upon to go back to Swanley Agricultural College and go on with a thorough training, which will be wanted after the war. The last war left too many half trained uppish women who thought they knew everything — especially V.A.D.s.

I am told that in the south there are almost as many girls in uniform as men! Jean is at home doing work for a Red Cross depot. She must take her chance. You and I have done our best! Also Betty and Dick I have put to trouble. I do not think physically this child emigration is now vitally necessary — (I agree with Mr. Churchill in weighing the risk of the crossing) — except there may be rather a scarcity of milk next winter. The authorities have not laid in supplies for animals on the same scale as for humans, but milk and eggs are important as well as bread and meat, especially for children. We have some amusing little people quartered on us, "Richard" aged 3 is a pickle.

The village is full of private refugees, mainly from the East coast because they were weary of the noise of *sirens* — rather than bombs. My visitors tell me their own house is full of soldiers and great trenches and fortifications in their fields. Here it is mainly a case of fortifying cross roads, and lookout posts on the hills. It's very exciting; will 'he' really come? I think he has missed his chance of a serious invasion, but we will have to keep on tenter hooks perhaps for months, and how cold it will be in winter; my shepherd said their hut was nearly blown over on Saturday night. There are shelters right away up the hills, where 4 men keep watch in turn, 2 sentries and 2 resting. And the rest of us 'carry on', and grow sheep and cabbages and rabbits.

I remain with much affection,

[P.S.] Wm. keeps at it; I doubt his standing the weather later on. He is only on near-by roads, looking for windows not properly black [ed] out, and motor offenders, to help the regular police, and to learn their duties in case they have to go elsewhere.

To Betty and Richard Stevens

Sept. 19. 40

You will be wondering how we are getting on. The cruelty of the destruction of working class homes is horrible. The percentage of casualties is very small considering the extent of London. Lancashire has been catching it too. We have been quieter here since the concentrated raiding in the South — as though the Germans may not have an indefinitely large supply of planes. There was however, another wandering "visitor" last night, who unloaded 15 bombs on wasteland, ten miles off — and I never woke up! It is most annoying. All I have seen is search lights, and one night an incendiary going out on a hill. Either the raiders are very bad shots, or else lost their way. We were rung up from the police station one night when a German plane was wandering round in a circle. The chance of being hit is infinitesimal, fortunately.

One poor child was killed in a neighbouring town by a single fire bomb through the roof over her bed. They do not make much mark on grass, but oily lines radiate from the centre. A road is closed today for fear any unexploded are on the peat moss. We cannot tell what to think of the risk of invasion. If the Germans got a footing in Eire there may be hot work on this coast. People are furious about the bombing in London. There is a funny old woman, a real Dickens character, who lives in this village, a widow; she is itching to go back to Woolwich, her native place and see what is happening. Other poor things have to come away; nervy women with nervous children.

It is very good of the Colonies and the Americans to be sending help. I think if the bombing of London goes on, something will have to be done to build wooden camps or move the timid ones further off. The villages are packed to overflowing, although there has not been the slightest general panic. Far from it. The civil population is splendid.

The weather has broken (opportunely); there have been violent gales, and welcome rain — to fill our water tanks and reservoirs. It has been a lovely summer, and perfect harvest weather. Now the leaves are coming off early after the hot season. I am going to dry some apple rings in the American way. We have a big crop, in spite of many blown off. We are both well. Wm's habit of snoring is very tiresome. I have put up with it for many years, but it drowns the noise of approaching planes! The Germans' make a different noise; an interrupted zoom er zoom er zoom as if they had a choke in their breathing; their engines do not run so sweetly as our aeroplanes. There has been a distant but very continuous thunder since I started this letter, possibly guns further south. We listen for noises, but it does not keep us awake like the poor towns people. How disappointing it's only thunder! a rumble over head and a thunder shower.

To Bertha Mahony Miller

October 11. 40

You have given me great pleasure by sending the *Colonial Furniture*. I study the illustrations over and over again, and I feel as though I would like to go through it page by page with Mr. Miller, in detail. Broadly — which is all that can be discussed in a letter — the Chippendale style chairs are more delicately fine (= slender) than ours. Some of the Chippendale and Sheraton settees look almost frail? The author seems to have this in his mind (with approval) when he says "the ideal was a delicacy of form sufficient to withstand the strain" etc. Perhaps I notice it because our more robust, familiar mahogany chairs (although of true Chippendale design and age) — were not made in his

workshop. Perhaps the real, London-made Chippendale is equally deli-
cate with the American. A great deal of northern mahogany, at the
timber or plank stage, came through Liverpool and was worked up in
Lancashire. The dates suggested by Mr. Lockwood for oak furniture at
first reading appear crazy? But upon reflection they are very interesting. The *patterns* are no guide to age where furniture is copied. For
instance the "press cupboards" with *pillars* supporting the canopy "last
quarter 17th century." In this district if an old court cupboard built
into the partition of an old farmhouse, has *pillars*, it is one of the earliest specimens. By the middle of the 17th cent., the pillars had become
droppers. Many of the press cupboards illustrated are very beautiful,
especially those with geometric panels and split-spindles — but they
are obviously inspired by older designs than their American dates. The
chests are inclined to be over ornamented. Fig. 8 which Mr. Lockwood
describes as "very beautiful" seems to be spoilt by too much carving on
the stiles. Ours never have brackets (only one in this book). Curious
that a date (unless spurious) seldom occurs on chests, but commonly on
court cupboards and bible boxes. The "joined stool" is exactly like the
one which I bought in Mr. Ellwood's sale. I wonder if our name
"coffin stool" is merely local? Its explanation is an old custom of resting the coffin on two stools in order to be safe from rats! I could go
through these volumes forever. Windsor chairs unknown in this north
country as antiques. We only see the very poor modern Windsors that
are used in meeting halls and assembly rooms. And, on the other hand,
this book does not show our common (by no means despicable) rush
bottomed cottage chair. The Lockwood "Turned chairs, Carver style"
are nearest, especially Fig. 412, a single chair; but it never struck me
that ours are as old as 1650? They have less elaborate finials, although
the front stretcher is turned; the finials are like this ⌐ on both
spindle and slatbacks, and where the back spindles are not full length,
the space is below with a plain rail above. No I am wrong. It's just
as common to have short spindles at top of the back. I have always
thought they were 18th cent. There is a good slat backed armchair very
similar to Fig. 429 amongst the American chairs at Belmont Hall, also
an old green Windsor chair that Miss Owen told me was made by the
Shakers about 1800. And 4 well-made wooden seated chairs that I cannot quite trace in the book. The spindles go through above the back
rest and are finished with knobs. The rocking chair is a particularly

125

nice one to sit in! I think most of the poor old lady's adored penates were of the Phyfe style, so these peculiar chairs may be late (early 19th) Windsor. The general design is pleasant, but the turning is clumsy. The simple chairs with the back spindles bunched might be inspired by Sheraton chairs.

The above is my favorite court cupboard. It is very plain, except the middle, fixed panel, which has good carving. It will be noted that by 1667 *all* pillars had become droppers. We own only one cupboard — out of a dozen — which has pillars. It is built into a partition in a farm house at Wray near Ambleside. The cupboard shown above was detached when I bought it, in a farm sale in Cartmel near Kendal. But like all others now detached it had originally been a fixture. It is unusually long in shape. The 4 doors fasten with thumb pieces, and the doors hang on pins — i.e. iron rods instead of hinges.

It is a curious fact that cupboards and bible boxes very often have dates but chests almost never (unless the date is spurious). Many of the patterns in Mr. Lockwood's book are like ours; for instance, the fleur-de-lys on the large board above.

But candidly — without intending any reflection upon the beauty and workmanship of the pieces illustrated in Mr. Lockwood's book — the style of the cupboard and the patterns of the decoration are chronologically such a confused muddle that I am inclined to look upon them as excellent *reproductions* rather than historical developments. He is open minded and just in what he says about styles overlapping, and old fashions surviving — for instance what he says about Chippendale, Hepplewhite, and Sheraton. But the dates attached or suggested for his oak are — well — "reproductions" of a sufficient age to be interesting, but quite wrong historically. Fig. 163 is an instance; Elizabethan if it were English; and suspiciously over ornamented.

I have been trying to rub up my judgement — such as it is — by a call this morning (Oct. 17th) at an old yeoman house in Troutbeck belonging to the last spinster descendant of an old family. Alas! old Miss Brown's old father was an enthusiastic carver in the bad Victorian days when amateurs "improved" old oak. Fig. 163 is just what the late Mr. Brown achieved on the stiles and lovely plain wainscoting.

I wanted to look again at a pattern, a genuine design which he had reproduced "ad lib" all over his house and furniture.

In Mr. Lockwood's photographs our most frequent design — foundations — occur, but our eight ∞ has turned into hearts in your patterns and his ⌒ is foliated.

I have a theory (only my own) that the craftsmen who carved our designs were imitating the runic interlacing. It would be too much to say that their patterns were developed from the Scandinavians because there is a complete gap between the early civilization of High Furness and the return of prosperity after the union. Everything was swept away by the Border Wars and by the Scottish free booters' burnings. I do not claim that the patterns are traditional; but I do think some one of the old joiners and carvers must have been familiar with such patterns as those on the Gosfirth Cross. Our figure of ∞ when elaborated is not a heart — it is ✱ twists and in one of the panels of the Brown bedstead there ✱ is "the worm Misgurd" clear enough (though to be sure he may be only an ordinary local adder) — ?? a foreshadowing of Hitler ??) The next panel is a complicated strapwork *quite clearly*. The foot boards of the splendid old bedstead have been covered with copied patterns by the tiresome Mr. Brown. Likewise the cradle, like 799, only spoilt. She has a living cupboard, with spindles, unspoilt. Also a very fine table, with the original long benches beside it; one hinged to a wall and letting down, the other on legs. My joined stool that I bought at Ellwood's is like that in the book. Miss Brown's is a little clumsier (heavier turning). I took notice it was higher than the long side benches. Perhaps the person sitting at the bottom of the table might be perched higher than the side folks? But I am inclined to revert to the "coffin stool" theory. She has a fine buffet chair, a child's high chair.

As to *tables* Mr. Lockwood portrays one with the Elizabethan bulbous leg. It is a vexation to me that there is a legend that a "table with balls on the legs" once existed in a farm house and was so large it would not go through the door after it had been sold away by the farmer. I once saw similar legs in Ulverston, remains of a similar table that had been in use in a tool shed. I have a large chest that is interesting from having belonged to a well-known Ulverston family named Fell, iron masters. The chest is an example of copying. I do not think it is earlier than 1700, but the patterns were 16th, early 17th. the round   Norman arch — the pomegranate, and the roundels, and the tulip or fleur-de-lys. The pomegranate is traditionally the symbol of Katherine of Arragon, but I have never met with the Tudor rose, which is rather strange as High Furness is so near Lancaster. This Ulverston chest has a running vine, a leaf-and-bunch-of-grapes design which occurs on Ulverston cupboards. I should be inclined to derive this pattern from the influence of Furness Abbey. I think it occurs on tiles.

Now you will be tired of this — it is my hobby. It is all wrong to say old oak turns a rich color through light and age. If you saw an old beam, the centre will be found to be darker than the outside. Cumberland and Westmorland oak furniture though equally old is light, a golden gray, compared with our rich brown. The old stain must have been rubbed in, perhaps with oil, before the bees wax and turpentine polish. It may have been bullocks' blood. I have a fine old chest from Shropshire which appears to have been partly treated with madder, it is almost as warm as mahogany. By "swamp oak" Mr. L. presumably means bog oak, dug out of peat; it is nearly like jet. Hard and heavy. Bog oak and white holly wood was used as inlay.

I received your letter of Oct. 9th and the two volumes the day before. They have given me great pleasure; thank you so very much for sending them. I don't deserve it when I am so slow at doing what I say I will do! I really wish and intend to rewrite the piece in *The Horn Book* of 1929. [" 'Roots' of the Peter Rabbit Tales." *The Horn Book*, May 1929]. Not that it is inexact, but one's outlook alters a little as one grows old —

Peter in the garden. Early pencil sketch for almanac.
Gift to Henry P.

Rabbit digging out.

Variants of these watercolors, almost certainly designed as Christmas cards, were used years later as "December" and "January" in *Peter Rabbit's Almanac for 1929.* Gift to Henry P.

Rabbits bringing home wood.

Mrs. Tiggywinkle ironing. Watercolor and pen and ink. Nov. 1904. Gift to Henry P.

Mrs. Tiggywinkle and Lucie on a hillside path. Unfinished. Watercolor, pencil, and pen and ink. Gift to Henry P.

The arrival. Watercolor. Victoria and Albert Museum. London. Linder Bequest.

A Rabbit's Christmas Party. The four scenes that open and close the festivities were given by Beatrix Potter to her aunt, Lady Roscoe. The two middle scenes were gifts to Henry P. in 1927.

Christmas dinner. Watercolor. Victoria and Albert Museum, London. Linder Bequest.

Rabbits dancing to a piper. Watercolor. Gift to Henry P.

Rabbits playing blindman's buff. Watercolor. Gift to Henry P.

Roasting apples. Watercolor. Victoria and Albert Museum, London. Linder Bequest.

Departure. Watercolor. Victoria and Albert Museum, London. Linder Bequest.

Lady Mouse from *The Tailor of Gloucester*. Watercolor. 1927.

Gentleman Mouse from
The Tailor of Gloucester.
Watercolor. 1927.

Beatrix Potter did many small paintings to aid in the purchase of a piece of land on the shore of Lake Windermere. Four were drawn especially for Marian Frazer Harris Perry.

Peter and camomile tea.
Watercolor. 1926.

Mrs. Rabbit. Watercolor. 1927.

Peter and his red pocket-handker-
chief. Unfinished. Preliminary
sketch for *The Tale of Benjamin
Bunny*. Watercolor and pencil.
Gift to Henry P.

Rats holding holiday and dancing the hays. Original
Manuscript of *The Tailor of Gloucester*. Watercolor.
1903. Free Library of Philadelphia.

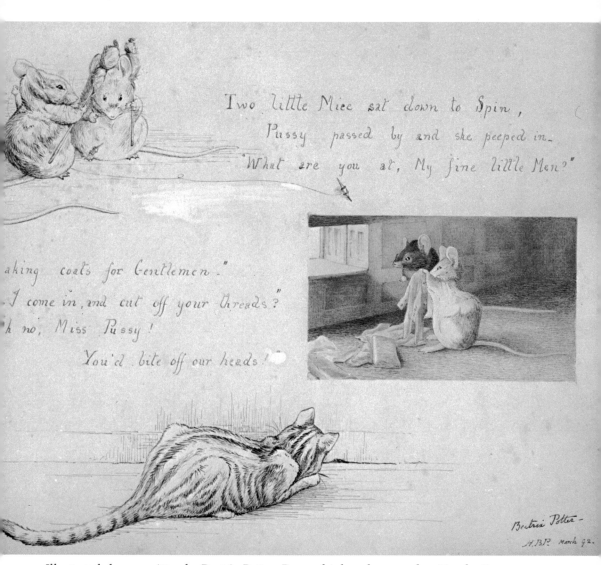

Two little Mice sat down to Spin ,
Pussy passed by and she peeped in.
"What are you at, My fine little Men?"
...aking coats for Gentlemen."
"...I come in, and cut off your threads?"
"...h no, Miss Pussy!
You'd bite off our heads!"

Beatrix Potter
H.B.P. March 92.

Illustrated rhyme written by Beatrix Potter. Pen and ink and watercolor. March 1892.
Gift sent to Bertha Mahony Miller.

The Fairy Caravan. Watercolor and pen and ink. Given to Henry P. in 1929.

Herdwick sheep. Pen and ink. Given to Mary F. Gill and the Field family on Beatrix Potter's 58th birthday, July 28, 1924.

Castle Cottage, Sawrey. Watercolor and pencil. Gift to Henry P. Sept. 28, 1927.

Fungus. Watercolor. Gift to Henry P.

and it seems a pity to reprint exactly the same? I looked through my portfolios without finding anything that seemed very suitable for reproduction. My studies made for backgrounds, whose quantities impressed Henry P. are very scribblesome. I will look again, if you will be patient a little longer. This war preoccupation does not conduce to steadily directed work. Only the active works that must be done, and the hobbies like my furniture and old china, which are in the sense of that tiresome new term "escape."

Talking of escapes, if it is permissible to say so, a German prisoner was loose for 5 days in the north of England, an exciting hunt; caught in a barn by a farmer, got away, and caught again. There was also a while ago a bombing 8 miles away which killed 2 sheep — drawn down by a farmer, who went out with a lantern to attend a calving cow. Nights have been quieter since the heavy raids further south which gives hope that Hitler has not an unlimited supply of bombers. It is not safe to show any light if a plane is over at night; and people are heavily fined for carelessness. There is no food shortage whatsoever for food supply. Bacon and butter are temporarily short, but last war I remember I was all round hungry, which is far from the case this war. Everywhere is crowded with evacuees, but no official billeting here, as it is a military area. One is awfully sorry for them. But the countryside is "cluttered up." Where any more can be placed is a problem, and some of them are a bit of a *nuisance*, to be candid. The best sort "stay *put*" and bear it. They complain most of noise. We have a friend from Liverpool who could scarcely keep her eyes open when she came a fortnight ago. She is going back tomorrow, with cheerfulness and unconcern although Merseyside has caught it as badly as the Thames, less spectacular than the capital, but much destruction of house property. Our friend is a Queen's district nurse; she has carried on. She has no nerves. Some of them are pathetic; a young man, leading a child about the village, his head bandaged, his wife and his tradesman business blown to bits in London. Compared to what people are bearing in the large towns, we have nothing to complain of here.

The spirit of the people is wonderful, magnificent. There is perhaps one defect — a certain hardness that resembles the reckless equanimity with which the public has come to regard road deaths — a toll which would have horrified us in the old days. It is different to the last war; no hanging back; and if a son is killed it's bad luck — but just bad luck, and accepted. I will try to write something, and to copy out an old story for Nancy.

[P.S.] There has been sound of heavy guns all afternoon — either practicing or firing off the coast. I do not think now that any invasion is likely, the weather has broken.

Nov. 25th 40

I hope this is in time for *The Horn Book!* It is my own fault if you have not waited. I found the old copy; and somehow in these times it read a little petty and egotistical. We are still unbombed here, and there are fewer planes at night.

Perhaps I will post a duplicate in a week. Some letters go lost. And having got a going, I had better write out Nancy's Christmas story before the scribbly fit passes.

I have been asked to tell again how *Peter Rabbit* came to be written. It seems a long time ago, and in another world. Though after all the world does not change much in the country, where the seasons follow their accustomed course — the green leaf and the sere — and where nature, though never consciously wicked, has always been ruthless.

In towns there is change. People begin to burrow underground like rabbits. The lame boy for whom Peter was invented more than forty years ago is now an air warden in a bombed London parish.

I have never quite understood the secret of Peter's perennial charm. Perhaps it is because he and his little friends keep on their way, busily absorbed with their own doings. They were always independent. Like Topsy — they just "grow'd." Their names especially seemed to be inevitable! I never knew a gardener named "McGregor." Several bearded horticulturalists have resented the nickname, but I do not know how it came about, nor why "Peter" was called "Peter." It is regrettable that a small boy once inquired audibly whether the Apostle was Peter Rabbit? There is great difficulty in finding, or inventing, names void of all possible embarrassment. A few of the characters were harmless skits or caricatures, but "Mr. McGregor" was not one of them, and the backgrounds of *Peter Rabbit* are of mixed locality.

"Squirrel Nutkin" lived on the shore of Derwentwater Lake near Keswick, and "Mrs. Tiggywinkle" in the nearby village of Newlands. "Jemima Puddleduck," "Jeremy Fisher," and others lived at Sawrey in the southern part of the English lake district.

The earlier books, including the later printed *Pig Robinson*, were written for real children in picture letters of scribbled pen and ink. I confess that afterwards I painted most of the little pictures to please myself. The more spontaneous the pleasure — the more happy the result.

I do not remember a time when I did not try to invent pictures and make for myself a fairyland amongst the wild flowers, the animals, fungi, mosses, woods and streams, all the thousand objects of the countryside — that pleasant, unchanging world of realism and romance, which in our northern clime, is stiffened by hard weather, a tough ancestry and the strength that comes from the hills.

To Marian Frazer Harris Perry

Dec. 24th. 40

This is the first Christmas for many years that I have not a single letter from America. Perhaps they will arrive delayed; — perhaps they are being wasted upon the deep sea fishes! Of one thing I am certain; my friends are still thinking about us and wishing us more pleasant times. The sun is shining and the sky blue — too clear, when one sees the lights flashing up amongst the stars. There has been a renewal of raiding after a lull; every night this last weekend we have heard guns. In the main, there is very little damage, but when they get over a large town like London or Liverpool, they cannot miss hitting something. It is sheer wanton mischief and cruelty, for the worse a town suffers the more determined are the survivors to go on fighting.

Our satisfaction about the eastern successes over the Italians was a little dampened by the report of the way the news was received in the States — that the Americans were delighted *because* they had begun to doubt? Nobody here doubts. We have *got to win*! It will be a slow and painful task; the issue for us is too serious for risks to be taken in too great a hurry. There is not much risk in attacking or respect for the Italian fascists' army. I cannot remember Garibaldi; I remember one of them; I think it was Garibaldi's friend Mattzindi (however is it spelt Mattsini?) [Mazzini] in London in the 70's, and the liberation of northern Italy from the Austrian rule. My parents coming back from a tour, and describing Venice under the Germans. We have never had any quarrel with the Italians. Except the horrid cruelty of their commanders in Abysinnia.

147

I am afraid Hitler will use gas if he makes a desperate attempt to land. I am amused to hear that an old lady whom I used to know, has returned to Sussex sea side home. She was evacuated on account of gun fire across the Channel, unwillingly. Old people are more afraid of invasion than bombs. We could not stand the cold if we were turned out of doors. It is uncomfortable not knowing what is going to happen next; most peculiar pause. The U. boat sinkings are an unpleasant actuality. We shall all have to grow more and eat less, if they cannot be stopped. Probably the losses have reached their apex, as on previous bad periods. If it gets worse the U.S.A. Navy ought to convoy some of the goods from U.S.A. You cannot afford to let us be beaten by hunger.

We were very lucky with our little harvest which was got in before bad weather. But the main contribution of this hilly district is wool and mutton. We were reckoning up the farm accounts. W. says I have marketed just over a thousand sheep in the twelve months — not fat of course, except a hundred or two. Most of them store sheep for fattening in the low lands. I do hope it may not be such a hard winter as last. I have a very big stock of sheep and young cattle. W. goes to the Agricultural Committee meetings; more and more ploughing wanted. None of the farm men taken so far; one or two in Home Guard, one off ill.

It's a strange world. I went to see a shepherd in the County hospital. Windows covered with fine wire netting, blackouts, etc. "George" told me with amusement that there had been a plane over the night before, and the nurses had run into the ward. "George", when there is a specially bad thunder storm amongst the fells, says it "reminds him of Wypers" — Ypres. He also has a disagreeable anecdote of seeing a Canadian regiment marching down an avenue in Flanders and falling into the first experience of gas. He got a whiff himself. What madmen to have another War!

We are very well here. We shall be extremely glad to welcome Spring and day light. It's not pleasant to hear a plane overhead on a long dark night, although well blacked out.

I wonder what's come of the mail?

I am enjoying rereading some books, and they improve with it. I didn't care for *Dew on the Grass* at first reading, but it grew upon me. Cornelia Meigs I like very much. Anne Carroll Moore sent me one or two. *Here I Stay* you sent me. We stay put!

With best wishes for New Year to you and to Betty and family —

~~~· Part III ~~~·

"Omens of Better Times"
1941 – 1943

To Anne Carroll Moore

The first Christmas for many years without one greeting from America! Perhaps the mail may arrive late, or perhaps the letters have been destroyed. It is officially said there was a lull in the raiding at Christmas; it was very bad during the preceding week. Our friend at a large sea port wrote that [censored] the Sunday before Christmas and the centre of the city was like enclosed view of Manchester; the centre and suburbs — not military, but horribly cruel.

As for Christmas peace — I myself saw 2 shells explode in the sky behind the outline of the Langdale Pikes on Christmas Eve! — a Cumberland outpost firing at planes. They go over our quiet fells and valleys. There have been no more bombs dropped in the district. The plight of the large towns is pitiable.

While the long nights last there is no cure. One still occasionally meets with people who disapprove of war-fare in the abstract; but they don't offer any suggestion of a cure for it. Nothing but increased strength seems any use. There is no shortage yet of food; except cattle "cake." I have enough home-grown to see my animals through winter; but I do hope it will not be so severe as last January as the snow was very trying for the sheep, and they are no use for killing in winter while they are thin, and lambs inside them. Farmers have made a great effort and will do still more in spring. We have some snow on the low ground today. There has been some lovely weather — to look at —. The clock being forward — we come out of our "black out" and see the sun rise, a very golden flush upon the snowclad fells, towering above frost fog in the dark valleys. May it be an omen of better times! We are both well; some what "edgy"; but much to be thankful for. With kind regards and best wishes for 1941,

P.S. If your country is dragged into war you will at least have the advantage of being further off from German bases than we are.

To Marian Frazer Harris Perry

March 21. 41

I was so pleased to receive your letter dated Jan. 23rd. It came on the same date as the news of the passing of the great "Lease and Lend" — better late than never!! I never thought for a moment that my friends had forgotten me when not one greeting arrived punctually on Christmas Eve. A few have come belated since, including yours and 2 from Boston, early in February, but a big mail undoubtedly was lost, in the Western Prince and other ships.

We have got through the winter and we welcome signs of Spring. The snowdrops have been lovely. Now it is fine dry weather for preparing to sow corn, a lot of extra ploughing; and we hope for a fine harvest like last year's. Things have been lively, but one cannot write much or Mr. Censor will black out. Surely I may be permitted to say that the last bomb heard of, on the outskirts of this district fell appropriately in a 'middenstead' — i.e. a receptacle for manure. If it were not so painful to think and know of the suffering which is taking place, a distant raid is rather fine — droning of planes very high overhead, gunfire and shells like falling stars — not at all near here — a cock pheasant shooting in the woods; our air warden, a fussy old man, blowing a whistle and ringing a hand bell; the special constable vainly requesting females to go indoors, which nobody did on a fine moonlight night. We are still waiting to see a dogfight. There is still plenty to eat; though sugar is precious. I have made a little marmalade. W and I have had a good winter as regards health, much better than last year. Give my love to Betty and her family if you see them and with love, believe me,

[P.S.] I don't know about courage. It seems to me the town populations have become like ants which continue to carry on even while a gardener puts his foot upon their activities. They don't know fear. I confess I went to bed in my clothes, but I slept like a top between noises. One becomes hardened to it. I have not taken my stockings off all winter expect of course to wash. I wish I might.

Ap. 14. 41

It is difficult to settle to anything. The news has been dreadfully anxious the last few days. Belgrade occupied — and can we save Greece? Surely Turkey will have to fight, but I suppose if she intervenes, the Japs will attack America and Australia.

I have been going through some remaining papers and books that belonged to my old American friend Miss Owen. The house is likely to be used for a hostel for Land and Forestry girls; it is a fine old Georgian house, very suitable, but wants a good deal doing to it. The dregs of the accumulations are at once curious and perplexing. The clearing has certainly provided interesting work. She collected autographs and pushed them between the leaves of books. In a volume of Kipling's there was a piece of thin note paper with two early poems, unpublished; not good; but with an unquestionable pedigree. Now I have found a scrapbook with portraits and autographs of Bishops — quantities, so many that it must be an almost comprehensive collection. Are they of any interest in the states? They are chiefly between 1860-70, a few older.

There is an air raid warning on, but I cannot hear any firing. We have some disturbed nights as this seems to be on a route. No bombs have been dropped near, and we are still waiting to see a dogfight. The destruction in the towns is cruel, yet the people stick it; there are not flights of evacs. like last autumn, when one saw cars with a mattress fastened over the roof against shrapnel and frightened women and children inside.

Some Girl Guides from Cheshire have been in the village for Easter weekend. They gave lively accounts punctuated with giggles. It's lucky people can take it that way; except not so praiseworthy that I think it is like road accident statistics, — people have become rather callous? As long as people are not hit — they laugh. It is clearing out a quantity of slum property that wanted clearing. The wind is still chilly; a late Spring. Daffodils are coming out and there are welcome showers. We have kept well in this house. On the farm there have been several laid up with a cold that is part flu — part whooping cough. Most of the corn has got sown, under difficulties. It has been a rather tiresome winter, so raw and changeable, though less severe than the winter before. I fancy many letters go lost.

[P.S.] Tanks are the nightmare. We can laugh about bombing; but if German tanks got a hold in this island — God help us! It's an asset that our road system is old fashioned.

One of the Guide's anecdotes. She was crossing some fields in Cheshire, a short cut home, and the planes came rather low, so she lay down under a hedge and a bomb dropped in a ditch without exploding, but she was splashed all over with black mud.

I had a welcome letter from you written Jan. 23rd and I answered it last month. Many are lost, apart from risks at sea.

I enclose two old scraps of American Bishops' writing. Most of the letters relate to visitations and accepting invitations for sleeping.

To Alexander McKay

Ap. 28. 41

I am obliged for the cheque $63-68 safely received this morning. We are still undamaged. Eleven killed in a farm house recently — the farmer, his wife, 2 children, his old mother, a servant girl and 5 evacuees. The two farm lads were blown through a window on their mattress and only received scratches; but one of them who was not very bright has lost his mind with shock. One of the children lost her head. Heads seem to get blown off!

Nice state of affairs in the 20th century in a civilized country? It is maddening to think of Greece. It is only an incident. But to think that if we had had enough aeroplanes, we might have saved them. There is one of ours zooming overhead as I am writing — our airmen cannot be everywhere.

The men say they were bombed out of France — bombed out of Norway — now it is bombed out of Greece.

To Marian Frazer Harris Perry

Nov. 11th. 41

I am afraid I have left this letter too late for Christmas and New Year, though a recent letter from U.S.A. took only 5 weeks. We are well here, and settling down to cold weather and "black out." Spring will be welcome! There is one satisfaction when the weather is bad with a biting east wind; we hope it is worse in Russia! There have been no raid alarms in this part recently; stray planes have dropped bombs in remote places without causing damage. There has been a depressed feeling over the Russian falling back. Really we ought to remember that we doubted if Russia would be able to stand at all; although one did not then realize what strength Germany was capable of bringing into the assault.

I trust and hope the seriousness of the position is realized in America. I have never been one who complained of the States. Your country is just in the same humiliating position that patriotic Englishmen had to suffer while watching other countries go under, and unable to help them because we were not sufficiently armed. Hitler has such a reserve of slave labour to make tanks, that it will take a big effort to outbid him.

The crops have been very good. There has been some waste owing to a spell of wet weather in early September — and shortage of farm machinery — such as binders. We waited for a tractor binder to come, and our little crop of oats stood up well through the rain and was cut late in *fine* weather. There is no shortage of food. Sugar and fish and eggs are the scarce articles. I had saved sugar and was able to make a nice supply of jam — mostly blackberry — as plums were a poor crop!

There are not many evacuees now. They have gone home; they don't like the country in winter. It seems unwise to have taken so many children back to towns — not only on account of the risk of bombing, but because many town schools being closed and parents busy, there is very little discipline. War brings out the noblest and the meanest qualities of mankind. The effect on the morals of young people is disastrous. So much drinking — partly through excitement and dissipating; and in the case of factory girls, through too much money. I wish labour had been conscripted at a fixed moderate wage! When girls and boys can earn five or six pounds a week, and soldiers' families can scarcely pay their way — it's all wrong. All very wrong. One hoped that the mistake of the last war would not be repeated; but it has. The factory workers are paid more than is good for them, and the dependents of the service men not enough.

I often think of your — and Betty — and Dick's great kindness. And I hope you got our thanks, letters go lost. It would have been awkward if the girls had gone, when the end is so slow of coming in sight. But that does not alter the fact that you "showed willing"! I have not seen the Dukes for a year; Kenneth is changed to another area of ordnance inspection. Jean is living with her parents and doing child welfare work in connection with the school board, elementary school, and the older girl Rosemary joined the WRENS as soon as she was old enough. That branch of the Women's Services (Naval) has a better name than some others. A friend who has 'joined up' with the ----s writes that 14 of her company have been given 6 months leave to go home and have babies. One way of keeping up the population! They are worse than the last war. If America has to come in, it's a pity it cannot go 'Pussy foot' again; much of the trouble originates in cocktails. As for the small boys, Mr. Heelis is non-plussed. They break into houses whose inhabitants are out working and they behave like Germans. The magistrates have tried whipping and special schools, but there is no keeping them quiet.

We have had a pleasant summer — apart from difficulties and alarms. Prisoners escaping from the camp in one excitement; they do not usually get far. You would be amused to see W.H. in a police rig out — he looks a mile high. He is very well at present; very busy. The Agricultural Committee has a great deal to arrange about ploughing. The sheep fairs have been good this autumn. So far I have enough labour, only very hard worked, especially men who have joined the Home Guard. With love and best wishes from us both,

At the top of this letter a bit of silvered material was attached and marked "Blitz."

To Anne Carroll Moore

Nov. 12. 41

We have not been feeling very cheerful; but it seems as though wind and snow and winter frosts may save Russia. America is going through the stage we did at first — talking a little too big, but not ready or able to save other countries from going under. *You* who visited devastated France after the last war will know what a fate it is. We have had noisy nights even in this remote district, as the German planes go over on passage elsewhere, and some times unload their bombs when running for home; but there has been very little damage. They usually fall in fields or water. There was one bad tragedy, a lonely farm house, where the farmer, his mother, his wife and 2 children, maid servant, and 5 evacuees were all killed. There have been none near this village. If it were not for pity one might say it is a fine sight! The red glare of Liverpool and Manchester burning last spring. The search lights and flares when towns on the coast are attacked. People take it calmly; with temper, not fear. Also animals; I had 2 horses in a field next to a pasture where 11 bombs dropped and my man found them grazing quietly when daylight came. We thought those bombs were dropped because the German suddenly realized that he was heading straight into the fell side in the darkness. They were only small bombs; it is interesting to look at the holes amongst the turf and rushes. Next morning there were little bits like tinsel on the grass; there did not seem to be any heavy metal — a thin bag of explosives? We have had a pleasant summer apart from the war, and good crops. It has been very hard work for farmers. This is really no suitable district for much ploughing and corn. We have plenty of food, and plenty of fodder for the cattle. I do hope it may not be such a severe winter as the two last — which were terrible for the hill sheep. I did not lose so many in the snow, but they lost their lambs in spring, they were so weak. As regards ourselves we are both very well — of course feeling older.

I don't know if you will get this by Christmas; I ought to have written earlier. This paper has done some travelling — it was sent to me by a friend in Australia! You will have heard Mr. Churchill say in Parliament that there is plenty to eat! We here personally feel cheerful about a Christmas dinner. We are going to kill a fat pig!! We are allowed 2 pigs a year amongst us; but may not kill any other sort of animal, except hutch rabbits. The rationing is very just; a bit inconvenient for country people far removed from shops. I have received a wail from Bedford Street — orders without cease, and enough paper, but they cannot get books bound. The Warne business has not been bombed. A large edition was lost last Spring at the printers. Other things have gone that matter more! It is sad to think of the City. And the same in Europe; senseless waste and destruction. The blitz has done one useful purpose, it has opened the eyes of the British trades unions; well if the Americans realize in time. With our kind regards,

To Helen Dean Fish

Nov. 13. 41

I write in anxious times. One knows not what to expect in 1942. Hitler must and will be beaten, but it will take some doing yet. It is an unkind thing to say but I wish the American trades union could have a taste of 'blitz' and understand what it is like. Unless frost and snow help the Russians it looks like being a very long war. We have plenty to eat. Personally we look forward to a Christmas feast, we have a fat pig to kill and eat amongst us! A household is allowed 2 pigs a year; they are the only animals that may be killed at home except hutch rabbits. The rationing is very strict, — but just. It wastes time in the country where we are so far from shops. We have had good crops and get them in better order than further south where the early harvest got wet in September's first week. There are still some potatoes to lift — it is such a difficulty to get through all the work. You mentioned garden seeds, I asked the local Girl Guide Captain and she could make good use of some seeds. I think I have enough to stock our garden. I have some that were sent from Australia too late for this season; and also what I saved, ripe — carrots, onion, leeks are useful. I wonder if you grow winter spinach? The spinach seed was bad (though beet seed which is similar was good) last season. We have lots of the cabbage tribe which ripen seeds in profusion. I was able to save sugar for jam; there was not much stone fruit but lots of blackberries.

I have a lamentable wail from Warne & Co! overwhelmed — not by bombs but by orders which they cannot accept. They have enough paper, but not enough book binders. There is certainly no occasion to reprint the black and white *Peter Rabbit*. We get an occasional noisy night but there have been no bombs dropped near this village. I picked up this little bit like tinsel in a boggy meadow where 6 bombs had fallen in a row. We think the German planes unload at random when going home from raids on the coast and on northern Ireland. Some sheep got killed, and there was one terrible disaster at a farm house, all dead.

We keep well; but feeling rather old and tired. There is variety in the size of bombs. A friend who is here describes an abyss large enough to take a house in a NW town last week, probably land mine. The local bombs have mostly been holes 12 feet across by 6 deep, in fields and on moors. [Have no] metal with them, only explosions.

This paper came from Australia. With our kind regards,

To Bertha Mahony Miller

Nov. 24. 41

The winter's cold and bad weather is here again. I hope it has not brought any more bronchitis to you? I have only got a cold in my nose; and let us both make good resolutions that "a stitch in time saves nine." With colds that are obstinate! stay in bed.

I happened to look through a packet of old letters from U.S.A., and I have reread some questions which you asked about the books. "Stymouth" was Sidmouth on the south coast of Devonshire. Other pictures were sketched at Lyme Regis; the steep street looking down hill into the sea, and some of the thatched cottages were near Lyme. The steep village near Lynton is called Clovelly. I have never seen it, though I know parts of the north Devon coast. Ilfracombe gave me the idea of the long flight of steps down to the harbour. Sidmouth harbour and Teignmouth harbour are not much below the level of the towns. The shipping — including a pig aboard ship — was sketched at Teignmouth, S. Devon. The tall wooden shed for drying nets is (or was?) a feature of Hastings, Sussex. So the illustrations are a comprehensive sample of our much battered coasts.

Old John Taylor was the Sawrey joiner and wheelwright; his wife, and later his stout elderly daughter "Agnes Anne," kept the little general shop for years and years. After their deaths, a daughter-in-law took it on. In turn she became old and invalidish and made it over to a niece-in-law — who has closed the long chapter; Ginger and Pickles is no more. Multiple stores had about killed village shops before the war. We were very vexed; indeed, I would have put in a friend who was anxious to take it on. But the Taylor niece-in-law sat tight! She kept on the cottage, made the "shop" a parlour to let, and threw away the good will and connections because, being a young person, she would not be tied keeping shop. Agnes Anne was a big, fat woman with a loud voice, very genuine in her likes and dislikes, a good sort. Old John was a sweet, gentle old man, failed in his legs, so he kept his bed, but was head of the family and owned several cottages. He professed to be jealous because I had put his son John in a book as John Joiner. [censored] When I saw old John, who was very humourous and jokey, I asked him how could I put him — old John — in a book if he insisted on living in bed? So a week afterwards, enclosed with an acct., there came a scrap of paper, "John Taylor's compliments and thinks he might pass for a dormouse."

It really is too bad to have closed Ginger and Pickles. The village blacksmith's is gone; turned into a bungalow for a Taylor daughter-in-law. And the village post office is gone [censored] 2 miles from Hawkshead P.O. And nearly all the older generation — all that were "old" when I was younger, are dead. To be dead is in the course of nature — and war — but [censored] we are alive seems to me to be generally for the worse, disagreeable.

I have heard lately of the death of an old cousin. She had been living in a country hotel since her London house was destroyed; she was 80 so it doesn't matter; but can you wonder the Germans are hated? Her daughter writes me that a [censored] frightened her into a stroke, followed by pneumonia. "She was ill only 4 days, but the night she died there was another raid and guns and bombs going all the time. There is nothing I would not do to those murderers. She could not even die in peace."

Another cousin of mine was killed in London last spring. The raids have been only small affairs for many months though more serious than might appear from the news reports, and evacuees have gone back to towns. Indeed there is as much in the country; but of course, less chance of being hit. One night there were 4 planes, on the way home, unloaded their sticks over [censored]; some sheep were killed. I had two farm horses in the next pasture to a bog where there is a line of small craters. The German would have flown into the fell side of the dark, if he had not tipped out his load; [censored] but only small ones. The horses were grazing quietly when daylight came. There were the saucer shaped holes, about 4 foot deep, and quantities of shining flecks like tinsel on the grass and rushes. The bombs probably weighed only about 50 pounds each. Thin, light bags of explosives.

A friend (evacuee) from a south Lancashire town tells us frightful tales — a shelter containing 300 people got a direct hit. Some bodies were got out and the rest sealed down with quick lime. Only 10 days ago she looked down into a chasm large enough to hold a lofty building. It had fallen on vacant ground; she found her friends in a nearby house undamaged, though a whole row had collapsed. The effects of blast are most peculiar; windows may be unbroken on one side of a street and *everything* gone on the opposite side. Everything literally. A young woman from a village went to Barrow to look for her sister last spring, and there was not a shred. It's a pity the U.S.A. strikers cannot realize, by seeing and feeling, what it is. Destruction and beastly cruelty.

We have had a fine summer; enjoyable but for the overwork and anxiety.

I am too late posting for Christmas. I wonder whether Nancy will care for the stories? ["The Solitary Mouse" and "Wag-by-Wall"] Of course, I wrote the introduction for my own pleasure — and it might appeal to Anne Carroll Moore because she knows the Lake district. I cannot judge my own work. Is not "Wag by the Wall" rather a pretty story, if divested of the "Jenny Ferret" rubbish? I thought of it years ago as a pendant to *The Tailor of Gloucester* — the old lonely man and the lonely old woman — but I never could finish it all; and after 9 months occasional nibblings, it seems likely to go into the post — unfinished yet!

What a pity you didn't come to Sawrey! A.C.M. came and Miss Gould and Miss Davis and Mary Haugh and Mrs. Coolidge, all delightful. Why not Bertha Mahony?

I do not know of any treatise upon credit; ask Mr. Micawber of *David Copperfield!*

I think both *Ginger and P[ickles]* and *Pie and Patty* are feeble in plot. The ovens are absurd, quite wrong.

My books are off the market — wails and lamentations from F.W. & Co. They have enough paper, but they cannot get book binders, so they have to refuse the whole Christmas market. It would hit me also, but farming has looked up; hard work but fair pay at last.

With kind regards,

Dec. 28th. 41

It seems an age since "Dec. 7th." We could hear your President's every word distinctly. His speech was fine; direct and forcible in its simple statement. Only, all the time I listened, I kept thinking — how many "Dec. 7th's" there have been in Europe? Did he ever read a book called the *Rape of Holland?* [Probably *Rape of the Netherlands* by Eelco Nicholass Van Kleffens]

There are beginning to be local reports of sailors — saved and lost. A good many Barrow lads saved from the Prince of Wales, and their relations informed. There is just one thing to be said in favour of the Japs — they did not machine gun the rescuees, which the Nazis would have done! They, the Nazis, certainly choose to waste bullets in wanton cruelty.

Here is an extract from a letter from east coast. "I don't think I have written to you since we were bombed last January. Barbara and I were walking on the heath when a plane swooped down and machine gunned us — (2 women, mother and daughter). It made 3 dives — of course we were lying flat! Then we heard a bomb. We were not touched. But when we got home we found it had fallen in the garden and half the bungalow was gone!"

Often they have machine gunned factory girls on their way to work. But there are seldom hits. There are more shooting casualties from our own shrapnel falling or ricochetting in raids. We have been quiet here lately; very different to last Christmas, when the sky was lighted up with a reflection of fires.

I posted you a transcript of 2 old unfinished tales belonging to the Caravan series, on Nov. 26th. I wonder if the letter survived. One has come to me from Milton, Mass. on Dec. 22nd — so some Christmas mail has got through, and there may be more to come yet. Our own postal arrangements are dislocated a good deal. And the public has travelled in spite of being told not to do so.

It has been a bright windless Christmas. More and more men are being called up. We have cause to be thankful to the Russians who have a large population to draw upon. I am lucky in having an aged — not strong domestic, too old for factory. I was never afraid of house work or outdoor work while I could do it, but I am rather infirm being so badly ruptured. There is plenty to eat and much to be thankful for — not least a relief that U.S.A. has at last realized and woke up before too late. I hope you are both well — as we are here — and may we all see the dawn of Peace in 1942.

[Dec. 29th] I have reopened my letter to tell you that your welcome message came this morning by cablegram. I am so glad you got my little Christmas message safely and thank you again and again for good wishes. *The Horn Book* has come also — I always enjoy it.

Jan. 18. 42

I have received a somewhat perplexing letter from Margery McKay, now Mrs. Cridland (how the young grow up!). She wants to write an article for *The Horn Book* about the animals in my books. Do you really think there is occasion? I hate to say "no" or discourage young people (though for that matter the young are become unsnubable on this side [of] the Atlantic!). I remember she wrote to me when she was a schoolgirl, and I wrote some "explains" on the margins of *The Fairy Caravan*, which was a book that must have required explains for American readers. Unless, as I sometimes think, your New England country folk are more *old English* than our English modern town and suburban population who have done much to swamp old-fashioned speech, customs, and manners over here.

I have put her off just now with the excuse that I rather expect to hear from *you*. *The Horn Book* has been more than kind with notices of my books. I cannot see what occasion or reason there is at the moment for referring to them? She seems to suggest bringing in the P[eter] R[abbit] series animals as well?

I suppose the reception of the *Caravan* in America was like the *Tailor's* in this country. Some people — people that I cared about pleasing — liked *The Tailor* best of all my books. It was not everybody's book; compared with several others, it fell flat. It does not seem as though any of the books published by David McKay have sold in large number* — of which I am not complaining. "A[.nne] C[arroll] M[oore]" was disposed to suggest another publisher might have turned them out in a more attractive shape. I did not agree with her objection to *Sister Anne* (which I reread with enjoyment and detached interest, whereas I am sick of *Peter Rabbit*!!).

I am trying to say that while wishing her well and happy, I'm not sure what ground Margery has for jumping off an article? I have suggested that she should wait for an obituary article of the author! I did once begin to write an article myself about pets, but I tore it up — which is what we are enjoined to do. There is a drive to pulp superfluous literature.

Your cable spoke of a letter coming, so I may be hearing from you.

---

*Whoever had published the later books, they would not have had the numerical success of the P R series.

[P.S.] On reading through again, this letter sounds ungracious. I do not mean anyone to think I grudge Margery writing the article because her father did not sell many copies. I don't think anybody but myself has claim to write a full account of my animals in the Peter R books. She can only have any claims to the "explains" relating to Caravan animals? I doubt whether they have enough interest to enough readers to be worthwhile, though a few readers like them very much. And there is no particular reason or excuse that I can see for another at present?

To Mrs. Charles Hopkinson

Jan. 19. 42

How very kind of you to post a Christmas parcel! I am waiting — waiting — ? ? Last Thursday one arrived with a delicious smell, and a hole at one corner. I don't think anything had been abstracted except shavings for packing — the contents were loose. But it was not from you! It was from Betty Stevens posted from Philadelphia. There was chocolate and dried fruit (no not dried, the apricots are fat and juicy) — and a curious cheese sausage quite unknown to us, and tea. Which makes me think of Boston harbour? America may be short of tea presently! We have never felt our tea ration short in this house. I fancy the war workers complain of tea shortage because they are drinking immoderate quantities. What old people feel the worst of is sweets and fruit. The beet sugar is not really sweet. I do hope your illness has passed off with a rest in bed; it is the warmest place. It required firmness to make myself get out of bed this morning. There is wet snow and a biting east wind. I got over that severe operation well. I am an old woman now (and rather badly ruptured which cripples me a bit) but I am able to get about and look after the farm in the working season, though I cannot work with my own hands like I enjoyed doing in the last war. We have had no bombs falling near this house and village, though we have heard and seen plenty of raiders when they pass over the Lake district, and unload on the way home. They usually fall on waste places and do little damage. This has been a very quiet Christmas compared to last year's, when the sky was lighted up with the red glow of fires in northern towns.

Mr. Heelis is very well. Of course we are all tired and over worked one way and another. You will excuse paper; it is shortest of anything!

Quite possibly your parcel may yet come. Our own post office is very remiss and in arrears.

With kindest regards and thanks for your good intentions

[P.S.] I wonder — was your newly married daughter abroad?

To Anne Carroll Moore

Jan. 19th. 42

The *Library Journal* has come. It was not a complete surprise as I had heard a rumour — in a round about way, which is an instance of your far spread influence for usefulness. A friend — Mrs. Ivy Steele, who emigrated years ago to Canada and subsequently married in N.Y. has a girl, nearly grown up now, who has enjoyed the benefit of children's branch activities. She told me in a recent letter that you were going to retire from the Public Library.

I am sure you will never cease to be an inspiration and a guide to those whom you have taught how to carry on the good work. I hope the reviewer is right in saying your influence has extended to England. I am so completely out of the world I don't know. Our shops did not look very promising a year ago. This year they cannot offer cartloads of fat rubbish because there is such a dearth of paper! Let us hope when book publishing revives the output may be quality rather than quantity — for — money as in the past.

I do hope you are very well and that your retirement is not due to fatigue. Long may you be spared to enjoy well earned leisure.
With kindest regards from my husband and myself,

[P.S.] The Christmas mail has come in irregularly. Some Nov. letters are still arriving, after later-posted ones.

Jan. 31. 42

Your letter and the snowy trees reached me two days ago, in a world equally white. I am so very glad to hear you are lecturing. I was half afraid your retiring from the Library might mean ill health. *The Library Journal* was not implicit on that point. Your country is truly in the war at last! How glad we are to know the American troops are in Ulster! I have never thought that invasion of Britain could be success- ful; but while any landing was being beaten off it would be horrible for people living as near the coast as we do here. The orders have always been to "stay put"; we would not have stampeded like the French; but the choice of sitting indoors — or taking to the woods is not attractive to the aged! There is about a foot of snow at present — no doubt it has come from Russia, the wind has been in the east. It is the third severe winter in succession. I feel the cold a bit; but I have had the luxury of breakfast in bed some very cold mornings, as we have an evacuated friend here, for the winter months, who is helpful. This paper is a bit off an old proof sheet. I have been sorting papers and books this afternoon — a perplexing task as regards books. "Salvage drives" are a craze; at the present moment being overdone. Things are being destroyed that ought not to be. There is a drive for old iron and the local council has made such a muddle of listing railings. Pretty old fashioned light work on walls is listed to go, while a next door heavy gate is not on the list. It is causing much annoyance; they are taking so many garden railings which are not of sufficient weight to balance the wreck. There is any amount of modern ugly bar fencing, but the Council unfortunately selects "*old* iron". I am sure mine is Georgian. I am trying to ransom it by offering a pump, a stove, a field gate and some hurdles. Nearly all the little old railings in Hawkshead are scheduled; the square will look bare. I have been telling the sanitary inspector (!) who is the author of the list that he should have taken many hundred tons of horizontal bars from the black modern fencing which disfigures our widened roads, for miles and miles. The middle and lower bars could be drawn out, and replaced by sheep netting. Books are also perplexing.

Books of reference that one cannot scrap. Books that one is fond of, though one does not constantly reread them. What about *The Horn Book* for many years? which I dip into with pleasure. What about little old books for children which I have collected? I have shelved the question with regard to a quantity of general literature by sending it to the Sailors Home at Barrow. The port missionary is anxious for books for the ships, and he can "salvage" what is unsuitable, though he does say they "will read any thing." How quaint and pretty to drop into a back water of old France in 'Arcadia'. I think some parts of the states must be as charming as other parts must be as unpleasingly modern. In this small island we have not room for back waters, and the few that still linger are to be listed and swept away by sanitary inspectors!

Some one sent me Rachel Field's *All This [and Heaven Too]*. The "second volume" — the New England sequel is delightful, and the American historical personages are alive and natural. The French part has no atmosphere, rather flat.

My husband keeps well — touch wood! There is a good deal of influenza about. It is going the round of the farms. Not severe; but if William gets it he — does get it — with depression. I am fairly cheerful about things. This snow — 4 falls since New Year — is becoming serious for the sheep, but it has done a good turn in Russia.

With kindest regards from both of us,

To Mrs. J. Templeman Coolidge

Feb. 12. 42

I had a delightful surprise this morning. I received the gift parcel — quite safely and intact. I did not expect there would be any more gift parcels when America is in the war. But your country has more room, and more diversity of climate. Do what we will we cannot grow lemons! The lemon juice is most acceptable. Lemons have disappeared, and oranges are strictly reserved for children. We were fortunate in having a good crop of apples which are keeping well. So far nobody is taking any harm, or losing weight like last war time. But these presents containing chocolate and real cane sugar are a treat.

We are directed to grow more and more. At present work is held up by snow. It has been the third snowy winter. "Sauce for the goose is sauce for the gander!" A hard winter has done a good turn for us in Russia. I am more sorry for the sheep than for the Germans! Four weeks of snow on the ground makes the hill sheep weak and thin. It is impossible to feed flocks of many hundreds with sufficient hay. The shepherds have been cutting down holly bushes and ash branches for them. We are both well here. I have been indoors a good deal owing to the weather; but ventured out this morning as there is a thaw. There are such stacks of snow where the yard has been dug out — it will take a lot of thawing.

I cannot tell you what satisfaction it is to know there are United States troops in Ireland. We are too near the Irish Sea to feel safe here. Bombing is nothing (unless you happen to be hit!) but the idea of invasion is a nightmare. I scarcely think it is likely to come; he has missed his chance.

I still have labour on the farm, as long as the shepherds don't all get flu at once; they are older men except one lad, their ploughman horse; so far he has not been called up. Of course he is in the Home Guard. William has retired at seventy, but still keeps his policeman's helmet and big boots. He couldn't stand night work in winter, but he is on call in winter for the police station. We have not been turned out of bed for a long time at night.

I hope you are quite well and Henry P. and his brother. Also I hope the news will improve; it is a rough time at present. The Japs will inevitably be beaten. They are so recklessly spread out; but it has been a shock, and so many people seem to have men in the East.

With thanks again and love,

To Bertha Mahony Miller

Feb. 17. 42

On your own head be it! "Wag-by-the-Wall" is a good story, but surely the mouse is most awful rubbish? Do you mean to say you would print all that tea party stuff in *The Horn Book*? Xarifa's conversations with the mouse improves; but the preparations are dragging.

If you really decide to use it I should like to alter a few sentences. I happen to have been copying the old loose pages into one notebook, and I thought there were some disjoints in the descriptions, especially the Grasmere festival. I will try to compress others, but *not* compress the description of Troutbeck Tongue which is a curious formation, for England. I daresay similar occur commonly abroad. Of course, the shepherds thought it was haunted. It is the water running through rocky canyons and through underground channels in the peat that carries sound — though my own funniest experience was a *smell*, an unromantic strong whiff of twist, "Kendal twist" tobacco! I was on the very top of the table-land and could see a mile around in absolute solitude. (NB I do not smoke myself.) It is the configuration, and the numerous ancient remains.

Joseph is a delightful person. I would not hurt his feelings for anything, but he is not likely to see *The Horn Book*. He is a Scotch shepherd, an old bachelor, who has come with a dog every spring for 16 years to help us at lambing time.

Think it over, and do as you think! If *The Horn Book* printed it, from my point of view it would have the benefit of safeguarding the copyright, in case Sally were worth making into a separate book, and she might be useful to children's library storytellers. The terms 50 dollars for serial rights would be satisfactory. I don't know about forwarding through F.W. and Co. They were *not* pleased about the *Caravan*. I will ask the bankers whether there is any difficulty about a direct payment. We may not send money out, but I did not know it was wrong coming in, if done openly and disclosed.

As regards rationing, it is difficult to describe because it depends on the individual. W.H. grumbles and H.B.H. doesn't! I never eat eggs; they make me bilious. We have been allowed to kill and cure our own large pig. There is no hunger like the last war, and food is excellent. What we miss is cane sugar. There is a reasonable sugar allowance; I was able to save enough to make ⅔ of my usual jam last summer, but it is *beet* sugar — *beet* root — and it is not really sweet. I never knew we had such a taste for sweeties — such as peppermints and chocolates until missing them. What are on sale are not really sweet. Soap is going to be very scarce. Children get oranges, nobody else. Mrs. Coolidge most kindly sent a parcel; there was some lemon juice in it, also cheese which is abundant — and tea. So far our tea ration has been sufficient; because I don't drink much I was glad to give hers to a dear old lady of 87 who was lamenting for her morning cup, and I had some lovely dried fruit, Californian. We have had a good crop of apples which are still keeping well. I cannot say we are necessitous, but the sweet things are a real treat! I have had 2 gift parcels, through Pierce and Co. — a third went missing. I am sure I shall be delighted to receive yours — it won't be wasted!

There is no telling how things may be next winter. Personally I am not downhearted. The Russian success counts for so much. I fear they are disappointed that *we* don't invade Europe. We have had too many fiascos, and we have too much to lose if beaten. Ireland is such a risk; it is the greatest relief to know there are U.S.A. troops in Ulster; to us personally. We are much too near the Irish Channel for comfort.

I do not think either nation can blame the other about Jap war failures. The Dutch seem to have done best, to start with. No doubt America will catch up and beat Japan. The loss of prestige is the lasting evil in the East. I hope you are not bombed!! I cannot help being a little amused; hunger and bombing are a commonplace, but we have had quiet nights for some time. It's remarkable how people get used to raids, so long as they are not hit. But the risk of invasion is a nightmare.

I shall not read *The Horn Book* number if you print that rubbish! At all events, don't print anything of Miss MacKay's gushing flattery.

[P.S.] Your letter came Feb. 16th. No parcel yet — one went lost at Christmas. 2 pages herewith.

If it is printed I should like some changes. I think the art of essay writing is to balance the main theme by ruthlessly cutting, no matter whether the incidents sacrificed are pretty or not. Cut out (1) Candle-light and firelight to pipe and tabor. (2) Lady Henry Bentinck. The sentence doesn't please and it is redundant. (Lady Henry is dead, and another much loved noble lady died last week, Lady Richard Cavendish at Holker Hall. The old order is passing away.) (3) Cut out the little children of St. Ann at Grasmere and also their red cap dance. (One of the prettiest distant sights I ever saw; it was quaint but too far off to hear any music.) (4) Freya Holda, she is an interruption. By the way, the word really is "bellying" before the wind, which would be some-what coarse speaking, like Titania's "swimming gait."

I will now go through small details seriatim. Long drive, etc., and Broughton-in-Furness (too many geographicals); running *set* (not step); the toddler and his gray-haired *gran* — all dancing (i.e. the modern child calls his grandmother "gran"); Kirby Lonsdale meadows; the band fiddling — *under a tree, a lime in scented bloom*. The Grasmere I wish to rewrite, leaving out the colours of the dance frocks — "kaleido-scope." "In spite of the rough turf, I have never seen more perfect Morris, or prouder beauty than the Durham reels danced by girls in corn-coloured smocks. The reels pleased me especially. Folk dancing if it is to take real hold ought to be an indigenous survival. 'Three reels,' 'Petronella,' and the 'Triumph' were traditional in this Border country. My farm servants danced them at our Christmas suppers, long before Morris was introduced from the south. Well-trained Morris dancing is a miracle of graceful agility; a display for international meet-ings. But give me the swinging, roaring reels — the sparkling pretty long sets — the maze of intricate dances surprisingly remembered. Follow the fiddle, forget your feet! or dance with style and bend and sway — a bow and a curtsy for man and maid, and an inextricable

tangle of laughter for beginners! Give me reels and spontaneous, unsophisticated country dancing all the time for dancing in a north country village." Delete children of St. Ann's. Another time all by myself
alone, etc., etc.

I don't know what to do with the tea barn party twaddle. [In the
original manuscript, Jenny Ferret, Sandy, Xarifa, Tuppenny, and Paddy
Pig, characters from *The Fairy Caravan,* have a tea party at High
Buildings.] If you want to shorten, I suggest that *you* as editor in
slightly different type interpolate that "after a long march in the rain
and wind they reach High Buildings, a barn high up the valley where
they camp and make themselves comfortable. They notice 'someone
has been camping here before.' They guess it was the shepherds and
Mistress Heelis at lambing time. At tea time, Sandy says, 'What are you
two looking at' " etc., etc.

That would mean cutting out mine from the point when Pony Billy
plodded on until the Xarifa and Joseph dialogue started?

I am afraid my alterations on this sheet are not shortening. "Troutbeck Tongue is uncanny: a place of silences and whispering echoes. It
is a mighty table-land between two streams. They rise together, north
of the Tongue, in one maze of bogs and pools. They flow on either
hand; the Hagg Beck in the eastern valley; the Troutbeck river on the
west. They meet and reunite below the southern craggs, making the
table land almost an island — an island haunted by the sounds that
creep on running waters which encompass it. The Tongue is shaped
like a great horseshoe, edged by silver streams, and guarded by an outer
rampart of high fells. From" etc., etc. "on Caudale moor in a mist. Usually I saw nobody, the long day round.

"I think mist is beautiful, though troublesome for sheep gathering. It
takes strange shapes when it rains at sunset. During storms it rushes
down the valleys like a black curtain, billowing before the wind, while
the Troutbeck river thunders over the cauldron. Old unhappy" etc., etc.
A weird place. The sights and sounds largely due to configurations of
the ground and water and — as regards sights — to a diet of cheese and
apples. There was one very sad happening; when the fairies (?) got
"Bobs." He was a favourite sheep dog. The 3 shepherds were gathering
sheep the east side of the horseshoe outer fell. One man in the valley
bottom, one half way up the mountain side, one on the skyline. They
had 7 dogs when they started. Each thought Bobs was with the other,

but when they got to Dalehead, Bobs was not. I lost a valuable ram on the same hill sides — simply vanished.

Sink holes — quarry or mineral trial holes — are horrible. According to an old plan there are 2 in the quarry pasture, but we have *never been able to locate them*. When abandoned, they are supposed to be covered with branches. They get grown over with moss and bracken.

I hope to think Bobs was killed outright. I went up next day, calling and whistling; the dog was much attached to me, but I never heard a whimper.

There was a forgotten sink hole on another farm in Eskdale, that a dog fell into, but it was only 15 feet deep; it was heard whining and fetched out with a rope unhurt. There are some on Coniston Old Man Mountain; the old copper mines that were worked in [the] 16th century. They might be 80 to 100 deep. Nasty places!

The Troutbeck quarries are not worked — owing to accidents from stones falling. The underground slate quarries have high ceilings like large caverns. The miners refused to continue. It is like projectiles (which the public does *not* understand.) A little bit of shrapnel falling from a great height can kill — whereas large bombs dropped most high have not much penetration. If I have patience, I will copy this again and duplicate by air mail. Can't get [to] post office today.

Beatrix Potter wrote to Mrs. Miller again on the following day, February 18, 1942. Much of the second letter repeats information included in the previous letter. There are, however, some additions and some second thoughts about the revisions. These are presented in excerpts.

February 18. 42

It seems funny to write this again. I posted a letter yesterday. I think some go lost so I will duplicate by airmail. I told you I think the *Mouse* is *twaddle!*

I think "Wag" is a pretty little story. I should like to print it someday in book form. There are a few changes I should like to make, principally in cutting — though I fear, not much shortening. There seem to be a few open joints; for instance, Sally Benson's cow is not alive. And some secondary incidents in the *Mouse* introduction spoil the balance of the essay. Although picturesque in themselves, I would advise cutting them out *ruthlessly*. I *like* the introduction and the peroration (I mean I like writing them!), but such a jumble has the disadvantage of making book neither "child" ('s) nor "grown up's" . . . .

If you receive both lists of corrections, please compare them. Like Mr. Turveydrop, I "polish! polish! polish! to the last revise. . . ."

It is difficult to know how to deal with the arrival and unpacking at High Buildings. *I think it drags.* Could not you, *as editor* perhaps in brackets or different print, say that after a disagreeable journey they arrive and find shelter in a nice dry stable where they notice somebody else has been camping? They think it must have been the shepherds and Mistress Heelis (It was a Scotch shepherd gave me that name.) They light an oil stove and make tea. Xarifa and Tuppenny fidget, "What are you looking at" etc., etc., etc. . . .

There is a description of Troutbeck Tongue which does not quite explain the very curious terrain. . . .

Sorry! but delete "Freya Holda"; she is an interruption; (delete) "between" (before) "sunset" (which) is followed by "during storms". . . .

I wonder if your Nancy's copy had the word "celestial?". The sheep glided up "to mingle with celestial flocks, a myriad fleecy clouds overhead". It was a strange, beautiful sight. I was belated walking down King Gait on the west slope of a narrow valley when I saw the mist on the opposite side, as distinct as any spectre of the Brocken. She had no dog, and the sheep were lamb size compared with the towering figure. I felt an inclination to run!

About "Wag-by-the-Wall" I have time to recopy it before July. But there is not much to alter. I would like to add "As the little owls grew older and greedier, the hen owl came out to hunt for mice by daylight. She looked like a great creamy white moth flitting over the bog. The peewits wailed and swooped at her, although she was only seeking for mice. Nancy Cow, knee-deep in sedge grass and meadowsweet, blew warm breath. Her big feet squelched among moss and eyebright and sundew. She turned back into firm turf and lay down, until Sally's voice called her home to milking." Those difficult verses? Wealth, power, and glory? "Now summer is smiling mid roses beguiling/ With haycocks and harvest and 'taties to store,/ Brave Autumn advancing with fiddles and dancing/ Leads in the kern supper with jigs on the floor./ Sing little *black* kettle" instead of patched.

I do not remember what I wrote down for the bees singing, so I will copy that bit again from my copy book (over leaf).

"So Sally went on using her old kettle, and it sang to her. The kettle sang on the hearth; and the bees sang in the garden, where Sally grew old-fashioned flowers as well as potatoes and cabbages. Wallflowers, pansies and roses, balm for her own herb tea, and thyme hyssop and borage that the honeybees love. Sally knitted by the cottage door and listened to the bees. 'Arise, work, pray. Night follows day. Sweet summer's day.' The bees drowsed and hummed amongst the flowers. 'Honest toil and cheerful labour,/ honeycomb of sweetest savour./ To bed with sun,/ Day's work well done.'

"The bees went home to their hives. Indoors the kettle began to sing gently and softly at first, then faster and more loudly as it came to boiling and bubbling over. It sang to the tune of Ashgrove, the words have gone from me" etc. I think "wealth" is a better word than "pomp."

At the end Sally "grew potatoes and balm for her herb tea, and sweet flowers for the bees in her garden, and the white owls nested in the woodshed" etc.

Do you think it is good taste to put in the Shepherd Boy's song in a story book? *Pilgrim's Progress* is next to the *Bible*; one would not wish to make it commonplace.

If it is included, I wrote 2 sentences following "Sally Benson, with the open book upon her knee, sitting by the warm turf fire on a winter evening, listened to the song of the kettle, and she was content." In the description, the "cottage was whitewashed without and within; it was spotlessly clean. There was no upstairs, only the kitchen, with cupboards and a box bed in the wall, and another tiny room and a pantry behind it."

To Anne Carroll Moore

March 12th 42

I was so glad to read your letter and to know that you are well and carrying on. Mrs. Mahony Miller also told me you are lecturing on children's reading. I have been corresponding with Bertha M. Miller! About a year ago she mentioned that a grandchild Nancy wanted news of the *Caravan* animals. I confess for many years I was plagued with child messages and letters — I daresay you have had the experience?

How to answer all — or not — or which? The stream has slackened — not run dry — but abated; and I have a weakness for the name of Nancy — and she asked about the *Caravan*, not those wearisome rabbits. In short I copied out two chapters, being much confined indoors by the weather.

Mrs. Mahony proposes to print them in *The Horn Book*. It did cross my mind when I was posting them — I mean to say if I did not want to do so it was unwise to post them? I think the second story "Wag-by-the-Wall" is very pretty; and the first story about Xarifa and a Mouse is rather silly. But I suppose she knows what she is about! I have told her she must do as she thinks best. She proposes to pay for serial rights. I wonder if Mr. McKay will say anything — I do not think he could object.

The shorter story — "Wag-by-the-Wall" — could make a little independent booklet, if the *Caravan* frame work were pruned away, as was done with *Sister Anne*. I remember you did not care for the "get up" of *Sister Anne*. It did not sell well; but I think that was due to the story, which was unlike my others. The English book-trade is almost at a stand still. Mr. Stephens writes that they are now producing a few copies of the Peter books and supplying a small proportion of each order received, which he finds "irritating". I should think so! The parcelling and forwarding must be more bother than it is worth. And here I have a letter from a dear old friend in U.S.A. who mentions you cannot buy "coloured cotton" — sewing cotton forsooth! It was time that America realized there is a war on. Neither nation can reproach the other nation for blindness about the strength of Japan. Your country will *have* to face up and beat them. America will never be safe on the Pacific with the Japs unbeaten and in possession of the oil and rubber of the East Indies — nasty beastly brutes! We had been thinking they were a little less ruthless than the Nazis, because several local sailors were saved from the Prince of Wales and they reported that the Japanese planes had not machine gunned them in the waters, which is the German custom;* but it seems they are one as cruel as the other — I do not think continents like Australia and America are in the same mortal peril as islands. Continents have space for maneuvering, and for

---

*We know a young man, a ship's engineer, and when his ship was lying on its side sinking the German plane fired another bomb into it. He was a very strong swimmer, in the water 40 minutes.

civil evacuation. This is a little island. When we drive over the Pennine range one can see on a clear day the North Sea visible in the east, and behind on the west — only 75 miles between 2 seas — the Irish Channel — bad neighbors both. When there was a farm house destroyed there were 5 evacuees from Newcastle killed, who could have been in no worse plight if they had stopped at home on the east coast. If we have to take to the hills, I hope it may be warmer weather! I was partly thinking when I copy these chapters — they are not perhaps worth printing now — I am very willing to retire into obscurity! but it seems just worth while to send them in duplicate to America. I suppose Mrs. Miller thinks them suitably worth while printing; it seems lengthy. We keep well — but snow week after week; another fall today. I am afraid there will be disaster amongst the hill sheep; they are getting weak and hungry. We are taking no harm. May be short next winter. And whatever this hemisphere will be like after the war, there will be some tidying up to do. The misery and ruin which you saw in France after the last war multiplied over and over. A very weary world at present; but the snow is doing a good turn in Russia.

With kind regards,

To Bertha Mahony Miller

March 12. 42

I have received 2 letters from you safely, of Jan. 5th and Jan. 31. 1942. In one of them you ask if I received the May *Horn Book*. I apologize for not acknowledging. Now you will think me very childish, but I did not read what you said about *me!* What you say in the latest *Horn Book* about Anne Carroll Moore — I think it's most difficult to write 'to order' (feeling one must) so I understand your difficulty — but I like your paragraph about her and her work very much; it could not be bettered. The paragraph about St. Nicholas visiting the stricken countries does not rise quite successfully to the situation. The conditions are so terrible that it is past expression.

I wrote to you and suggested cutting down "The Solitary Mouse" a little; it seemed rather long. The weather is still severe; while I am a good deal confined to the house, I may find time to copy out some other chapters — *not* with a view to immediate publication, but they might as well be preserved in duplicate in a continent that is safer than this little island. I wonder if people realize that it is only seventy-five miles from sea to sea in this narrow part of Grt. Britain. One thing is certain; your nation will *have to* beat Japan — same as we *have* to beat Germany — if we want to ever live in peace and security.

With kind regards,

[P.S.] I wonder what Mr. McKay will say? It's your doing anyway. I'm sure F.W. and Co. think they have copyright in all pertaining to Peter R[abbit] books but the *Caravan* is of less consequence.

March 19. 42

I received your letter of Feb. 16th yesterday and about at same time the Jan — Feb *Horn Book* with your fine tribute to Anne Carroll Moore. It could not be better. What a wonderful, purposeful life of achievement — purposeful because she has had an aim all throughout her career. I have just made stories to please myself because I never grew up! Your letter of Feb. 16th is so understanding that I gladly leave the question of how much or how little should be printed entirely to you. I see Nancy has come into *Horn Book* mention. I am very glad! And I cannot help whispering that I think she is a more human 'interlocutor' than Nicholas — wooden doll — though he seems to have been successful with children, and it was an inspired idea, for Miss Moore could not have carried a little girl about with her in her handbag.

The news has been most distressing lately. But there is great hope from Russian success. I cannot think (and I don't want to think) that Australia is in peril. The Japanese are spreading themselves so far. And America and Australia have room to maneuvre in open lands, unlike small islands. The loss of the Exeter and the Houston is serious indeed. But we will win in the end. I am hurrying to get this letter to post. Thank you for your letter,

March 23. 42

We overlap and cross letters. Two days ago I received your cable, which I think intended to convey that you had received one — or 1 + duplicate — suggested compressions and corrections. The cable said 'prices,' meaning précis? I am perfectly satisfied to leave *everything* to your judgement. If the thing were printed exactly as it stands in your today received typed copy — it would not disgrace me. It looks better typed. The rhymes are more intelligible in type. If you get this in time, I still think the essay would be better balanced by some ruthless cutting out. And I think the reference to *a solitary mouse* is slightly lunatic, rather *bathos* ? unless you, as editor, explain that it has connection with a story? The "names" have fared well. *Hird* wood, not third. ("Hird is good old Norse, like swain, and "Hall" — Hallilands.) You have marked Bentinck, perhaps ? the *ck*. It was correct; the first Dutch Bentin*ck* was a soldier of William of Orange, a Dutchman. In the corrections, I cut out Lady Henry.

I agree with you that the introduction and ending make quite a decent combined essay — except the mouse which is rather an absurdity unless a reason is given for its inclusion. In fact, I favor retaining Nancy and the mouse; but do as you like. I am glad you sent any descriptive bombing letters to Miss Moore. Make any use you like of them.

Sally Benson is a dear! Put in the extra about her cow and her flowers for the bees, if you can.

Surely the tag — the moral — if not too long a heading is "The Peace that is amongst the lonely hills" — or "The Lonely Hills" — from Wordsworth's shepherd lord, Clifford, of the "Feast of Brougham."

I have so often thought of those lines, since the silence of the starry sky has been interrupted by aeroplanes, which at first we detested as an intrusion, but since the war we delight to see them, which is my meaning about the golden Hurricanes against the blue. They are infinitely finer flyers than they used to be; though there are still a few disasters in the mist; and a few lucky landings, like the American airman who landed a Spitfire in quite a small pasture; he skillfully taxied on the turf in a semicircle instead of going straight and running into a field wall. The plane was not even scratched. The wings had to be removed; the pilot wanted to take off on his own; but it was considered too risky. It went away on a lorry with a trailer. Another pilot flew round and round in a fog over Coniston and knocked off some splinters on trees in a hedge, but got down all right. Another in Troutbeck was burnt to cinders. My head shepherd heard the crash and hurried up the fell side. He said a very short swerve to the left would have cleared the rocks, blind work in a mist.

Surely Hitler will be too hard pressed to invade us here in any force.

Your parcel never came! But it might be our own Post Office. There is much thieving, like the aftermath of the last war. Thank you just as much for posting it. We have plenty of plain food still. And thank goodness the snow disappeared last week except a little on the fells. It lay 9 weeks, which is most unusual here. Now the ploughs are at work again.

With kind regards and best wishes,

April 6. 42

I received your letter of March 17th today. We have both had the same feeling that the essay should close at the words "mantle of peace." The piece about the mouse would be (an) anticlimax at the end. You have probably received my suggestions about the title. "Lonely Hills" or "Among the Lonely Hills," instead of "Troutbeck Memories." Wordsworth's verse signifies *peace*, but then the correct quotation is *"sleep* that is among the lonely hills" (take care the printer does not get it among*st*). I do hope I did not suggest that the original price was unsatisfactory? I did not mean to do so. I get confused over dollars — and indeed *all* my arithmetic is a blank, usually wrong!

We were puzzled by the cable "Prices satisfactory"; we thought it must be a mistake for "précis," meaning my sheet of corrections and compressions. And perhaps my reply cable "Proceed Lonely Hills" may not have been delivered? as it seemed to perplex the post office! I explained that it was the name of a book, not code. *Not* a lonely raid of the Three Jovial Huntsmen! What a pother about a tangled skein of words.

Do you call the wall clocks "Wag *on* the wall" in America? We call them "by the wall" here (it doesn't matter). I looked in the *Colonial Furniture;* there is not one picture with open works, like a longcase clock without a case. It is pleasing to see the pendulum swing solemnly "en plein air."

Someone will have enjoyed your delicious parcel — evidently not the fishes, as the other parcel reached its destination.

The newspapers lay rather much stress on food and clothing. It is reported that some refugees (mercifully escaped from Singapore) were surprised *not* to find the English in rags and starving. We are very far from that yet. The regulations are trying, especially in the country. The latest is about coal. We are 12 miles from the depot at Windermere station, and I have hitherto fetched six weeks' supply. Now we will get same quantity; but to be fetched each week unless the rule is relaxed in remote districts.

News has been sad lately. The Japanese must be stretching their lines recklessly; in the end they will crash — but it's a pity they do not kill their prisoners outright.

The aspersions on this country hurt me. There was a map that might be more widely known. It showed the comparative size of *Great* Britain inset on the map of Australia; our little island inset on the Timor Sea between New Guinea and Australia. How can we fight Germany and police the world? There are still some idle, selfish people, but the majority are doing their best.

And Mr. Churchill is still the Prime Minister, if less in evidence at the moment. He has been right — through and through. The war cannot end this year, even if we staked everything on one desperate throw.

There is no flinching or faltering — we have got to win. As for India — it is a second Ireland; fortunately it is rather further off!

This war is different to the last. The boys go and not a murmur if they are killed; it cannot be helped. It's like Lady Macbeth, "She should have died hereafter." Our favourite nephew went last week — we don't seem to mind. But I do think the women in the East ought to have strychnine pills like the Russian women are said to carry.

The weather is very wet, cannot work the land, but the snow is gone, and the grass is growing, lambs and spring calves coming. One old cow had twins! Good luck to the Hills!

Jacqueline Overton was a protégée of Anne Carroll Moore's and children's librarian at the Bacon Memorial Library, Westbury, Long Island.

To Jacqueline Overton

April 7th 42

I received your letter of March 2nd. It renews an old regret. I never met Caldecott. My father bought some of his work, through a dealer, and he could easily have made Caldecott's acquaintance; but he did not do so.

We bought his picture books eagerly, as they came out. I have the greatest admiration for his work — a jealous appreciation; for I think that others, whose names are commonly bracketted with his, are not on the same plane at all as artist-illustrators. For instance, Kate Greenaway's pictures are very charming, but compared with Caldecott — she could not draw. Others who have followed him were careful, correct draughtsmen, but lifeless and wooden. Besides; Walter Crane and Caldecott were the pioneers; their successors were imitators only.

Caldecott and Crane's *Baby's Opera* were engraved by Edmund Evans; wherein they were fortunate. The Racquet Court Press turned out fine work. The last pair but one of the picture books were not so well engraved, an unpleasant mealy stipple spoils *Come lasses and lads* and in *Ride a Cock Horse*. I seem to remember that Evans tried an experiment with the engraving. The last pair of all *Mrs. [Mary] Blaize* and *The Great Panjandrum [Himself]* were strong and clear again. No doubt Caldecott's health affected his work — he was consumptive. How sorry we were to hear of his breakdowns. He went to Florida I believe one winter; and to Switzerland or Northern Italy? I have a little Swiss picture of cows in a mountain landscape. He painted a small number of oils, tentatively. This "Swiss Cattle" is about the size of the paper I am writing on; it is painted on a bit of paste board, with a small brush. The cows are very good, but the general effect is wanting in light — as though it has been painted on brown paper and sunk in. On the back of the cow's picture is an unfinished view of Caldecott's house, in Surrey (or Sussex). A red brick house with a foreground of untidy garden flowers. It was bought at the sale after his death. Another larger oil painting was bought by one of my Manchester cousins. I doubt if she was acquainted with him; and anyway she is dead. We were all interested when he achieved success, because he had been a clerk in a Manchester bank. He must certainly have had some art training, for instance in perspective, but I gathered that he was an original genius. No doubt Blackburn's *Life* will give you particulars of his training and career, with dates. What one remembers is the tragedy of his lungs. But he had reached the summit. He would never have done finer work than *John Gilpin*. The later picture books declined a little; though there is one of my first favourites in the last — the *Great Panjandrum* — the maid and the cabbage leaf. I *know* — because *I* tried to draw cabbages when I drew *Peter Rabbit*.

I remember Sir John Millais saying it takes an artist to appreciate an artist's work — (he was speaking not of Caldecott but of Charles Keene, who drew in *Punch* —). Keene used a peculiar scratchy style of ink work, but a splendid draughtsman. Caldecott had 2 drawings in *Punch*. One of hay makers sheltering under umbrellas; I forget the other.

There used to be a small gallery in Bond Street called the 'Fine Arts Society'. It was a good class dealer's, not "society" like the "Water Colour Society" etc. — The Fine Arts used to have a one man show; several of the *Punch* artists; Miss Greenaway; other water colourists and etchers; and Caldecott at the height of his picture book fame. My father bought at different times. Perhaps there were 2 shows? as well as the sale after his death at Christie's, I think. His work very seldom comes up for sale now. There was never a large output. And at the sale after his death the greater part of his pen and inks were bought for the British Museum print room.

Anyway we had the color pictures of *The Three Jovial Huntsmen* (8 in one frame, but not the cover that is used for *The Horn Book*) and a frame of coloured designs for the "Curmudgeon's Christmas" which appeared in the *Graphic*, and 4 *Brittany Folk*, and most of the pen and inks of *The Mad Dog*, and 4 little pen and inks of a frog a wooing. They came into my possession after my Mother's death. I gave them with other water colors to a Manchester Art Gallery — except about a dozen. The ink has faded sadly — though I kept them out of strong light. He did a lot of correcting with white paint, which has stood alright, but it's a pity he used Indian ink. It's much easier to work with, for free flowing work, than the stodgy process black. His water colour has stood well. He was fortunate in having his work reproduced by Edmund Evans before the advent of process colour-photography and horrible clay faced paper.

I do not know if Wilfred Evans is still alive; he must be an old man if he is. All three sons of Frederick Warne (and Co.) are dead. Warne succeeded G. Routledge. When I gave the Caldecotts to the Manchester Art Gallery — the curator Mr. Lawrance Hayward, Curator, spoke of him with affectionate regard, but I scarcely think Mr. Hayward is old enough to have known him; I am afraid it is too late. I distrust my own memory. I seem to remember my father saw him at a private view and he was like the poor sick gentleman in the *Babes in the wood*; tall with a reddish beard? or am I thinking of someone else? The pretty maid hanging out the clothes was the Caldecott's maid at the house in

Surrey.* The other oil painting is a hunting piece; good, but rather flat and finicky as a painting. It is sad that I cannot give more help. He was one of the greatest illustrators of all. I hope you will succeed — try Mr. Hayward — and write to A. L. Stephens, F. Warne and Co., Bedford Court, Bedford, Strand WC2 to ask if they can put you in touch with any elderly person who knew Caldecott.

---

*Which was the maid's picture? Which was his wife's? My memory is not clear. I think The Queen of Hearts was a portrait of his wife.

To Bertha Mahony Miller

April 27. 42

I received a cheque safely two days ago, and I have paid it into the bank. I should think it is lawful! There are so many regulations in these days — it's perplexing.

The weather has improved, glorious sunshine although the wind is cold. The plum and damson blossom is coming out; and everyone is sowing and planting in field and garden.

Further literary efforts can wait for wet days. I shall be interested to see how the essay looks in print. I have had such a nice letter from A[nne] C[arroll] M[oore], but she regrets I never talked to her about folk dancing.

With kind regards,

June 18. 42

Your charming present arrived unexpectedly this morning — *Lemon Juice!* Also butter, dextrose, onion flakes, chocolate, bacon and cheese. I was very thankful for a tin of lemon juice in a Christmas parcel — I think from Mrs. Coolidge. It helped my cough when I had bronchitis, all through the month of May (which is too good a month to waste when one is nearly 76). I am not coughing now, so I shall save your lemon juice till next winter, and sprinkle the dextrose on my breakfast porridge, to promote energy as promised on the label. I have nobly given the tin of bacon to a friend who was lamenting the smallness of the ration. We have half a pig hanging up here, and I am not altogether glad, as it proves hard. And it will be very hard indeed if we are nibbling at it for twelve months. I do not think the pig itself had been so well fed as poor Pig Robinson. We usually pride ourselves on home-cured hams. The onion flakes are welcome; this season's onions are just beginning to grow as seedlings.

The May number of *The Horn Book* has not come, perhaps it might have traveled with a gift parcel, and it may arrive yet. I am curious to see how the essay looks in print.

I thought I might have written out some others, while I was a prisoner, but my energy only went so far as sorting books — rereading once — before consigning to the pulp collection. I dislike the task, even if one does not read them often, they are friends. As regards old letters, they are usually best burnt — no that's a fine! — best torn up. I have been surprised at the number — and the friendliness — of the packets of dozens of letters from [the] U.S.A., and they are only a few tied up in bundles from amongst the numbers received through many years. I don't receive English letters like that — a good many from children, some wanting autographs, some enthusiastic, grateful parents (also in U.S.A.). But never does anyone outside your perfidiously complimentary nation write to tell me that I write good prose! It's a wonder the censor does not cut it out. I think he might have suppressed *The Horn Book*, if it does not come by next post.

I eat your chocolate at the moment. We are getting a fair amount of chocolate here, but it does not taste very nice. I had 2 oranges when I was ill; I had nearly forgotten the taste. The crops are looking well; it is not much like summer, such cold nights.

With renewed thanks.

[P.S.] The chocolate is *good!*

July 13. 42

I received *The Horn Book* on Saturday 11th — much interested. My essay has had the honor of appearing in an exceptionally good number. It reads quite presentably, I think — though to me, of course, it is a bit dislocated by the cutting out of its raison d'etre. The footnote giving Warne as the publisher of *The Fairy Caravan* is an oversight — McKay, Philadelphia. The illustrations would be used by Mr. McKay's permission? I am still looking for the ponies in the tangled, deserted garden of my "Blackermoor in Hertfordshire"? Why? — oh why? — did you plant a cedar in the middle of a paragraph about a stunted thorn??? It is a favourite picture of mine so it does not matter.

The third picture of the hogbacked bridge — Ing's Bridge — is in the lane below Troutbeck Park. Tell Nancy we had a cattle hunt there recently, worthy of the Wild West. The county veterinary and assistants have been at the Park, conducting an experiment on sheep doctoring. (A bunch of 60 lambs, marked with green, blue, red, and yellow "pops" of paint, dosed from green, blue, red, and yellow labelled bottles once a fortnight and weighed.) All very interesting in the cause of science; but when he departed in 2 cars (waste of petrol?) he left two gates open.

I came away presently and missed some cows. We tracked them over Ing's Bridge and down the lane. Troutbeck village is a maze of ancient lanes. I sent the car round one way, and they were headed off the main road, having gone a mile probably in 20 minutes. I had the satisfaction of cornering them in a lane which is a cul-de-sac but had to send for a man and dogs to drive them back to the farm.

The ring leader was a dairy cow bred at Sawrey. (We send up a cow to Troutbeck periodically for the use of the shepherd's family.) The remarkable thing, to my mind, was that the cow had traveled there in a covered car, 15 miles. She could not have seen the road, but unerringly she was taking a short cut home. And determined, she set her head and horns. Her company of black cows and their calves were out for a lark; it was pretty to see them kick up their heels and gallop.

There is a small misprint on the first page. "Black" should have been "blank." Possibly I wrote it wrong myself. What the Danish woman complained of was the absolute blank ignorance of the fate of her relations, except her parents, who had escaped at the last moment to Sweden.

Thank you very much for the interesting copy of *The Horn Book.* We are busy in the hay here; I have enjoyed a bit of haymaking.

To Alexander McKay

July 17. 42

Thank you very much for the cheque received safely.

$59.11 in payment for royalties. The book trade is in a funny state here, great difficulties about labour and printing — a provokingly large opportunity waiting to be supplied. My evergreen "works" were unobtainable at Christmas. I suppose the demand was largely due to scarcity of toys.

We are busy in field and garden, and crops are promising. Which is well for it looks like at least another winter of war. With kind regards.

Beatrix Potter's comment about not knowing "what to put" refers to the filling in of a form sent to her by Mrs. Miller requesting information for a new edition of Contemporary Illustrators of Children's Books, *that was to be called* Illustrators of Children's Books in England and America.

To Bertha Mahony Miller

Nov. 10. 42

I have been rather slow to answer your letter and enclosures of August 19. It has been such a rush this season — everyone so very busy with farming and work. The autumn fairs are over at last, and settling down for winter. I am so delighted with the little photograph of Anne C. Moore. It's so like her, quite charming.

The war news is exciting. There will be some severe fighting yet, but the war seems to have taken the right turn at last.

I think you had better put as little as need be — I don't know what to put! Married name, married a lawyer, farms own land in Lake District.

I hope it will not be so much snow this winter. At all events, we here are able to get plenty of logs to burn.

With kind regards and best wishes for Christmas to you — also to Nancy — and also to Mr. Miller.

[P.S.] I wonder if artistic furniture survives as a trade in U.S.A. Second-hand is not controlled in price and sells enormously here, but real antique pieces have not gone up in proportion.

To Marian Frazer Harris Perry

Nov. 18. 42

The time has come for posting Christmas letters. There does not seem much to write about — except the weather, which has been disappointing all through the so-called summer; the real fine sunny weather was in May. Now we are having frost at night and damp mists. The country has been beautiful with autumn colours, but crops have been a struggle. There is *plenty in the barns*, but some sad stuff lying about. I even saw a big field of hay in Langdale yesterday. We never seemed to get a whole fine 7 days on end in haytime or harvest. It has been very hard work for everybody; and rather a worry, though interesting and profitable to run a sheep farm in these days. I had more than 3 tons of wool to sell.

We have kept well, except small colds. You did not sound very well when I had the last letter from you. How pleasant it must be to go up to the hills in summer, and see Betty and her children. I do hope her boy is growing stronger; it must be a great anxiety. Is he the boy baby who arrived in Aug. [19]36. Little boys are said to be stronger when they have attained 6 or 7 years of age.

We have had peaceful nights for a long time up here — though raids still occur in the south — described as 'nuisance' raids; but very unpleasant for the places and people who are hit.

There is plenty to eat. Not so much meat of course, but we are quite accustomed to vegetarian days; in fact I felt rather nauseated one day when there were fat greasy mutton chops! We have hutch rabbits which are a welcome change. And now things are improving I hope we will not require to part with the little pet dogs. The elder Peke, Susie, is 7 and growing middle aged and stout. They are good company; and she keeps my feet warm in bed. Petrol is strictly rationed. I doubt if I shall get about at all in winter. I was only allowed 13 gals. for 3 months, and I have deliberately used 8 the first month — while the roads are open, and while there is so much doing on the farms; spring and autumn are the busy time — sheep fairs, and other sales. I went on a lovely drive to Keswick to the sale of Herdwick rams. I have not been to Buttermere since the war. That would be "joy riding"! I went to Langdale about tenants' repairs. There seems to be an epidemic of smoky chimnies, and "raining in" from dislodged slates. It has been a wet windy autumn. Perhaps if we have frosts before Christmas it may be a favourable spring — not lingering snow like the last two winters. There is plenty of firewood.

I hope you are feeling better and that we shall meet again when there is Peace, and safe crossings. I am afraid you will find sad holes in the towns — but nothing can change the beauty of the Lakes Hills.

To Anne Carroll Moore

Nov. 19. 42

I salute you and Nicholas and I nibble a taste of his maple sugar heart! bless him. It was too pretty to eat, so I nibble a taste occasionally for luck.

Do you remember leaving it here a long time ago? I heard from you in the lovely surroundings of spring flowers in California — and Bertha Mahony Miller sent a charming picture of you in your academic robe standing beside a big tree. We are well here; only feeling rather old and tired. There is no hardship. We have been very lucky and have plenty to eat, but it's worry and hard work for thoughtful older people — though we should not grumble when one sees and hears of others in anxiety and grief? A lot of local men and boys are in the Middle East.

Americans will be feeling their share now. It was pretty to hear the church bells ring; only some of us think it would have been in better taste to wait. War is going the right way at last; but there will be bitter fighting yet; and the misery in Europe does not bear thinking about.

There has been a big harvest and a struggle to get it in; the weather has been unsettled all through summer and autumn; it is finer now. We have actually 7 days on end without one shower of rain. There is sharp frost at nights.

We have both been much occupied with farm affairs. Wm. on the War Ag. Committee is mapping out — instructing the movements of a govt. threshing machine which is wandering from farm to farm — every farmer clamouring for it out of his proper turn — all in a hurry for the oats, which we are permitted to have crushed for cattle food, with the object of increasing milk production. It's rather a gamble to grow oats amongst the hills and valleys. We have a tractor plough and corn binder to hire out. They don't always ripen; but even a moderate sample of grain is very useful for the cows. Wheat is not satisfactory up here. I was able to make some marmalade. There was a ship load of oranges at a port — going to waste, so adults were allowed a few. The children at the Waifs and Strays evacuated home have had regular supplies from America.

There is a fine crop of apples here which will keep until March — or longer — in the cellar.

I am enclosing a photograph of me and my little dog Chulegh; the child, Alison Hart, was staying in the village; her father had a good lens and was taking pictures — especially of *Peter Rabbit* backgrounds.

With our kind regards and good wishes for Christmas and New Year, —

[P.S.] This letter is nothing but food I'm afraid.

Helen Dean Fish and her friend Polly Street visited Beatrix Potter first in 1930. "Dear Short Fish and Long Street," the salutation of the following letter refers to that visit.

To Helen Dean Fish

Nov. 19. 42

Or is it the other way round? It's a long long way to Tipperary! And a long long lane that has no turning? We hope that the tide of war has turned at last; though there will be hard fighting yet — and a dreadful mess to clean up in Europe; and in the Far East too.

How strange it seems to go back to the tapes of one's infancy instead of elastic! Everything was tape, and buttons, when I was a child. And I remember I had a pair of leather strap garters with buckles that made red marks on my little legs.

Beyond small inconveniences we are not seriously short of anything. We are burning more wood than usual. I had intended to get some peat last summer — but nobody had time — and I doubt if it would have dried. It has been a wet season — making the hay and harvest very hard work — nearly dry and then damp, and all to shake out again.

We are well here — feeling rather tired and old — but hopeful for better prospects next year. It reminds me of 1917.

With kind regards and good wishes for Christmas and New Year,

189

[P.S.] I wonder if it was you that sent me a calendar last New Year? Not a very big one, but large enough numerals to read 2 yards off on the wall. I used to pin up a tradesman's calendar of the advert't sort — but none are printed now.

To Mrs. J. Templeman Coolidge

Nov. 19th. 42

A happy Christmas to you and Henry P. With War the world over it cannot be merry, but I hope it has not brought trouble to you and yours. We have one nephew in Africa but fortunately he is not in the North. The news has been heartening; though the ringing of bells seems premature. It was pretty to hear again, amongst the hills and valleys, but in doubtful taste, when many local men are at the front. Up to now none of the village wives have heard anything; and no news is good news.

We have had a wet chilly summer — making haytime and harvest a great struggle. There has been abundant crop, and continual showers. We are facing winter with plenty to eat, both for us and for the cattle. I have saved up some sugar so I was able to preserve a good deal of fruit, and the apples are a great standby. Tell Henry P. I have no guinea pig, but numbers of piebald rabbits. We eat one a week to help out the meat ration. . . . .

My husband and I are both well, and very busy. There has been so much to oversee and direct, if one can no longer work with one's own hands like the last war. Now there is much more machinery. We have a tractor outfit for self and neighbours. I cannot say the steep small fields are easy to plough and reap, but it's got to be done!

With our kind regards,

The letter of November twentieth refers to biographical material requested by Mrs. Miller for Illustrators of Children's Books: 1744-1945. *It also answers questions Mrs. Miller had asked in earlier letters to Beatrix Potter.*

To Bertha Mahony Miller

Nov. 20. 42

The wireless says this is the last day for Christmas greetings. I send hearty good will to *The Horn Book* and to you.

I posted back the book form a week ago. I didn't seem to know what to put in it! Only the date of birth and that I had a governess — not school. At bottom of page I got scribbly (which you can cut off) for it was only what crossed my mind, looking back to roots and reasons. I think sometimes — not always — children born in a town are more alive to the fresh impressions of country life than country children bred and born. In the same line of thought we may compare the thoroughness with which you Americans explore every corner of Old England and the tireless energy of country cousins on holiday in London, who wear out their London hosts in pursuit of "sights." I am sure my brother and I hated London, although — or because — born there. I mean while we were too young to know the real interest and romance of London through the ages.

I wonder what it is like. Accounts conflict. Some people tell me it is shocking devastation, and others go falteringly to see surviving friends and old haunts, and then report they saw no ruins at all. I guess it's worst in the centre (city) and in the suburbs and east end.

I kept some letters from friends, which one may reveal now — this was from the mother of the Peter Rabbit boy: "I must let you know about our terrible adventures of last Monday (Sept. 40). About 9:30 p.m., just an hour after the siren had sounded, we had a whole salvo of bombs dropped about 30 yards away from our house, bringing down 1 house just four houses away from us on our side of the row and another one opposite; blew out our dining room windows, made a hole in our front verandah and 2 holes in the roof. It also burst the main gas pipe in front of our house, and the gas came pouring in nearly choking us. Our opposite neighbor's house was so badly damaged that they all had to come here. There are about 15 huge craters on our Common. You can imagine how much we dread the nights. 3 of us have our beds in the drawing room where we have wooden shutters" — *wooden* shutters??! Nevertheless, the old lady and her large cheerful family have continued to live unhurt at Wandsworth Common, London SW 13.

Truly the war has caused some upsets. The news is heartening, but there will be more fighting to do yet. And what a mess to rebuild and clean up!

There were one or two inaccuracies in Helen Dean Fish's account of her visit, but they are too trivial to deserve correction. For instance, it was not the terrier "Sandy" who was killed down a quarry hole, it was the sheep dog "Bobs," while he was working — not "hunting" sheep, a shocking crime amongst dogs. And it was the first book — *Peter Rabbit* — which could not find a publisher. It is true that I printed a small, private edition of *The Tailor of Gloucester*, a private printing which was already in progress when *Peter Rabbit* came out publicly. The instant success of *Peter* made it easy to place other books. In fact, I was plagued with inquiries, but I preferred to deal with one publisher only.

My reason for arranging publication by another publisher in America, much later, was that they were stories of a rather different sort which I had no wish to publish in this country (too personal — too auto-biographical — what do you call it?) You may ask "Why print them at all then?" I suppose vanity and a desire to see them in the dignity of printed type without the expense of myself paying for printing!! I have always disliked the idea of *The Fairy Caravan* being on sale here; and the other stories — *Sister Anne* is one of the Caravan tales, which was too long! Another reason for allowing the *Caravan* to be published in U.S.A. was to save copyright there. The first book, *Peter*, was not copyrighted, and it was extensively pirated.

Compared with the Rabbit series, the Caravan tales had no great numerical success, but I was quite satisfied. I just wanted to have them in print and not on horrid clay-faced paper. Also I had pleasure in choosing a plain, artistic binding for my English copies of the *Caravan* — not gaudy, ugly, toy book style. I believe my attitude of mind towards my own successful publications has been comical (?); at one time I almost loathed Peter Rabbit. I was so sick of him. I still cannot understand his perennial success.

I have just been reading "The 'Roots' of the P.R. Tales" in 1929 — with amusement. It is frank and downright, but accurate. I see no reason to change my view 13 years later.

It is very hard work, but I am still managing 2 sheep farms and the small home farm, and a tractor outfit. I cannot work with my own hands now, like the last war, but I'll do my bit till I drop — and enjoy it!

I was terribly cockered up last August. I got a phone message if I would be on Kirkstone Pass. Mr. Hudson, the Minister for Ag[riculture], was motoring through from Scotland to Lancashire, and he would stop 10 minutes to talk to me — which he did, a fine man. He looked down into the valley, a bird's eye view of Troutbeck Park farm, but, also, there was a very, very thick white mist, so he did not see my sheep and cattle. But he saw I seemed to have a nice crop of turnips, so he got into his car and drove on, after a pleasant conversation about hill farming. He was very cheerful and jolly. He promised us fine weather in September, which did *not* materialize in the Lake District, but there is plenty of fodder here, in spite of some wastage, and I suppose the crops and harvest is marvellous further south — so we are alright for food.

The extract from *Horn Book* [July] 1942 ["Jack Darby on Writing Books for Children"] is very understanding — very. I appreciate what Walter D. Edmonds says. I am amused by the "taboo" — "alcoholic" rendezvous. In the privately printed edition of *Tailor* there was a picture of the rats carousing in the cellar under the Mayor of Gloucester's shop — one of them drinking out of a black bottle. For the life of me, I could not see why Mr. Warne insisted on cutting it out? I've a mind to post him a copy % *Horn Book*?

Thank you so much for the snap of Anne Carroll Moore. It's lovely — like herself.

To Marian Frazer Harris Perry

Jan. 23rd 43

I had your nice letter for Christmas, and now I think your delicious parcel has followed it — when I had given it up for lost. I had two parcels, packed by T. Fluke and Co., Chestnut Street — one containing a card from "Dick and Betty" — the other had no sender's name, but it was probably yours? The good things are very good, indeed, especially the figs and other sweeties. The tongue will be for a special occasion.

It is very tiresome for you to have had a knee, and I do not need much telling that it would make you feel *ill*. The wife at the farm — the dairy woman — had a knee last summer and autumn that went on and on; she declared that it started with kneeling on a cinder when she was 'doing' the kitchen range. The skin did not seem to be broken, until the doctor lanced it; but it made her very weak and ill — and even yet it is stiff. I hope yours has cleared up completely.

W. and I have kept well, only feeling the chilly damp as we get older. It is a comfort that the wet has come down in rain, week after week, instead of snow, which is inconvenient for supplies, and bad for the sheep. I often think we must be backward in our winter arrangements in this country, when one reads of other lands undergoing vastly more severe winters with equanimity. We have plenty of logs for burning. There is some influenza in the village, but it is not a serious type, only heavy colds with aches and pains, which can be cured in bed. I shall be glad when spring comes; the garden is too sodden with rain to do any work. A few snowdrops are peeping through the wet dark earth, showing white buds. The yellow aconites and yellow winter-flowering jessamine are cheerful. The war news is heartening. Except the indignation against U.S.A. which is possibly more serious than U.S.A. is aware of.

It may be more easy to forgive wrongs inflicted upon others. The French have double crossed us the whole time; it is incomprehensible how anyone can countenance Vichy.

I have not had any servants called up yet; they are doing essential work on the land; never ending work with extras; the actual ploughing itself is not so much difficulty as the cultivating and harvesting. We have got a tractor outfit here, which does quick work on suitable ground, but many fields are too steep and slippery. It has partly ploughed the old pasture next to the cottage, and might finish it when the turf is less wet; at present ploughing for neighbors who hire it — at a charge! Some fields it does in a day — other fields no bigger are a very out-of-pocket job, but it's useful.

I hope you will get my thanks and love. Several letters came by Christmas mail, but I miss some who usually remember.

Annis Duff, editor of Viking Press, also wrote Bequest of Wings, *which describes the many books the Duff family enjoyed. Mrs. Duff asked a relative in Edinburgh to get Beatrix Potter's permission to use quotations from* Peter Rabbit *and* Mrs. Tittlemouse *in her book of essays.*

To Professor David Duff

May 27. 43

I have received a letter by this morning's post from Mrs. Annis Duff, who says there is haste about a matter of quotation and printing for a new book which she is about to publish; and that *you* will cable to her. As regards her letter I may say, "You do me proud and make me blush!!"

Her compliments are too well chosen to be satiating or nauseous (there's fine words for you). She really does appreciate what I tried to say, and understands that my little books were written carefully. As regards Mr. Treble (of N.Y. branch of F. Warne & Co.) saying that I object to quotations, he must be under some mistake? I should be sorry to see Peter and his friends perverted to vulgarity. I suffered real anxiety for six months when a film company had an option to turn them into a "Talkie"; but it was F. Warne & Co themselves that took up the idea. When we found later that the film company proposed to expand the text I didn't like it; fortunately it fell through.

I am quite sure there could be no possible objection to Mrs. Duff's quotations from *Peter* and *Mrs. Tittlemouse*. I give my consent. I don't think it is necessary to get Messrs. Warne's. The other from *The Fairy Caravan* is a longer quotation. She does not say whether she consulted Mr. Alexander McKay of D. McKay & Co., Philadelphia? I cannot imagine any reason for him to object; it would be a good advertisement for a book which is much liked by a few but not a very good seller. Mrs. Duff's letter is very pleasant, I will write and thank her.

Yrs. sincerely,
H.B. Heelis
"Beatrix Potter"

To Mrs. Ramsay Duff

[June] 1943

I am ashamed of not having answered your pleasant — and reasonable letter at once. I did write immediately to Professor Duff in Edinburgh, and I hope he received my assent in time to be useful. I do not understand why Mr. Treble should take upon himself to say that? Messrs. Warne are rather stiff about copyright (though it's quite in vain so far as 'copying' is concerned) but a simple extract, with source acknowledged, is not in any way objectionable. The extract about Paddy Pig and the tartlets strikes me — the responsible inventor — as slightly tedious. But that's my fault, not yours.

Your idea of a book about children and their books is a very good one. One's memory works back as one becomes an old woman. I am thinking of what I liked as a small child of 3 or 4. Trash, from the literary point of view — goody-goody, powder-in-the-jam, from the modern standpoint! I liked silly stories about other little girls' doings; there was a story called *Little Sunshine's Holiday*. She went by train at night, just like the journeys I was taken, and when she got there at some unearthly hour, instead of having bread and milk to supper or breakfast, she was given a basin of cream with a large spoonful of strawberry jam floating in it. I have *not* been a greedy person; perhaps it is because my own upbringing was so spartan, I have always remembered that jam — which I dislike now. I did not have *Alice in Wonderland* when it came out. I think simple happenings appeal to children, and that is why they appreciate *Peter* etc.. Your book should be a success.

I have a good many well-worn — dropping to pieces — American books for girls, which belonged to an old American lady who lived in this neighbourhood for the latter part of her life. No one was interested in her remaining books and odds and ends after the better ones had been sent away for sale, so I bought them for a moderate sum, and I have been gradually sorting them — paper salvage, books for sailors' home, canteens — and there remain a number of old-fashioned girls' 'novels' — such as first editions of Louisa Alcott's and *Queechie* [*Queechy* written by Susan Warner although her pen name, Elizabeth Wetherell, appeared on the title page]. *The Wide, Wide World* is not first edition. There are a few children's books, but not some that I would like to see again, such as *The Silver Skates*. Perhaps that was later than Miss Becky Owen's youth in the 60s. She had the J. H. Ewing books, she would buy them later. *The Horn Book* is most interesting, I very much appreciate receiving it. But this last two or three seasons I begin to be disturbed by the illustration? I hope I am able to appreciate 'style' (which I have never had myself) but need style involve downright out-of-drawing? Some of the really beautiful illustrations are feebly bad if their anatomy were not covered up by striking, arresting style. Could you say it nicely to Bertha Mahony?

Yrs. Sincerely,
Beatrix Potter
(Mrs. W. Heelis)

To Alexander McKay

June 10th 43

Thank you very much for your letter and draft for royalty account $41.38 safely received. I am afraid received a week ago. I get slow in my old age! and so many things to attend to. We seem to spend half our time filling in forms. To be sure the rationing etc. is very much better done than in the last war — but it's some Red Tape! Now on top of our own farming there is semi-public work re agricultural committees. You would laugh to see ME in the chair at a meeting of old sheep farmers, discussing prices and subsidies with a young gentleman from the Board of Agriculture. It has been a good winter and spring for sheep, very little snow.

It is a wonder how any books are printed in these days. The sales of the Peter Rabbit books have been hampered by short supply of paper. There has been a good demand because there is a shortage of toys for presents to children. We are all excited listening for the news. What will happen and where?

With thanks and kind regards,

Elizabeth Booth was a school friend of Isabella Halsted, a daughter of Charles Hopkinson.

To Elizabeth Booth

June 12th 43

Thank you for a very pleasant letter. Yes! the Peter Rabbit books seem to have filled a gap! In spite of paper shortage they are circulating after 40 years; indeed they are more useful than in normal times because there are fewer toys to give to children.

"Toys" makes me think — and try to say — what real pleasure I have had in return from American unknown correspondents' letters. You really appreciate my little books; whereas in this country it is the popularity of a "best seller" toy book — enormous sales, but mainly *toy* book; a convenient present. For instance, in this country *The Tailor of Gloucester*, my own favourite, has never sold so well as in America.

I am interested to know that your father recognized the archway into the precincts of the Cathedral. I remember I sat on a door step on a blazing *hot* day to sketch it. The Tailor shop was copied from a print of houses in old London city — probably destroyed. I do not know what happened in Gloucester. I used to stay with cousins who lived on the Cotswold hills between Gloucester and Stroud; dead long ago.

How funny about the nurse and the rat! She would not have liked "Sammy." I have memory of him waddling along the floor, wanting to be picked up by my aunt — a stout elderly lady who did not altogether appreciate his friendly advances. Poor Sammy. White rats are not very long lived; and he was always wanting to be petted in his declining months. But not everybody liked him. One of his scrapes was to cut a neat round piece size of our ½ crowns out of the middle of a sheet. He carried a curious collection of stolen articles to his box.

I remember the Aunt providing a hard boiled egg, and watching the rolling of the egg along a passage; but she requested that his neat box might be kept firmly fastened. Like your nurse she was not fond of rats!

I reciprocate your good wishes — and agree with you, you and Timmy Willie, in preferring the country — there is more room for bombs! We have not had any for a long time near here, and in the worst times they always fell on rough land.

> Sincerely yours,
> 'Beatrix Potter'
> = Beatrix Heelis — Mrs. W. Heelis

To Bertha Mahony Miller

Aug. 18. 43

Your very interesting letter of July 20th arrived today — curious about wool — though perhaps too technical to go into the question. Briefly, our Herdwick sheep with their *hard* water-proof jackets are the only sort that can thrive on the high fells; but the demand for their wool almost ceased when linoleum came in and carpets went out of fashion. At present, the price is fixed by govt. 15½ pence instead of 5 to 8 pence, and there is also a subsidy to help hill sheep, so hill sheep farms are paying reasonably well. But we farmers are apprehensive of what will happen after the war. The rate of wages goes up; no one grudges the shepherd his high wage, but if wool drops and the subsidy *ends*, it's doubtful if Herdwick sheep farms can survive another slump *unless* a fresh market can be found for the harsh, hard wearing wool. Govt. is buying it *all*, reported to be for khaki and a rumour that the cloth is going to Russia. I wish very much it may be true; and last-ing! Your tailor, Mr. Aho, would find it bad for his trade because Herd-wick cloth *never wears* out! I should think it's suitable for Russia. I am in the chair at Herdwick Breeders' Association meetings. You would laugh to see me, amongst the other old farmers — usually in a tavern(!) after a sheep fair. We are serious enough, about the future.

The first thing is to win the war — and make sure there will not be another. Begging your pardon, the Americans are the risk. Uncle Sam has not lived near enough to hxxl. In spite of Pearl Harbor, it is doubt-ful if U.S. yet realizes. I hope we are properly grateful for help, but the attitude has been irritating at times. They say they are winning the war for *us*. It's to be hoped *they* don't expect to dictate the terms of peace. Not like the last time.

About the photograph. It will be that one where little Alison Hart is holding my Pekinese Chuleh. Mr. Hart took many snaps and at last made that lucky shot. It's really a pretty picture (of a most ill-behaved little dog who looks as if butter would not melt in her mouth). Her elder sister Tzu Zee refused to pose — too proud. I am quite willing for it to be reproduced. I have written by this post to ask Mr. Hart whether he regards it as copyright. I cannot think he would object — probably pleased to have the child included. I am not very sure if I have his right address. They are visitors who sometimes come to lodgings in the village on holiday.

I think it's a fine idea to make Sally Benson's letter come at Christ-mas, making her story a companion to the Christmas *Tailor*. I like to think some of your storytellers may use it. I wonder how it will look in type, — the posts don't leave much time to see, before November? One difficulty of uncertain crossings is that one never knows what got across — whether you received any copy of an amended version? You will not want to include Jenny Ferret. I had better write it out again and post it in case the U boats got an earlier copy; it is a very good sign that the Atlantic crossing is growing more safe. We have had no night alarms here for a long time. A live bomb was found this last spring in a field above this house, but grass had grown over it, so it must have been there for some time. They are nasty things; some boys had an accident in another village — no amount of warning will teach them to leave such things alone. We are waiting for fine weather to begin harvest; the haytime was grand, a big crop carried quickly.

My love to Nancy and tell her 4 young owls have been hatched and reared in the loft this summer. They are flying about now, shouting to each other, sometimes on the bedroom window sill.

We keep very well here, I am glad to say, and no discomfort or shortage. Miss Moore will have come and gone from Mass. I am sure you would enjoy her visit. With kindest regards.

Aug. 23. 43

I posted an airmail letter to you two days since to say I had no objection to the use of the photograph, and I am trying to get at Mr. Reginald Hart, who took it. I should think he would make no objection or change. His little daughter Alison Hart is holding my Pekinese dog Chuleh in the picture. I wish it had been the other, Tzu Zee, but she is very proud and objects to being photographed.

I hope you will think old Sally's story is improved by being shorn of some trimmings? It seems better balanced without the longer verses — one too good, and the last, too doggrel.

About the name. Have you any reason in U.S.A. for always referring to the clock as "Wag *on* the wall?" I have looked in the history of *Colonial Furniture*, and it is not mentioned therein. I think I have once heard that form of clock mentioned as *"at* the wall" — but never *on?* I went to see Mrs. Cookson, Gallowbarrow, Hawkshead yesterday, who has a fine specimen, and I asked her what she called it. She replied without hesitation "Wag b' t' Wa." The nearest phonetic pronunciation would be "Wag by twa — Wag-by-the Wall." Mrs. Cookson said never *on!!* They are uncommon, older than the long case.

The sequence was first the brass "lantern" clock. I have one, imperfect, date 17th century; then "Wag-by-Wall," then Wag acquired a hood, a wooden head cover to slip on; and 18th century invented the long case. No doubt some overlapping of dates. The wag is, of course, the pendulum. The weights on Mrs. Cookson's are this shape, instead of the normal cylindrical in a grandfather.

Unless you have strong reason for contrary, I would like the old clock to be "Wag-by-the-Wall" — or "Wag-by-Wall." [Final title was "Wag-by-Wall"]

We have a big crop of corn; we are waiting for settled weather to cut it. It is scarcely ripe yet in the north.

My lantern clock had a curious history. A man in Ulverston who buys secondhand furniture at sales bought a long case at an auction. When he got it home and looked inside, he found this much older brass clock was fixed in, in such a way as to use the face and fingers of the grandfather. I bought the old one, which he pulled out; unfortunately its own face is missing. It has the brass dome which was the bell and the pretty pierced brass fret, with dolphins, which is usually considered about 1650-70.

The "Wag-by-Wa's" were plain, a plain face in a plain wooden border frame or merely a face unframed. With kind regards,

Aug. 28. 43

I wrote to you on 23rd following receipt of your letter of July 20th to say I was willing for the photograph of myself and little Alison Hart and my dog Chuleh to be used in *The Horn Book* and that I was writing to Mr. Hart — uncertain of his address, but I don't think he would be likely to object or charge. It was a snapshot — they were visitors to lodgings in the village.

I sent the letter by airmail. Today, 28th, I am posting (ordinary post) a write-out of "Wag-by-the-Wall," with some pruning, which I hope you will think is an advantage? The longer verses left out — John Bunyan's too good, and my own too bad, at the end! Also a learned antiquarian discussion about *clocks*. Why do you call it "Wag *on* the wall?" Unless there is some strong reason, American usage, it's not correct. I have been to see Mrs. Cookson, Gallowbarrow, Hawkshead, who has a fine specimen and she said without hesitation "Wag b' t' wall" — "Wag-by-the-Wall" — when I asked her what she called it. I never heard that form of old clock called "on." I think I have once heard it called "at." They are older than the long — case-grandfather clocks.

Posts are still rather uncertain, so I shall post this duplicate presently, in case the other copy miscarries. I don't think our own inland posts are reliable; the postmen are greatly overworked. Several local letters have failed to arrive.

The corrections in the text are small, but I am always inclined to go [on] polishing. It was a very good idea to think of making it Christmas Eve.

[P.S.] I have had enclosed letter from Mr. Hart (which you need not return). I am posting this Sept. 2nd.

[P.S.] I had a tiresome cough, but hardly amounts to bronchitis; such terrible, wet weather, and stuffy dampness. I posted you a copy of the story by ordinary post on 28th Aug.

Mrs. Miller had asked if "Wag-by-Wall" could be delayed until May and be printed in The Horn Book's *Twentieth Anniversary issue. Beatrix Potter agreed. She did not live to correct proofs or see the story in print. Later Mr. Heelis gave Mrs. Miller permission to publish* Wag-by-Wall *as a book, illustrated with wood engravings.*

Nov. 5. 43

I cordially agree with the delay until May for printing the story in *The Horn Book*. It leaves time to see proofs, and I would like to make it as nearly word-perfect as I know how, for the credit of your 20th anniversary.

The winter's snow will be over by then. Would you desire to drop "Christmas Eve"? I am inclined to *leave it in*, with perhaps an added sentiment about the return of spring (how the sad world longs for it!). I liked your suggestion of Christmas Eve because I like to think some of your storytellers may read the story turn about with the old *Tailor of Gloucester* at Christmas gatherings in the children's libraries. Twenty years is soon vanished. I was turning out a drawer, sorting waste paper, setting aside, and I found an old draft of *Pig Robinson's* first chapters dated 1893 —! I remember that story stuck on board the Pound of Candles; and Sally's story stuck because the kettle was obstinately dumb.

Mr. Hart's name is Reginald. Reg. S. Hart he signs himself. He is an immensely tall, thin man with lengthy limbs like a gibbon monkey. He hung up some plates — old blue delph — opposite my bed last time he and his family were on holiday. It was comical to see him reach up to the picture rail without the stepladder. Mrs. Hart is short and shy; Alison is a little dear. He is an architect, on civil service job at present, interested in books and china.

I have spent more than enough time upstairs; I had bronchitis, and the doctor forbid me coming up and down. I am out and about now, when the rain stops — which is seldom. My heart has never been normal since I had rheumatic fever as a young woman, so my prolonged bronchitis cough upsets it, but I hope to do a bit more active work yet — and anyhow I have survived to see Hitler beaten past hope of recovery!

No letter has come except dated Sept. 18th. I am interested to read about your woman minister. The *right women* are exercising an increased and hopeful influence in all spheres here. The majority of the young ones are going through a horrid phase, but I think it is a phase, and that there will be a reaction of common sense and decency, though it may take another generation to achieve it.

[P.S.] Amongst old papers I found a nice letter from Marcia Dalphin, Rye, N.Y. [Librarian of the Rye Free Reading Room in Rye, New York] I wonder if she is still at the library? I will write to her on the chance. I am afraid I never answered her letter.

With kind regards.

To Marian Frazer Harris Perry

Nov. 13. 43

Your delightful Christmas remembrances have arrived safely, first the parcel and then the letter four days after. The ocean passage is safer now, but our domestic posts are haphazard! I was so very glad to hear from you again; and your hand writing looks firm and well. I had a bad time with bronchitis in September; I am going about, much as usual now, but rather feeling the weather. The hills are white with the first snow, and a bitter wind. There has been scarcely any sunshine in the Lake district this summer; and although there have been no big floods, there have been few days without a shower. We were lucky on this farm; we mowed the hay grass and got it quickly in a fine interval in July. Some farms are very short of fodder for the cows, but there will be plenty to share out. Eggs have been a scarce article. We are enjoying a very good cake from the dried egg in your package, a delicious cake. We have always been able to buy Sultana raisins "on points." Now there are dates in the shops, and oranges and lemons are expected in good supply before Christmas. It seems there would have been plenty of lemons already from the Mediterranean but for want of packing cases. I was so lucky having 2 tins of lemon juice when I had a cough; one was from Australia and one in an American package without sender's name last year, probably from you.

As regards eggs, I set a hen, and we have 7 fine pullets which should be in lay by New Year — if they don't get stolen. We are allowed to use our own oats for feeding a small number of hens, and what is called "a domestic pig." It sounds like a greedy boy?! Thanks to breakfast bacon the domestic breakfaster here is well fed — overworked, and rather tired and deaf — but most truly thankful and hopeful. When we think what we have escaped and survived compared with other lands — I don't know how we have got through alive.

I had a letter from Betty 3 weeks ago; she sounds very busy indeed. There is no such thing as young servants. Our elderly maid is faithful, but not strong; and I am sure I would not find another. It is sad about the little boy. I wonder if he will outgrow his delicacy; it is getting time. With our kindest regards and good wishes for New. Year,

To Anne Carroll Moore

Castle Cottage
Sawrey
Ambleside
Nov. 30. 43

Dear Anne Carroll Moore,

This may reach you early in the New Year. May next year bring peace and relief to a very wicked harassed world — which seems to go from bad to worse. I have just been reading a letter from an old friend, well over 70 — who tells me she has been in hospital after a direct hit on the flat where she lived, which took fire. It's a horrid way of waging war. We have had no bombing for some time back; but so tired. I was laid up with bronchitis in Sept. October, and the coughing made my heart bad; it has never been normal since I had rheumatic fever as a girl, so I do not bother myself; but I am worried about our old maid servant, who is also shaky. I doubt if I could ever get another, and I could not run the house now with only occasional help. So I have been less cheerful than usual lately.

Mr. Heelis is fairly well; over worked at the office; everyone is short handed. But surely the War is on the turn. We are enjoying a bright sunny day; snow on the hills. We were lucky to get the hay early here; and the oats are not so bad; out a long time, but very useful. With kind regards,

Yrs. sincerely,

Beatrix Heelis

[P.S.] I may pick up in spring. I was pretty bad.

~~~ Epilogue ~~~

Beatrix Potter died on December 22, 1943. The bronchitis which had been so severe in September and October did not clear up, and by December she was again seriously ill.

When news of her death reached America early in January, only The New York *Herald Tribune* took immediate note of it in an editorial published on January 6, 1944.

When on Friday morning the news came to America that Beatrix Potter was dead there must have been a great hurrying to bookshelves and nursery cupboards to see if there were still there a well worn copy of *Peter Rabbit* or *The Tailor of Gloucester*, or any of that score of little books so dear to English and American children. And perhaps some mother sat down with one of them before she went off to market with her ration book, and leafing through it remembered how many times she had read it to a boy overseas now, in Africa or New Guinea, and how she once in awhile rebelled, knowing it almost by heart, but was never allowed to leave out one word or skip one picture. For little children too, have them by heart, and long before they know their letters will pretend to read the story. "And their names were Flopsy, Mopsy, Cotton-tail and Peter," they chant.

Who can say what makes a book great? For that these nursery classics are great is indisputable. What is it in them that has made for them a body of readers so fond that when it was known that books were in danger in England, many public libraries and many individuals rushed to get new sets of Beatrix Potter lest they be without them some day.

Is it because the books are so little, just right for the hand? Because their illustrations are so charming? Because they are full of delicious fooling that children understand, and of a salty common sense, and the sweet reasonableness of characters like Xarifa in *The Fairy Caravan*.

We do not profess to understand, and only know that glimpsing for a moment a bonneted head and foolish face on the street corner, we think, "Who was that woman? I know her," — and with a gasp suddenly sense that it was Jemima Puddleduck to the life. Or noting a strained pose and apprehensive eye, realize that it suggests nothing so much as Peter in red handkerchief, draped shawl-wise, on his second visit to Mr. McGregor's garden in company with his carefree cousin. "Benjamin, on the contrary, was perfectly at home, and ate a lettuce leaf."

Beatrix Potter, North-Country farmer, connoisseur of old furniture and china, lover of nature and animals, was an artist both with words and with brush. The perfect characterizations bear witness to it and are unforgettable. Her greatness lies in the fact that she was able again and again to create that rare thing — a book that brings grown-ups and children together in a shared delight.

William Heelis answered the many letters he received from Beatrix Potter's American friends in almost the same words. His letter to Marian F. H. Perry, the friend to whom Mrs. Heelis wrote most often and most personally, may stand for all.

Castle Cottage
Sawrey
near Ambleside
April 3rd 1944

Dear Mrs. Perry,

Thank you for your very kind letter. I knew you would be sorry to hear of Mrs. Heelis death. It is sad to think that her last few years were so interfered with by this awful 'war', but she was always cheerful and brave to the end.

I know that your friendship and interchange of letters with you and your niece was great happiness to her.

With kindest regards
Yours sincerely
W. Heelis

ˑ˜˜˜ˑ Appendix ˑ˜˜˜ˑ

'Roots' of the Peter Rabbit Tales

The first and most important essay Beatrix Potter wrote about her work appeared in The Horn Book *in May 1929. The essay was part of a letter written to the editor, Bertha Mahony Miller, who had asked for biographical and literary information. Unfortunately, the original has been lost. What follows is "almost" complete and is the text as printed in* The Horn Book.

The question of "roots" interests me! I am a believer in "breed"; I hold that a strongly marked personality can influence descendants for generations. In the same way that we farmers know that certain sires — bulls — stallions — rams — have been "prepotent" in forming breeds of shorthorns, thoroughbreds, and the numerous varieties of sheep. I am descended from generations of Lancashire yeoman and weavers; obstinate, hard headed, *matter of fact* folk. (There you find the downright matter-of-factness which imports an air of reality.) As far back as I can go, they were Puritans, Nonjurors, Nonconformists, Dissenters. Your *Mayflower* ancestors sailed to America; mine at the same date were sticking it out at home; probably rather enjoying persecution. The most remarkable old "character" amongst my ancestors — Old Abraham Crompton, who sprang from mid-Lancashire, bought land for pleasure in the Lake District, and his descendants seem to have drifted back at intervals ever since — though none of us own any of the land that belonged to old Abraham.

However — it was not the Lake District at all that inspired me to write children's books. I hope this shocking statement will not distress you kind Americans, who see Peter Rabbits under every Westmorland bush. I am inclined to put it down to three things — mainly — (1) The aforesaid matter-of-fact ancestry, (2) The accidental circumstance of having spent a good deal of my childhood in the Highlands of Scotland, with a Highland nurse girl, and a firm belief in witches, fairies and the creed of the terrible John Calvin (the creed rubbed off, but the fairies remained). (3) A peculiarly precocious and tenacious memory. I have been laughed at for what I say I can remember; but it is admitted that

I can remember quite plainly from one and two years old; not only facts, like learning to walk, but places and sentiments — the way things impressed a very young child.

Does not that go a long way towards explaining the little books? I learned to read on the Waverly novels; I had had a horrid large print primer and a stodgy fat book — I think it was called a "History of the Robin Family," by Mrs. Trimmer. I know I hated it — then I was let loose on "Rob Roy," and spelled through a few pages painfully; then I tried "Ivanhoe" — and the "Talisman" — then I tried "Rob Roy" again; all at once I began to READ (missing the long words, of course), and those great books keep their freshness and charm still. I had very few books — Miss Edgeworth and Scott's novels I read over and over.

I only cared for two toys; a dilapidated black wooden doll called Topsy, and a grimy, hard-stuffed, once-white, flannelette pig (which gradually parted with a tail made of tape). The pig did not belong to me. Grandmamma kept it in the bottom drawer of her *secrétaire*. The drawer had to be solemnly unlocked, and I nursed the precious animal, I being seated on a cross bar underneath the library table; the table cloth had a yellowy green fringe, and Grandmamma also had very hard gingersnap biscuits in a canister. I remember one of my teeth (milk teeth) came out in consequence (on purpose?) while I was under the table. Children were much better brought up in those days. Thank goodness, my education was neglected; I was never sent to school. Of course, what *I* wore was absurdly uncomfortable; white piqué starched frocks just like Tenniel's "Alice in Wonderland," and cotton stockings striped round and round like a zebra's legs. In those early days I composed (or endeavoured to compose) hymns imitated from Isaac Watts, and sentimental ballad descriptions of Scottish scenery, which might have been pretty, only I never could make them scan. Then for a long time I gave up trying to write, because I could not do it. About 1893 I was interested in a little invalid child, the eldest child of a friend; he had a long illness. I used to write letters with pen and ink scribbles, and one of the letters was Peter Rabbit.

Noel has got them yet; he grew up and became a hardworking clergyman in a London poor parish. After a time there began to be a vogue for small books, and I thought "Peter" might do as well as some that were being published. But I did not find any publisher who agreed with me. The manuscript — nearly word for word the same, but with only outline illustrations — was returned with or without thanks by at least six firms. Then I drew my savings out of the post office savings bank, and got an edition of 450 copies printed. I think the engraving and printing cost me about £11. It caused a good deal of amusement amongst my relations and friends. I made about £12 or £14 by selling copies to obliging aunts. I showed this privately printed black and white book to Messrs. F. Warne & Co., and the following year, 1901, they brought out the first coloured edition. The coloured drawings for this were done in a garden near Keswick, Cumberland, and several others were printed in the same part of the Lake District. Squirrel Nutkin sailed on Derwentwater; Mrs. Tiggywinkle lived in the Vale of Newlands near Keswick. Later books, such as "Jemima Puddleduck," "Ginger and Pickles," the "Pie and the Patty Pan," etc. were done at Sawrey, in this southern end of the Lake District. The books relating to Tom Kitten and Samuel Whiskers describe the interior of my old farm house, where children are comically impressed by seeing the real chimney and cupboards.

I think I write carefully because I enjoy my writing, and enjoy taking pains over it. I have always disliked writing to order; I write to please myself. I made enough by books and a small legacy from an aunt to buy a home at the Lakes which has gradually grown into a very large sheep farm; and I married very happily at forty-seven. What are the words in the "Tempest" ? "Spring came to you at the farthest, in the latter end of harvest." I have always found my own pleasure in nature and books.

The reason I am glad I did not go to school; it would have rubbed off some of the originality (if I had not died of shyness or been killed with over pressure). I fancy I could have been taught anything if I had been caught young; but it was in the days when parents kept governesses, and only boys went to school in most families.

My usual way of writing is to scribble, and cut out, and write it again and again. The shorter and plainer the better. And read the Bible (*unrevised* version and Old Testament) if I feel my style wants chastening. There are many dialect words of the Bible and Shakespeare — and also the forcible direct language — still in use in the rural parts of Lancashire.

Sawrey, near Ambleside.

THE LONELY HILLS

Bertha Mahony Miller wanted to publish "A Solitary Mouse," the story Beatrix Potter had sent to Mrs. Miller's granddaughter, Nancy. The tale about the small brown mouse who lived alone in the barn at High Buildings, Troutbeck Park, remained unpublished, however, until an earlier version appeared in A History of the Writings of Beatrix Potter *by Leslie Linder. What finally appeared in the May 1942* Horn Book *was an essay, "The Lonely Hills," which contained significant changes from the original manuscript. Almost all of the introduction was kept, but only three paragraphs from the story itself were retained as an ending for the essay.*

I have been listening to a Danish girl distilling melody from an old spinet. Her fingers caress the yellow ivory keys. Notes come tinkling forth like the sound of a harp; like a hesitating breeze, away, far away amongst hemlocks. The limpid undertones are the song of a brook that ripples over pebbles. J. Sebastian Bach composed his minuet for such an instrument; an old-fashioned piano propped against the wainscot on seven fluted legs. The maker's name, "Clementi," is painted above the keyboard in a wreath of tiny flowers.

Music strikes chords of memory. Big golden-haired Ulla spoke of Copenhagen; of Hans Christian Andersen; of the little bronze mermaid sitting on her stone upon the strand where Danish children bathe and play beside the summer sea. She spoke of long frosts in Denmark; of skating on lakes and canals. No letter — another month and still no letters from Denmark; poor Denmark; poor Europe; silent behind a blank curtain of fear.

For me the pretty jingling tunes bring memories of Merry Nights and of our English Folk-Dance Revival twenty years ago. The stone-floored farm kitchen where first we danced "The Boatman" and heard the swinging lilt of "Black Nag." The loft with two fiddles where country dancers paced "The Triumph," three in arm under arched hands. The long drive home in frosty starlight with a load of rosy sleepy village girls wrapped up in rugs. Coniston, and the mad barbaric music of the Kirkby-Mazzard Sword Dance, when a beheaded corpse springs up and holds a wheel of wooden swords aloft. Chapel Stile in Langdale where we came out into deep snow from a dance over the store. "Haste to the Wedding," "Pop Goes the Weasel" and "We Won't Go Home Until Morning!" The Morris bells and baldricks! The plum cake and laughter. Fat and thin, and high and low, the nimble and the laggard, the toddler and the gray-haired gran — all dancing with a will.

There were summer festivals, also, most lovely to remember. Quivering heat and smell of trodden grass, the lawns of Underley Hall, a stately setting. Deep below the woods and hanging gardens the River Lune meandered in wide sweeps through Kirkby Lonsdale meadows. The "County" perched precariously upon a grandstand made of planks. A fine wind and string band with big drum and bassoon, very hot and thirsty, fiddled furiously under a tree, a lime scented bloom. At Underley the dancers were marshalled behind lilac bushes and azaleas. They danced on in converging strands of colour to weave a tapestry that glistened like shot silk.

I remember another unforgettable pageant, held on the Sportsfield at Grasmere. The fells towered around like a wall, and white clouds were piled over Helvellyn and Stone Arthur, with distant rumblings of thunder. And the dancers! The merry dancers! They had come in their hundreds from all over the north, a rainbow-hued kaleidoscope. In spite of roughish turf I have never seen better Morris, or prouder beauty than the Durham reels danced by girls in corn-coloured smocks. The reels pleased me especially. Folk dancing, if it is to take real hold, ought to be an indigenous revival. "Three Reels," "Petronella," and "The Triumph" were traditional in this border country. My farm servants danced them at our Christmas suppers long before Morris dancing was introduced from the south. Well-trained Morris dancing is a miracle of graceful agility; a display for international meetings. But give me the swinging, roaring, reels — the sparkling pretty long sets — the maze of intricate dances surprisingly remembered — follow the fiddle, forget your feet! Or dance with style and bend and sway; a bow and a curtsy for man and maid; and an inextricable tangle of laughter for beginners! Give me reels and spontaneous unsophisticated country dancing all the time for dancing in a north country village.

Another time all by myself alone I watched a weird dance, to the music of Piper Wind. It was far away in that lonely wilderness behind the table-land on Troutbeck Tongue. In the midst of this waste of yellow-bent grass and stones there is a patch of green grass and stunted thorn. Round the tree — round and round in measured canter went four of the wild fell ponies. Round and round, then checked and turned; round and round reversed; arched necks, tossing manes, tails streaming. I watched a while, crouching behind a boulder. Who had taught them? Who had learned them to "dance the heys" in that wilderness? Oftentimes I have seen managed horses cantering round the sawdust ring under a circus tent; but these half wild youngsters had never been handled by man.

I stood up. They stopped, stared, and snorted; then galloped out of sight. While I was watching them I remembered how I had been puzzled once before. In a soft muddy place on the old drove road I had seen a multitude of little unshod footprints, much too small for horses' foot-marks, much too round for deer or sheep. I did not know at that time that there would be ponies on the Troutbeck fell; though I knew they were at Haweswater and Mattisdale. I wondered were they footmarks of a troop of fairy riders, riding down old King Gait into Hird Wood and Hallilands, away into Fairyland and the blue distance of the hills. Over the ferry where mountains are blue, the finding of those little fairy footmarks on the old drove road first made me aware of the Fairy Caravan.

In the calm spacious days that seem so long ago, I loved to wander on the Troutbeck fell. Sometimes I had with me an old sheep dog, "Nip" or "Fly"; more often I went alone. But never lonely. There was company of gentle sheep, and wild flowers and singing waters. I listened to the voices of the Little Folk.

Troutbeck Tongue is uncanny; a place of silences and whispering echoes. It is a mighty table-land between two streams. They rise together, north of the Tongue, in one maze of bogs and pools. They flow on either hand; the Hagg Beck in the eastern valley; the Troutbeck River on the west. They meet and re-unite below the southern crags, making the table-land almost an island, an island haunted by the sounds that creep on running waters which encompass it. The Tongue is shaped like a great horseshoe, edged by silver streams, and guarded by an outer rampart of high fells. From the highest point of the Tongue I could look over the whole expanse: Woundale and the Standing Stones; Sadghyll and the hut circles; the cairns built by the stone men; the Roman road; Hallilands and Swaindale, named by the Norsemen; and the walls of the Norman deer park stretching for miles — "Troutbeck Park."

Far away in Dalehead the black Galloway cattle were dark specks moving slowly as they grazed. Sometimes I came upon the herd on the lower slopes of the Tongue; which was a reason for not taking Nip. The little shaggy cows were quiet with me, but fierce in defence of their calves against dogs. Sometimes I timed my ramble to cross the track of the shepherds when they drove down a thousand sheep from the high fell for dipping. Rarely, I saw a hiker who had lost himself. Once there were two ravenous boys who had been out in a mist all night on Caudale moor. Usually I saw nobody, the long day round.

Mist is beautiful I think, though troublesome for sheep gathering. It takes strange shapes when it rises at sunset. During storms it rushes down the valleys like a black curtain billowing before the wind, while the Troutbeck River thunders over the Cauldron. Memories of "old unhappy far-off things and battles long ago"; sorrows of yesterday and today and tomorrow — the vastness of the fells covers all with a mantle of peace.

The following passage is the final paragraph from Beatrix Potter's reply to The Horn Book's *request for biographical material for* Illustrators of Children's Books: 1744-1945. *The reader may enjoy comparing this paragraph with her comment in her letter of November 20, 1942, written to Bertha Mahony Miller.*

As Americans on tour inspect every corner of old England — as country cousins on holiday are better acquainted with the sights of London than any native Londoner — so it sometimes happens that the town child is more alive to the fresh beauty of the country than a child who is country born.

My brother and I were born in London because my father was a lawyer there. But our descent — our interests and our joy was in the north country. It is immaterial to give the address of my unloved birthplace. It was hit by shrapnel in the last war; now I am rather pleased to hear it is no more!

H.B.H.

~~~ Index ~~~